Inflation Patterns and Monetary Policy

Inflation Patterns and Monetary Policy

Lessons for the European Central Bank

Johannes M. Groeneveld

Chief Economist,
De Nederlandsche Bank NV
Amsterdam, The Netherlands

Edward Elgar
Cheltenham, UK • Northampton, MA, USA

Published by
Edward Elgar Publishing Limited
8 Lansdown Place
Cheltenham
Glos GL50 2HU
UK

Edward Elgar Publishing, Inc.
6 Market Street
Northampton
Massachusetts 01060
USA

A catalogue record for this book
is available from the British Library

Library of Congress Cataloguing in Publication Data

Groeneveld, Johannes M., 1965–
    Inflation patterns and monetary policy: lessons for the European Central Bank / Johannes M. Groeneveld.
    Includes bibliographical references and index.
    1. Inflation (Finance—European Union countries. 2. Monetary policy—European Union countries. I. Title.
HG925.G76 1998
332.4'1'094—dc21   98–13465
                                                  CIP

ISBN 1 85898 853 5

Printed and bound in Great Britain by
Biddles Ltd, Guildford and King's Lynn

Contents

v

List of Figures

List of Tables

Acknowledgements

For the greater part, this book was written at the Monetary and Economic Policy Department of the Nederlandsche Bank. It resulted from a research project on the possible monetary strategies to be conducted by the future European Central Bank. My profession at this Department enabled me to carry out timely empirical research relevant to monetary policy-makers. In this respect, I am indebted to the Nederlandsche Bank for offering me the opportunity to work on this project and to present papers at various conferences.

This book would not have been completed without the involvement of a number of people. I would like to mention some of them, realizing that many more played a stimulating role during various stages of the project. First of all, I wish to thank Getty for her invaluable support. Moreover, I would like to express my thanks to Kees Koedijk and Clemens Kool, who provided me with many challenging ideas. I also would like to thank Lex Hoogduin for his willingness to read and comment on the first drafts of every part of this book. In addition, I owe a debt of gratitude Linda Keijzer and Leo de Haan for their moral support, particularly during the last phase of the project.

Hans Groeneveld
May 1998

1. Introduction

*the concerns people mention first regarding inflation are
that it hurts their standard of living .... Other concerns are
that inflation makes us feel good, but ultimately deceives us,
or allows opportunistic people to deceive us, that the social
atmosphere created by inflation is a selfish one and harmful
to national morale, that high inflation can cause political
chaos or anarchy, and that inflation and decline of currency
value is harmful to national prestige.*

Shiller (1996), p. 57

1 BACKGROUND

For European monetary policy makers in particular, the 1990s have been, and
still are, most exciting. First, the drive towards economic and monetary
integration in Europe gained enormous momentum with the adoption of the
so-called Delors Report at the European Council of Madrid in June 1989. This
report finally led to the signing of the Maastricht Treaty in February 1992.
According to the agreed timetable, the third and final stage of Economic and
Monetary Union (EMU) will start on January 1st 1999. At that date, the
national currencies of the participating countries will be irrevocably fixed as
a prelude to the introduction of the single currency, that is, the euro, in 2002
at the latest. As enshrined in the Treaty, the future European System of
Central Banks (ESCB) will decide and implement the single monetary policy
within EMU. The start of Stage Three of EMU will be marked by a sort of
'Big Bang' with a sudden shift from the coexistence of national monetary
policies, formulated in the pursuit of national objectives and implemented
through different procedures, to a single monetary policy, set by a
supranational institution with Union-wide objectives and operated in a
consistent way throughout the area (see Monticelli and Viñals, 1993).

For European monetary policy makers, the turmoil in the ERM just after
the adoption of the Treaty was another breathtaking event (Eichengreen and
Wyplosz, 1993). Somewhat ironically, severe exchange rate tensions emerged
at a very time when the credibility of the ERM seemed to be firmly
established. As a major cause for these tumultuous times, reference is often

made to the persistent inflation differentials between some ERM members, which culminated in substantial real appreciation of the currencies of the high-inflation countries (de Grauwe, 1994a). After the rejection of the Treaty by the Danish population in a referendum, financial markets suddenly started to doubt the tenacity of monetary policy makers to defend the exchange rate parity, triggering speculative capital flows which forced Italy and the United Kingdom to leave the ERM. Recently, only Italy re-entered the ERM.

Interestingly, the whole EMU project hardly suffered any delay following the exchange rate turbulence in 1992—93. On the contrary, the ratification of the Treaty necessitated quick preparatory action on many fronts simultaneously in the second or transitional phase of EMU. Under the responsibility of the European Monetary Institute (EMI), monetary policy makers started to design a viable institutional and logistical framework for the ESCB. Soon, the meetings of representatives of national central banks at the EMI were heavily intensified. These consultative bodies sought to pave the way for the resolution of numerous complex issues in order to enable the ESCB to conduct monetary policy effectively and efficiently from the very first day of Stage Three.[1] Fortunately, they did not have to bother about the primary objective of the ESCB. This issue had already been settled in the Statute of the ESCB, which states that the central goal of the ESCB is the achievement and maintenance of price stability.[2] Although the Statute contains neither a specific definition of 'price stability'[3] nor a rule to judge whether the support for other policies 'conflicts' with price stability, its aim is obvious: to avoid potential trade-offs when all the goals are at par. The importance attached to inflation also clearly comes to the fore in the Treaty. The convergence criterion on inflation formulated to assess the eligibility of EU countries to join EMU requires that:

> a Member State has a price performance that is sustainable and an average rate of inflation, observed over a period of one year before the examination, that does not exceed by more than 1.5 percentage points that of, at most, the three best performing Member States in terms of price stability.

The strategic and tactical question how to formulate and execute the future common monetary policy is left open in the Statute. In other words, the monetary strategy of the ESCB has not yet been selected. Here, the term 'monetary strategy' denotes the set of procedures according to which a central bank decides how to achieve its final objective, that is, price stability (EMI, 1997). On the basis of current central bank practices and taking into account theoretical considerations, several possible strategies can be distinguished for the ESCB. In principle, the ESCB can choose between real or nominal interest rate objectives (Barro, 1989), nominal income targets (Garganas, 1993), exchange rate targets, money (Issing, 1992) and/or other indicators as information variables (Friedman, 1994). Since the ultimate goal of the ESCB is price stability, it could also try to target inflation directly (Crockett, 1994). As opposed to the uncertainty regarding the appropriate monetary philosophy for the ESCB, there is somewhat more clarity on the strategy to be followed by countries of the European Union that plan to participate in EMU at a later stage; they are expected to peg their currencies to the euro (that is, exchange rate targeting). To this end, a modified version of the present ERM is being developed so as to minimize the risk of a recurrence of the huge exchange rate tensions of 1992–93.

From the above, the central theme of this book can be extracted. Basically, the dynamics of inflation and monetary strategies to reach price stability inside and outside the E(M)U are the binding ingredients of this book. I contribute to recent and future discussions about monetary policy in Europe from an empirical as well as a practical perspective. To this end, the patterns of inflation in various European countries are examined within the context of a theoretical model which is connected with monetary targeting. By extending this model, I subsequently investigate whether monetary links between ERM members have become tighter in the course of time. Since national inflation rates appear to be increasingly driven by European-wide monetary developments, the usefulness of European monetary aggregates as indicators for future price movements has obviously increased. Thereafter, I focus on the inflation dynamics of countries that have recently shifted to a direct inflation targeting strategy. Apart from these central issues, I also dwell upon many related topics such as the occurrence of (a)symmetric shocks and the stability of (national and European) money demand functions. Before presenting the structure of this book in detail, I first briefly pay attention to the general pattern of inflation in the European Union over the past decades.

2 A PRELIMINARY LOOK AT INFLATION

Judged by the quote presented at the beginning of this introduction, people dislike inflation, though their reasons differ from those usually put forward by economists. This inflation aversion emerges from a questionnaire survey conducted among 677 people in the United States, Germany and Brazil (Shiller, 1996). From this perspective, people from all over the world seem to support the choice of price stability as the key objective of a central bank.

Be that as it may, the universal negative attitude towards inflation presumably originated not very long ago. For instance, the inflation histories of the present member states of the EU are definitely not identical (see Table 1.1). This table records average inflation rates and their variability in all present member states of the EU, except for Luxembourg. For the sake of comparison, I also include Japan, Switzerland and the United States. The sample period begins just after the collapse of the Bretton Woods System in 1973 and ends in 1996. The full sample is broken down into three subperiods.

Table 1.1 Patterns of inflation

Sample	1973—1996		1973—1978		1979—1987		1988—1996	
	Mean	SD	Mean	SD	Mean	SD	Mean	SD
Austria	4.3	2.2	6.8	2.0	4.2	1.9	2.9	0.8
Belgium	5.2	3.5	8.9	3.4	5.5	2.6	2.5	0.8
Denmark	6.6	4.2	10.7	3.1	7.7	3.3	2.7	1.2
Finland	7.4	4.9	13.4	3.8	7.6	3.1	3.3	2.3
France	6.8	4.3	10.2	2.2	8.7	4.0	2.5	0.7
Germany	3.5	2.0	5.1	1.7	3.2	2.2	2.6	1.0
Greece	17.0	5.6	15.7	7.1	20.8	3.2	14.0	4.2
Ireland	8.9	6.8	14.7	4.9	11.2	6.4	2.6	0.9
Italy	10.8	6.2	15.9	4.8	13.1	5.6	5.2	1.1
The Netherlands	4.1	3.0	7.8	2.2	3.5	2.6	2.2	0.9
Portugal	16.0	8.5	21.8	7.7	19.8	6.7	8.3	3.7
Spain	10.9	5.8	17.8	4.6	11.8	3.5	5.3	1.1
Sweden	7.4	3.6	9.7	2.1	8.3	3.1	4.9	3.3
United Kingdom	8.6	6.1	15.0	5.8	8.4	5.1	4.6	2.6
Japan	4.5	5.3	11.4	6.2	2.9	2.3	1.4	1.3
Switzerland	3.7	2.6	4.9	3.8	3.5	1.9	3.0	1.8
United States	5.7	3.2	7.7	2.2	6.4	4.1	3.7	1.0

Notes: Inflation is measured as the twelve-month change in the consumer price index. I have used monthly data. SD stands for the standard deviation of inflation. The German data pertain to West Germany. The Irish inflation figures are intrapolated from quarterly data.

The table shows that inflation was highest in the first years of the sample. Thereafter, inflation dropped considerably in most cases. This overall pattern is also discernible for the variability of inflation. In the third subperiod, most countries have come close to what is generally considered to be a reasonable degree of price stability. Interestingly, the inflation dynamics of all industrialized countries thus exhibit the same evolution over the past three decades. Moreover, the majority of countries would qualify for participation in a 'virtuous' monetary union in terms of the convergence requirement of a high degree of price stability as demanded in the Treaty. This general feature brings us back to the central issue of this volume: whether and to what extent this phenomenon is related to the monetary strategies of central banks.

3 OUTLINE

The central theme of this book will be worked out in six chapters. The theoretical underpinnings of my empirical research as to the impact of money growth on price developments are discussed in Chapter 2. I have opted for a relatively new theoretical approach for predicting inflationary trends in an economy: the P-star-model. This conceptual framework was introduced by Hallman, Porter and Small (1989) as a new way to detect price pressures at an early stage. In this concept, it is assumed that a deviation between the actual and equilibrium price level — the price gap — indicates the short-run direction of inflation. Compared to existing models of inflation, the innovative element of the P^*-model is that the differential between actual and potential real output as well as the dispersion between actual and equilibrium velocity are hypothesized to matter for the future course of inflation. After having sketched the roots and methodology of the original P^*-model, I present an overview of the most salient modifications to the initial P^*-concept in subsequent studies. In the second part of Chapter 2, I highlight the statistical issues encountered when implementing this framework. In the empirical investigation of the validity of the P^*-model in subsequent chapters, I take a fresh approach regarding the construction of the equilibrium variables. I shall use the Multi State Kalman Filter technique developed and programmed by Kool (1989) to proxy potential real output and trend velocity. Compared to most other econometric methods, this technique offers a more flexible way for dealing with structural changes in the patterns of macroeconomic variables.

The P^*-model is empirically tested for four founding members of the European Exchange Rate Mechanism in Chapter 3. The countries include Belgium, France, Germany and the Netherlands. Chapter 3 also contains a discussion of related issues in the context of the relevant recent economic literature. Since this framework is connected with a particular monetary strategy, namely monetary targeting, I also discuss the history of monetary policy making in the countries under review when assessing the policy relevance of the empirical findings.

In Chapter 4, I extend the traditional P^*-model by allowing for the possibility that the domestic equilibrium price level in the aforementioned countries is determined by a European monetary aggregate instead of the domestic money supply alone. This could be the result of exchange rate links. This offers an opportunity to test various interesting hypotheses. For instance, in countries with an exchange rate target such as the Netherlands, the domestic money supply becomes theoretically fully endogenous under certain conditions. In this situation, national monetary authorities put their policy instrument predominantly at the service of the exchange rate objective and consequently lose control over total domestic monetary expansion. Furthermore, the existence of a statistical link between European monetary aggregates and inflation in Germany, the anchor country in the ERM, might have warranted more attention to monetary conditions in other ERM countries in the formulation and execution of the monetary policy of the Bundesbank in the past decade. In this case, the transition to Stage Three of EMU could be smoother as well, especially if the ESCB would also primarily base its policy measures on the development of Union-wide monetary aggregates. Chapter 4 also examines whether the impact of an ERM-wide money supply on domestic inflation rates is separate from, and more powerful than that of the countries' own national monetary aggregates. Finally, the applicability of the P^*-framework for the group as a whole is tested.

To investigate whether potential monetary spill-over effects only exist between original ERM members, the initial and extended P^*-model is applied to a former shadow member of the ERM, that is, Austria, in Chapter 5. Indeed, Austria's entry into the EMS and the ERM in January 1995 provides an added reason for exploring empirically to what extent Austria is integrated into Europe from a monetary perspective and whether a formal exchange rate commitment is required to establish firm monetary ties with other (ERM) countries.

Chapter 6 deals with another potential policy option for the ESCB. This approach is called 'direct inflation targeting' (see, for example, Leiderman and Svensson, 1995). Recently, several industrialized countries have switched from an intermediate monetary strategy to this new regime, which aims at influencing the ultimate goal of monetary policy in a direct manner. By setting explicit inflation targets, these countries actually seek to enhance or, in some instances, regain the credibility of monetary policy. After an explanation of this new strategy and how it is actually implemented in New Zealand, Canada and the United Kingdom, I compare the inflation dynamics in these three inflation-targeting countries with those in neighbouring countries that have not recently changed their monetary strategies (that is, Australia,[4] the United States and Germany, respectively).[5] Essentially, I try to figure out whether this new regime has helped to bring down inflation and has consequently improved the credibility of monetary policy. The final section of Chapter 6 merges the theoretical and empirical evidence and offers some preliminary thoughts for answering the question whether monetary or direct inflation targeting is preferable for the ESCB.

Chapter 7 sheds light on the evolution of economic convergence in Europe and aims at identifying potential candidates for the initial EMU group on purely economic grounds. In this analysis, all present member states of the EU and Switzerland are put to the test. Formally, the convergence criteria laid down in the Maastricht Treaty in 1991 are intended to determine which countries are eligible for participation in EMU.[6,7] The underlying notion is that 'virtuous' EMU candidates should have comparable inflation preferences and track records (Bini Smaghi, 1994). If not, conflicts could arise within the ESCB concerning the right course of monetary policy, which might lead to erratic and unpredictable behaviour (de Grauwe, 1996a). This would seriously damage the credibility of the ESCB and result in higher inflation expectations or uncertainty, thus threatening the economic viability of the whole unification project.

Chapter 8 briefly summarizes the main findings of this volume and suggests directions for future research.

NOTES

1. For example, money market instruments and monetary statistics have to be harmonized. Moreover, national payments settlements systems between commercial and central banks have to be linked.
2. The Statute also states that the general economic situation in the Union shall be supported as long as this does not jeopardize price stability.
3. The Bundesbank's figure for 'acceptable' inflation — typically 2 percent — is based on a goal of stable prices taking into account potential measurement errors.
4. Admittedly, Australia is effectively also a direct inflation-targeting country. However, compared to New Zealand, the Australian monetary framework is rather informal and untransparent.
5. Dueker and Fischer (1996) follow a similar approach.
6. Naturally, this decision will also be governed by political considerations.
7. The four main criteria for the transition to EMU are a high degree of price stability, sustainability of the government fiscal positions, observance of normal fluctuation margins in the EMS for at least two years without devaluation, and evidence of durability of convergence reflected in long-term interest rates.

2. The P^*-Framework: Theory and Backgrounds

*Economists have long been searching for the holy grail —
an accurate thermometer with which to forecast inflation....
Some think they have found it.*

Christiano (1989), p. 3

1 INTRODUCTION

In the summer of 1989, the Board of Governors of the Federal Reserve System introduced a new, experimental way to forecast inflationary trends (Hallman, Porter and Small, 1989). This approach was called P-star (P^*). The development of the P^*-model was inspired by the desire to detect potential inflationary pressures in the economy of the United States at an early stage. In short, P^*, or the equilibrium price level, can be interpreted as the price level resulting from the actual money supply, provided that the velocity of this monetary aggregate and real output are at their 'equilibrium' levels (V^* and Q^*, respectively). The essence of the P^*-concept is that a deviation between the actual price level and the equilibrium price level — the price gap — indicates the short run direction of the price level, and consequently inflation. The novelty of this framework is that the differential between the actual and trend velocity as well as the discrepancy between actual and potential real output levels are hypothesized to contain informative value for the future course of inflation. In most standard theories of inflation, only one of both gaps appears as an explanatory variable in the inflation equation.

The empirical application of this new conceptual approach for the US suggested that P^* was a better indicator of inflationary pressures than the criteria which had been used so far.[1] This feature attracted much attention and triggered a considerable body of studies testing the validity of the P^*-model for other industrialized countries (see for instance Hoeller and Poret, 1991; Kole and Leahy, 1991; Reimers and Tödter, 1994, among others). Generally, the findings of these studies are encouraging. For instance, it is concluded that 'In sum, the price gap can be considered useful as a simple yet comprehensive indicator of potential upward pressure on prices' (Bank of Japan, 1990, p. 5).

The interest in the P^*-framework was largely motivated by the need to find a reliable inflation indicator for monetary policy aimed at price stability. In effect, it contributed to the renewed focus on the quantity theory of money which had lost popularity in the 1980s. Its fading attractiveness was fuelled by increased doubts about the existence of stable relationships between money, prices and output. These doubts prompted several countries to abandon or downgrade the practice of monetary targeting in the 1980s (Goodhart, 1989).

This chapter can be neatly divided into two parts. Section 2 concentrates on theoretical and methodological aspects of the P^*-concept. Section 2.1 first discusses the underpinnings of the initial P^*-model in detail. Thereafter, Section 2.2 provides a concise overview of the modifications of the original P^*-framework in subsequent studies. The second part of Chapter 2 is devoted to the more technical features of the model. In Section 3, I highlight the statistical issues to be dealt with when implementing this framework (for example the identification of potential unit roots and the related question of stationarity of the variables under review). In addition, I describe the econometric techniques that are used in the existing P^*-literature to produce estimates of potential real output and trend velocity (Section 3.1). In the empirical investigation of the validity of the P^*-model in Chapters 3 and 4, I take a fresh approach with regard to the computation of potential real output and trend velocity. I shall use the Kalman-filter technique which has not been used in previous P^*-studies. Subsection 3.2 treats the basic ideas underlying this filter and provides an intuitional as well as a technical description of the working of this filter.[2]

2 THEORETICAL AND METHODOLOGICAL UNDERPINNINGS OF THE P^*-MODEL

2.1 The Initial P^*-Model

Hallman, Porter and Small (henceforth HPS, 1989, 1991) presented the concept of P-star (P^*) as a new indicator for potential inflation. However, as pointed out by Humphrey (1989), the P^*-approach is actually not a novelty, but elaborates on the premise that, in line with the quantity theory of money, the price level is determined by the money supply in the long-term. The ideas underlying the new approach can be traced back to the first advocates of the quantity theory of money, such as David Hume (1711—76). In their analyses, two common elements are discernible. First, changes in the money supply have a positive effect on the general price level. Second, and this is an empirical matter, most of long term fluctuations in the price level are assumed to be caused by movements in the money supply.

The basis of the P^*-model is Fisher's well-known equation of exchange identity (Fisher, 1911).

$$P = M \frac{V}{Q} , \tag{2.1}$$

where P is the actual price level, M represents the domestic stock of money, V denotes the velocity of some measure of money and Q stands for real output. Without further elaboration, no testable hypothesis can be derived from equation (2.1), since it simply pins down actual velocity for given observations on P, M and Q. HPS, however, assume that V and Q always tend towards their equilibrium values (V^* and Q^*, respectively) over time (for instance within two or three years). The equilibrium price level (P^*) is defined as the price level that is consistent with the actual money supply (M), the long-term equilibrium value of M's circulation velocity (V^*) and the potential real output (Q^*), or in symbols:

$$P^* = M \frac{V^*}{Q^*} \tag{2.2}$$

From (2.2), it follows that at a certain trend velocity (V^*), P^* is proportionally dependent on the money supply per unit of potential real output. Assuming that V^* and Q^* can be determined independently, and that both are unrelated to the actual money stock, the importance of expression (2.2) for conducting inflation forecasts is evident when it is placed alongside equation (2.1): P can only differ from P^* when V differs from V^*, Q from Q^* or both variables diverge from their long-run equilibrium values.

Taking into account the above assumptions, the equilibrium between the actual and the trend values will 'automatically' be restored within a few years. Any deviations between P and P^* will consequently also disappear over time. This is easy to see when both equations are combined and the result is expressed in natural logarithms, resulting in so-called price gap:

$$GAP = (p - p^*) = (q^* - q) + (v - v^*) , \tag{2.3}$$

where the lower-case variables are the natural logarithms of their upper-case counterparts. The price gap $(p_t - p_t^*)$ is composed of an output and a velocity gap. However, equation (2.3) does not give an insight into the dynamics of the equilibrating mechanism following a (monetary) disturbance, when p_t becomes unequal to p_t^*. As noted by Humphrey (1989), the first advocates of the quantity theory of money already had a clear vision of the outlines of this adjustment process. Their views can be readily explained by Figure 2.1. The 'classical' economists felt that prices react with a certain lag to monetary shocks. To these theoreticians such a lagged price response implied at least two things. First, a steepening of the time path of the equilibrium price level (caused by a jump in the money supply) would open a gap between equilibrium and actual prices. This is illustrated in Figure 2.1: the slope of line BD is steeper than that of BC. This discrepancy will last until the actual prices have completely adjusted to the equilibrium prices. Correspondingly,

Figure 2.1   P diagrammed: price gap presages
and rise in inflation*

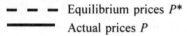

—— — Equilibrium prices *P**
——————— Actual prices *P*

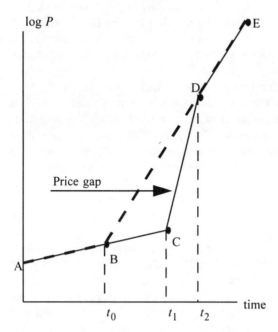

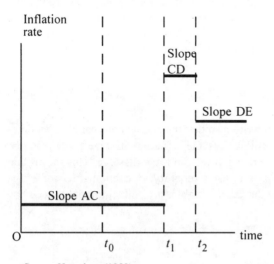

Source: Humphrey (1989).

real output exhibits a temporary rise and velocity perhaps a temporary fall. Hence, the quantity theory of money leaves open the possibility that a sudden increase in the money supply affects real economic activity in the short run. Second, during the adjustment period, actual prices have to rise at a faster-than-equilibrium rate, if they are to reach their equilibrium level. This explains why the line CD has a steeper slope than the line BD. From this, it follows that an emerging price gap augurs a temporary rise in inflation. In short, an acceleration (or deceleration) of inflation restores the equilibrium between p and p^* over time.

The next step is to incorporate these considerations in an algebraic expression, so that the short-term dynamics can be correctly forecasted. It is obvious that the estimated adjustment process must satisfy the long-term restrictions imposed by the P^*-model. Firstly, the P^*-approach explains, as in other prevailing inflation models, the (change in the) rate of inflation from the differential between the actual and equilibrium price level and the anticipated development of this equilibrium price level. The latter component, the so-termed forward-looking information, is included by definition in the P^*-model, namely in p^* itself. This way, the problem of adequate modelling of (rational) expectations is automatically solved.[3] To allow for backward-looking information, a number of lagged inflation levels is added to the dynamic specification.[4] An economic explanation for the inclusion of these lags is that shocks, in this case discrepancies between p and p^*, have not generally faded after just one period. Furthermore, the choice of the dependent variable (that is the change in inflation ($\Delta\pi$) or the inflation rate itself (π)) depends on its time series characteristics. If differencing is required to obtain stationarity (or, to put it another way, if the inflation rate has a unit root[5]), the endogenous variable should be $\Delta\pi$. HPS (1989) test for the appropriate specification by nesting the first differences and levels equations in the following way. They start with a levels version of the model with five lags of π.

$$\pi_t = \alpha(p_{t-1} - p^*_{t-1}) + \sum_{j=1}^{5} \delta_j \pi_{t-j} \qquad \alpha < 0 \qquad (2.4)$$

Then, equation (2.4) is rewritten so that the endogenous variable becomes $\Delta\pi$, while the price gap still enters the equation in levels since in the 'classical' line of thought a price gap will, in time, dissolve. This means that deviations between p and p^* are only temporary. In econometric words, the P^*-framework requires that the latter variables are cointegrated. I proceed by noting that

$$\delta_4\pi_{t-4} + \delta_5\pi_{t-5} \equiv (\delta_4 + \delta_5)\pi_{t-4} - \delta_5(\pi_{t-4} - \pi_{t-5})$$

$$\equiv (\delta_4 + \delta_5)\pi_{t-4} - \delta_5\Delta\pi_{t-4},$$

so that equation (2.4) can be rewritten as:

$$\pi_t = \alpha(p_{t-1} - p_{t-1}^*) + \sum_{j=1}^{3} \delta_j \pi_{t-j} + (\delta_4 + \delta_5)\pi_{t-4} - \delta_5 \Delta\pi_{t-4} \qquad (2.4')$$

Also valid is:

$$\delta_3 \pi_{t-3} + (\delta_4 + \delta_5)\pi_{t-4} \equiv (\delta_3 + \delta_4 + \delta_5)\pi_{t-3} - (\delta_4 + \delta_5)\Delta\pi_{t-3}$$

Substitution of the above in equation (2.4') results in equation (2.4"):

$$\pi_t = \alpha(p_{t-1} - p_{t-1}^*) + \sum_{j=1}^{2} \delta_j \pi_{t-j} + (\delta_3 + \delta_4 + \delta_5)\pi_{t-3}$$
$$- (\delta_4 + \delta_5)\Delta\pi_{t-3} - \delta_5 \Delta\pi_{t-4} \qquad (2.4'')$$

Repeating the same exercise for δ_1 and δ_2 finally yields equation (2.5), which is, in fact, a reparameterization of equation (2.4).

$$\Delta\pi_t = \alpha(p_{t-1} - p_{t-1}^*) + \gamma\pi_{t-1} + \sum_{j=1}^{4} \beta_j \Delta\pi_{t-j} \qquad \alpha < 0 \qquad (2.5)$$

with $\gamma = ((\sum_{j=1}^{5} \delta_j) - 1)$ and $\beta_j = -\sum_{i=j+1}^{5} \delta_i$

A test of the restriction implicit in going from the levels specification of equation (2.4) to the first-difference specification in expression (2.5) can be based on the t-statistic of the parameter γ in equation (2.5). When empirical tests indicate that the t-statistic for the coefficient of π_{t-1} is close to zero[6], an acceleration specification is preferable to a model that employs lagged levels of inflation as regressors (that is, equation (2.4)).[7]

From the above, it follows that the price gap $(p - p^*)$ gives an indication of the short run direction of the (change in the) inflation rate. The model predicts that the dependent variable will rise, fall or remain unchanged when actual prices P are below, above or identical to equilibrium prices P^*, respectively. On the basis of equation (2.3), a negative deviation between p and p^* is by definition accompanied by an actual production that surpasses potential real output $(q > q^*)$ and/or by an actual velocity that falls short of equilibrium velocity $(v < v^*)$. Equation (2.6) on page 14 combines both equations (2.3) and (2.5).

This 'unrestricted' version of the P^*-model allows the coefficients on the output and velocity gap to be different in magnitude. This formulation also conveys the innovative element of the P^*-model. By making assumptions about the αs, the P^*-concept actually collapses into either a simple version of an output-gap approach or a more monetaristic theoretical framework. Neo-Keynesian approaches towards modelling inflation centre primarily on the output gap $(\alpha_1 = 0)$ and the inertia in price adjustment, which is equivalent to the standard expectations-augmented supply curve. In this case, inflation tends to accelerate only as the output gap widens. According to this model of inflation, the long-term price level is determined by dividing nominal GNP by the exogenous level of potential real output ($P^* = Y / \hat{y} = p \, y / \hat{y}$).[8] Hence, the neo-Keynesian model of inflation is under certain conditions equivalent to equation (2.6).[9]

$$\Delta \pi_t = \alpha_1 (v_{t-1} - v_{t-1}^*) + \alpha_2 (q_{t-1}^* - q_{t-1}) + \gamma \pi_{t-1} + \sum_{j=1}^{4} \beta_j \Delta \pi_{t-j} \quad (2.6)$$

$$\text{with } \alpha_1, \alpha_2 < 0$$

In the monetarist approach, on the other hand, the equilibrium price level comes about by multiplying money per unit of output by exogenous equilibrium velocity ($P^* = (M/Y) \, V^*$). In such models, an expansion of the money supply would temporarily cause a negative divergence between v and v^*. Hereby, a process is set in motion that initially would raise spending, and subsequently prices, until equilibrium is reached. This view is generally consistent with the special case in which $\alpha_2 = 0$. To summarize, the P^*-framework for predicting inflationary trends is in fact a synthesis of both approaches: output and velocity gaps are assumed to be driving forces of inflation.

Finally, one could say that equations (2.5) and (2.6) can be regarded as reduced forms of inflation models embedded in (totally) different large-scale econometric models, which for instance bear a close resemblance to Keynesian, monetarist or 'business cycle' theories. However, this uncertain origin should not be disturbing. Indeed, the basic thrust of the P^*-model is that money is neutral in the long run, which simply means that the long term aggregate supply curve is vertical. The equilibrium price level is thus independent of the real side of the economy, except for changes in Q^*. Furthermore, the inclusion of lags of the dependent variable in the expressions corresponds to the view that the effect of a monetary disturbance on prices will dissipate over time. This is another similarity between the P^*-framework and large structural models. However, how much time it really takes before equilibrium is restored has to be investigated empirically.

2.2 Modifications and Extensions of the Original P^*-Model

The empirical success of the P^*-model for the US has inspired many economists to test its applicability for other countries. Some subsequent studies have not just copied HPS's approach, but also clearly contributed to the enrichment and deepening of the initial P^*-analysis. In a number of articles, the HPS outcomes are put in a broader perspective. Other subsequent P^*-studies have modified and extended the basic framework in various ways. This section presents an overview of the most interesting insights emerging from the existing P^*-literature. In Section 2.2.3, the relevance of these additional elements for the empirical research is summarized.

2.2.1 Technical comments on HPS's model specification

From an analytical viewpoint, Christiano (1989) notes that the core expressions of HPS (1989) can in fact be regarded as constrained versions of an error correction model (ECM) in the spirit of Engle and Granger (1987). As a matter of fact, in the P^*-framework the actual and equilibrium price level (p and p^*) must satisfy the properties of cointegrated variables: they must be integrated of the same order and there should be a long-run relationship between the two variables. Under these conditions, the price gap exerts a correcting influence on short-term inflation developments (and is therefore econometrically equivalent to an error correction term). The Granger Representation Theorem establishes that it is possible to adapt an ECM of the dynamics of adjustment of the actual price level to the equilibrium price level. For the sake of simplicity, I assume that p and p^* meet the above conditions and are I(1). In this case, a general dynamic specification of such an ECM is:

$$\pi_t = \alpha(p_{t-1} - p_{t-1}^*) + \sum_{j=1}^{n} \beta_j \pi_{t-j} + \sum_{i=1}^{m} \psi_i \pi_{t-i}^* \qquad \alpha < 0 \qquad (2.7)$$

$$\pi_t = \alpha_1(v_{t-1} - v_{t-1}^*) + \alpha_2(q_{t-1}^* - q_{t-1}) + \sum_{j=1}^{n} \beta_{j1} \pi_{t-j}$$

$$+ \sum_{i=1}^{m} \psi_{i1}(\Delta q_{t-i}^* - \Delta q_{t-i}) + \sum_{i=1}^{m} \psi_{i2}(\Delta v_{t-i}^* - \Delta v_{t-i}) \qquad (2.8)$$

$$\alpha_1, \alpha_2 < 0$$

The similarity with HPS's expressions is perfect when all ψs are zero. Under these conditions, the unrestricted ECMs have exactly the same format as equations (2.5) and (2.6).

Pecchenino and Rasche (PR, 1990) question the interpretation of HPS's specification. They feel that HPS present expression (2.5) wrongfully as the outcome of a model of economic behaviour based upon an inflation expectation mechanism. In their view, the price gap equation may alternatively just be interpreted as a model of the time series properties of the American price level (p) (or a reduced form model) rather than as a model of economic behaviour. In case HPS's specification is just a — slightly amended — time series model of the inflation rate, one has to be careful in using such an equation to investigate the outcomes of monetary policies that differ significantly from the way monetary authorities have historically conducted monetary policy. Under these circumstances, the time series properties of the inflation rate can change considerably, and a model such as equation (2.5) will be inappropriate and inaccurate. Thus, expression (2.5) can be seriously affected by the Lucas critique (Lucas, 1976).[10]

Ebrill and Fries (EF; 1991, p. 745) draw attention to the fact that it is sometimes difficult to determine the number of unit roots in the price deflator with great precision. In this case, there are no strong statistical arguments in favour of a level or first difference version of the model.[11] Apart from EF (1991), most P^*-studies only estimate inflation equations in either levels (for example, Hoeller and Poret, 1991; Tatom, 1992; and so on) or first differences (Christiano, 1989; Pecchenino and Rasche, 1990; and so on).

Furthermore, EF extend the benchmark model of HPS by including an extra variable to account for supply shocks (*rpgas*). Apparently, they feel that these distortions are not adequately captured in movements of potential output. All in all, their estimation equations look as follows:

$$\pi_t = \alpha_0 + \alpha_1(v_{t-1} - v_{t-1}^*) + \alpha_2(q_{t-1}^* - q_{t-1}) + \gamma \pi_{t-1}$$
$$+ \beta[(\sum_{j=2}^{5} \pi_{t-j})/4] + \delta(0.67\Delta rpgas_{t-2} + 0.33\Delta rpgas_{t-4}) \tag{2.9}$$

$$\Delta\pi_t = \alpha_0 + \alpha_1(v_{t-1} - v_{t-1}^*) + \alpha_2(q_{t-1}^* - q_{t-1}) + \sum_{j=1}^{4} \beta_j \Delta\pi_{t-j}$$
$$+ \delta(0.67\Delta rpgas_{t-2} + 0.33\Delta rpgas_{t-4}) \tag{2.10}$$

rpgas denotes the difference between the log of the implicit deflator for the consumption of gasoline and oil and the log of the implicit GNP deflator. Note that the lag structure of π in equation (2.9) and the energy price term in both equations look peculiar.

Reimers and Tödter (RT, 1994) and the Deutsche Bundesbank (1992) work with another inflation variable in testing the P^*-concept for Germany. In their setup, inflation is measured in a different time frequency, namely as the yearly change in the price level ($\Delta_4 p = p_{t-1} - p_{t-4}$). In addition, the specification formulated by RT (1994) explicitly accounts for the influence of changes in import prices ($\Delta_4 pim$).[12] Moreover, changes in p^* itself are added to the equation. Their final testing equation has the following format:

$$\Delta_4 p_t = \alpha \sum_{i=i}^{4} (p_{t-i} - p_{t-i}^*) + \beta_1 \Delta_4 p_{t-1} + \beta_2 \Delta_4 p_{t-2}$$
$$+ \beta_3 \Delta_4 p_{t-3} + \omega \Delta_4 pim_t + \delta \Delta_4 p_t^* \tag{2.11}$$

The Bank of Japan (1990) has amended the original P^*-specifications by regressing the GNP deflator on distributed lags of the price gap. As is apparent from the discussion above, all other P^*-articles assume that the price gap and its constituent parts only affect the endogenous variable with a (fixed) lag of one period. One might wonder if the most commonly used approach is realistic. The spillover of real or monetary disturbances into price movements can indeed take more than one period to materialize. In this respect, the organization and structure of an economy play a crucial role. In some countries it just may take some time before disturbances in the real or monetary sphere — reflected in positive or negative price gaps — have implications for inflation (or its change).

2.2.2 Economic interpretation of HPS's model

As Kole and Leahy (1991) correctly stress, equation (2.7) allows for the possibility that inflation is also affected by changes in p^* (that is, π^*). This means that inflation may still change if p^* accelerates, even when $p = p^*$. Up to now, there is little empirical evidence in support of the superiority of unrestricted ECMs and the existence of correlations between π and π^*. The coefficients of lagged rates of change — in the components — of p^* are mostly insignificant (see for instance Hoeller and Poret, 1991). My estimations appear to be consistent with those of the majority of existing P^*-studies, suggesting that a model specification in conformity with (2.5) and (2.6) is statistically preferable to equations (2.7) and (2.8). Therefore, the estimation outcomes of the latter expressions are not recorded in Chapters 3 and 4.

Ebrill and Fries (1991) provide economic arguments why one should select a particular form of the inflation equation. An economic reason to specify the inflation equation like expression (2.5) is that the inflation rate is stationary but the velocity and output gaps are functions of the inflation rate. Under these circumstances, the researcher is confronted with simultaneity problems, rendering the results from the ordinary least squares estimation technique inconsistent. Another reason is that the past rate of inflation may persist unless the stance of monetary policy is changed, while monetary policy may aim to offset changes in the inflation rate. If the relationship between money growth and inflation is fully summarized by the velocity and output gaps, the restriction of unity on the coefficient of the lagged inflation rate would be warranted. However, if the transmission mechanism of monetary growth is not completely reflected in this specification, and if the monetary authorities act to stabilize the inflation rate, the levels equation (2.4) would be the appropriate specification.[13]

The economic interpretation of both equations (2.4) and (2.5) becomes considerably more complicated if π^* (or its change) also depends on the lagged price gap. In this case, another form of simultaneity arises. Actually, this possibility is neglected in all existing P^*-studies. To test whether the equilibrium price level is linked to the price gap, the following equation can be estimated:

$$\pi_t^* = \eta(p_{t-1} - p_{t-1}^*) + \sum_{j=1}^{n} \lambda_j \pi_{t-j} + \sum_{i=1}^{m} \mu_i \pi_{t-i}^* \qquad (2.12)$$

If both η and the λ_js are statistically insignificant, the interpretation of the estimation results of the P^*-model (equations (2.4) and (2.5)) is straightforward. Otherwise, a complex interaction exists between p and p^*, which would also require a different estimation technique. On the other hand, the possible link between π^* and the lagged price gap does not constitute a problem when the P^*-framework is just used for forecasting inflationary trends. In testing the validity of the P^*-model for various European countries, I have never found η and λ_js to be significant parameters, though.

Frenkel (1994) extends the analysis of existing P^*-studies in a new direction. He applies the 'lag theory' to the empirical findings for the price gap model to analyse the lag structure of the price reaction function following shocks to the long-run equilibrium price level. It appears that the HPS results for the US indicate that an increase in the growth rate of money leads to a cyclical movement in the inflation rate. On the other hand, the empirical result for Germany obtained from Reimers and Tödter (1994) suggests that the price reaction function exhibits hardly any cyclical elements in the price adjustment path. Reasons for this different reaction pattern are presumably the less flexible wages in Germany compared to the US and/or the possibility that the German inflation expectations follow more the regressive expectation hypothesis.

Hall and Milne (1994) and Funke and Hall (1994) raise a point relating to all existing P^*-studies. They argue that the P^*-literature is in fact responsible for the rediscovery of the money supply as a simple monetary policy indicator after the emergence of instabilities in national money demand functions in the course of the 1980s, partly due to financial innovations and deregulation (Goodhart, 1989). However, all P^*-studies disregard the central question of causality, which can be considered the most fundamental drawback of this strand of literature.[14] Indeed, Hall and Milne (1994) found that for both the United States and the United Kingdom the causality within the system — contrary to the assumption of the quantity theory — moves from prices to money and not in the reverse direction.[15] In the case of Germany, however, the causality seemed to go both ways (Funke and Hall, 1994; IMF, 1994).[16]

2.2.3 P^*-estimation equations in subsequent chapters
In the empirical research in Chapter 3, I try to incorporate the notions emerging from the existing P^*-literature as good as possible. To this end, I consider two model specifications simultaneously. The first one employs $\Delta\pi$ as a dependent variable (see, for example, HPS), whereas the second uses $\Delta\Delta_4 p$ as an endogenous variable (see Reimers and Tödter, 1994). Following Ebrill and Fries (1991) and Reimers and Tödter (1994), both specifications will be augmented with a uniform energy price variable to capture 'imported' price shocks (p^{en}). As is standard practice in econometrics, I shall also iteratively test for the most suitable specification by employing a 'general-to-specific' approach, that is, starting with a benchmark specification and then sequentially deleting variables with insignificant coefficients. Finally, I take into account the possibility that the price gap (and its components) may affect inflation in individual countries with different time lags, thereby

explicitly allowing for differences in economic structures between nations. This approach corresponds to the view that the nature of links between economic variables largely depends on the structure of an economy in the broadest sense of the word. Some economies respond different to shocks than others, so that the statistical relationships between the gaps and inflation may be observable with different lags. In conclusion, the baseline regression equations are:

$$\Delta \pi_t = \alpha_0 + \alpha_1 PG_{t-n} + \gamma \pi_{t-1} + \sum_{j=1}^{4} \beta_j \Delta \pi_{t-j}$$

$$+ \tau \Delta p_{t-m}^{en}, \qquad \alpha_1 < 0$$

(2.13)

$$\Delta \pi_t = \zeta_0 + \zeta_1 VG_{t-n} + \zeta_2 OG_{t-n} + \gamma \pi_{t-1} + \sum_{j=1}^{4} \beta_j \Delta \pi_{t-j}$$

$$+ \tau \Delta p_{t-m}^{en}, \qquad \zeta_1, \zeta_2 < 0$$

(2.14)

$$\Delta \Delta_4 p_t = \alpha_0 + \alpha_1 \sum_{j=1}^{4} PG_{t-j} + \gamma \Delta_4 p_{t-1} + \sum_{i=1}^{4} \beta_i \Delta \Delta_4 p_{t-i}$$

$$+ \tau \Delta_4 p_{t-m}^{en}, \qquad \alpha_1 < 0$$

(2.15)

$$\Delta \Delta_4 p_t = \zeta_0 + \zeta_1 \sum_{j=1}^{4} VG_{t-j} + \zeta_2 \sum_{j=1}^{4} OG_{t-j} + \gamma \Delta_4 p_{t-1}$$

$$+ \sum_{i=1}^{4} \beta_i \Delta \Delta_4 p_{t-i} + \tau \Delta_4 p_{t-m}^{en}, \qquad \zeta_1, \zeta_2 < 0$$

(2.16)

where PG, VG and OG represent the price, velocity and output gap, respectively.

3 TECHNICAL ASPECTS

3.1 Statistical and Econometric Aspects of the P^*-Model

The critical step in making P^* operational as an indicator of the long-run price level is to determine V^*, the long-run velocity of money, and Q^*, potential real output. How these variables can be constructed depends predominantly on the econometric characteristics of the actual time series of velocity and output, V and Q, respectively. Before one chooses a method for determining the equilibrium variables, the actual time series of the key economic variables in the P^*-approach have to be subject to stationarity (or equivalently unit root) tests. Since these statistical features are highly relevant for a correct application of the P^*-model, I present a brief survey of recent literature on unit roots in appendix 2A. Here, the (econometric) techniques that are generally applied to uncover these time series properties are touched upon. When the statistical tests indicate that, for example, velocity is stationary, which means, among other things, that it tends to fluctuate around a fixed average (which may include a deterministic trend), I can simply take the mean of V for the estimate of V^* over the sample period. On the other hand, if velocity turns out to be non-stationary, it is incorrect to employ the mean of V as a proxy for V^* since this would yield non-stationary velocity and price gaps, which would violate the assumption of the P^*-model. In the latter case, an alternative 'technique' has to be used to proxy equilibrium velocity. Indeed, the theoretical assumption is that short-run inflation dynamics are influenced by the price gap because of the existence of an underlying equilibrating adjustment process. If actual prices do not converge to computed equilibrium prices, as is the case with a non-stationary velocity gap, the P^*-framework is rejected, implying that no theoretical foundation exists for including the gap in the inflation specification.

Existing empirical studies in the field of the P^*-model show that there are various ways to make the concepts of Q^* and V^* empirically applicable. A number of studies assumes that output and velocity follow a deterministic (growth) path in the long run. For instance, Christiano (1989) calculates potential output with the assistance of a linear time trend. Especially in the 1960s and early 1970s, this method was the accepted methodology for evaluating potential output.[17] The Bank of Japan (1990) also employs a linear time trend to determine equilibrium velocity of the main targeted monetary aggregate in Japan. A problem with this approach is that without a good understanding of the factors underlying the trend in velocity, it is impossible to tell if and when the trend will come to an end or change. On the other hand, in the study of both HPS (1991)[18] and Christiano (1989), equilibrium velocity (of $M2$) in the United States is measured by its average value over the sample period.[19] This choice was prompted by the results of unit root tests indicating that the hypothesis of a unit root could not be rejected. Because of this, the crucial assumption of the P^*-model was not violated. When velocity does have a unit root, the use of its mean as a proxy of the equilibrium value leads, however, to a non-stationary price gap. In this case, the hypothesis that P and P^* are cointegrated cannot be accepted, implying that the P^*-model is not suitable for forecasting future movements in the price level.[20]

In a provocative study, Nelson and Plosser (1982) demonstrate that macroeconomic time series in general contain a unit root. This finding refers in particular to velocity (V). In the situation of non-stationarity of real output and/or velocity, a measure for equilibrium values of both variables can be derived either from structural models or filters. Examples of the former approach can be found in HPS (1991) and Ebrill and Fries (1991). These studies use estimates of potential output from Braun (1990), who derives them by combining a Phillips curve-based estimate of the natural rate of unemployment with Okun's law.[21] Furthermore, Reimers and Tödter (1994) — like Kole and Leahy (1991) — apply a simple estimated long-run money demand function to assemble equilibrium velocity V^*.[22] Hence, in the latter approach it is necessary to make assumptions about the future course of the variables that influence velocity and this strand of research is therefore contingent upon a richer set of assumptions than the linear trend 'models'.

When real output and velocity are non-stationary, their equilibrium values can also be obtained by using a filter technique. Hoeller and Poret (1991) and Kool and Tatom (1994) among others use the Hodrick—Prescott filter (HP filter), which is an appropriate filter for stochastic trends (King and Rebelo, 1992). Since I shall apply another filter technique to generate V^* and Q^* (namely the Kalman filter), a few sentences will be devoted to the HP filter, so that the main features of both techniques can be compared. The HP filter is most extensively used by proponents of real business-cycle models, but it is just as useful in the context of the P^*-model. This filter can help anatomize an observed shock into a permanent and a temporary component.[23] Technically, the HP filter is obtained by minimizing the sum of the squared deviations of the actual series from its time-varying trend under the restriction that the sum of the squared second differences (that is, the acceleration or deceleration of the trend) does not exceed a certain value chosen by the user. This value is known as the 'smoothness' factor (λ in the notation of King and Rebelo, 1992). Choosing a large λ imposes the view that most variations in a time series stem almost entirely from transitory shocks. Choosing a very small λ is consistent with the opinion that virtually all variations in a time series can be attributed to changes in the trend and hence are driven by permanent disturbances. In extracting the low frequency component from the series, this filter uses both backward and forward observations. After application of the HP filter, time series which are integrated up to the second order ($I(2)$) are rendered stationary, provided that the smoothing factor is chosen correctly. As can be expected, a critical degree of smoothing exits below which the resulting trend leaves the character of an original non-stationary series unaffected, while the deviations from this trend are just still stationary. In Hoeller and Poret (1991), the selected smoothing factor ensures stationarity of the price gap, which is required by the P^*-approach.

From an economic viewpoint, the main drawback of the HP filter is the lack of a sound economic underpinning. It is a rather mechanical tool that hardly offers space for economic interpretation of the outcomes. Another shortcoming concerns the two-sidedness at the end of the sample, since future data are not available. As a result, the level of uncertainty in the estimates of Q^* and V^* will be greater at the end of the sample, because almost no information is available about the long-term effects of the latest shocks.

With the exception of the HP filter, all other approaches just considered suffer from important shortcomings for studying periods where structural shifts in macroeconomic equations or changes in the properties of time series take place. The main sources of instability in — the characteristics of — time series and in aggregate macroeconomic relations are various types of misspecification on the one hand and behavioural changes on the other. As an example of the latter source, one can think of the case where the (estimated) coefficients in an equation are different for some subperiods of the available sample due to, for instance, changes in (monetary) policy during the period over which the estimation was carried out. Thus, the estimated parameters at some period cannot subsequently be used to assess the impact of other policy regimes (the Lucas critique is an example of instability in economic relationships caused by shifts in policy regimes; Lucas, 1976). The point is that the determination of potential output and trend velocity is based on ex-post estimation and the economic relations are assumed more or less stable over time. To make things more concrete, one can for example think of the establishment of the German monetary union in July 1990. In the third quarter of 1990, all data, for example, the money stock and interest rates, were the first all-German economic data forthcoming. This event can be readily qualified as a shock hitting the German economy, which has also had implications for the assessment of German monetary policy (see Issing, 1992). Ignoring the possibility of breaks in economic relationships can lead to imprecise conditional out-of-sample forecasts or systematic forecast errors (rendering the P^*-model less useful and less reliable as a benchmark in forecasting inflationary pressures). In many cases, the answer to such instabilities has been to engage in an extensive specification search. Often, new explanatory variables (among which dummies) are added to the original specification. Mostly, the included variables only have a weak theoretical foundation and cease to be relevant for the specification and explanation as soon as another data period is considered. As will be explained below, the use of the Kalman filter technique offers an opportunity to obviate a large part of the problems of the ex-post approaches.

3.2   The Kalman Filter Technique: Theory and Backgrounds

At the heart of the Kalman filter technique lies the wide spread recognition among economists of the fact that estimated equations in macroeconomics tend to display instabilities over time and that the properties of time series are prone to changes over time.[24] By contrast to the ex-post alternatives, the Kalman filter method explicitly accounts for the effects of economic and/or political disturbances and allows us to analyse what happened shortly after the facts occurred. This is a satisfactory feature, because in reality the main problem economic agents face day by day is how to interpret new information and how to adjust their views and expectations accordingly, irrespective of the stability of the past and current economic environment. In this respect, economic actors must have some notion about the nature of new observations.

For example, new facts may be interpreted as permanent or temporary changes in economic variables. Because the perception of new information is surrounded by uncertainty, it is logical to represent this uncertainty by a probability distribution of the possible character of new information. Given the prior probabilities for all conceivable circumstances, people will eventually detect the true nature of new observations. Hence, learning takes place and is, technically speaking, the result of the confrontation of the realization of the variable under review in period $t + i$ $(i = 1,2,...)$ with the expectation at period t following from the prior probabilities. The resulting posterior probability leads to a new prior distribution and to a new expectation. This also implies that the character of economic relationships is sometimes — thoroughly — revised. Continuing on the same line of thought, if the economic environment really changes over time, observations from the remote past may contain information that has become obsolete. In such situations, old observations should have a low impact on the establishment of a better understanding of the present state of economic affairs.

The Kalman filter technique offers an opportunity to cope with the above considerations. In short, the Kalman filter combines both recursive estimation techniques and Bayesian learning processes and therefore appears an appropriate tool for analysing economic relations. Recursive estimation, where each additional observation is processed at the time it becomes available, mimics on-line decision making and thus corresponds more closely to decision-dependent economic models (Kool, 1989, p. 32). For my purposes, this on-line property is very useful for computing potential output and trend velocity as will be demonstrated below. Bayesian learning, on the other hand, is closely connected with a view of the world in which changes take place all the time. For this reason, it appears to be a suitable tool for analysing structural shifts in a recursive framework.

More technically, I apply the so-called multi-state Kalman filter (MSKF) algorithm developed and implemented by Kool (1989) to proxy the equilibrium variables.[25] The starting point for the MSKF method is a general state space framework. This formulation explicitly accounts for the time-dependency of the model's parameters. Suppose a variable y is related to a k-dimensional vector x of explanatory variables (including an intercept and/or a time trend). Such a state space model may look like:

$$y_t = \zeta_t x'_{t-1} + \epsilon_t \qquad (2.17)$$

$$\zeta_t = \Gamma_t \zeta_{t-1} + v_t \qquad (2.18)$$

with: ϵ, v =   white noise

ζ =   vector of k parameters describing the state of the system

Γ =   transition matrix linking ζ_t to ζ_{t-1}

The state space model consists of a measurement equation (2.17) and a transition equation (2.18) describing the dynamics of the state parameters ζ (in other words: the transition of the old parameters to the new ones). The stochastic vector ζ_t follows a k-dimensional normal distribution. The k x k matrix Γ describes the dynamics of the transition equation. The elements of the transition matrix have to be specified by the user before running the algorithm. The scalar measurement error ϵ_t and the transition error vector v_t are supposed to be independently distributed. Here, ϵ_t is assumed to be normally distributed with mean zero and variance $\sigma^2 h_t$, where the multiplicative factor h is assumed to be time-invariant. By allowing the variance level to change gradually in time, it is — like the other model parameters incorporated in ζ — treated as an unknown stochastic variable. Consequently, this procedure explicitly takes account of the phenomenon of heteroskedasticity and is in line with the Bayesian methodology.[26] The vector v_t follows a multivariate normal distribution with mean vector zero and covariance matrix $\sigma^2 M_t$. The assumption of constant parameters ($\zeta_t = \zeta_{t-1} = \zeta_{t-2}$, and so on) is now equivalent to the assumption that the relationship does not change in time, which implies that the transition matrix is the identity matrix ($\Gamma = I$).[27]

The time-variation in the parameters linking elements of x to the endogenous variable y can be clarified by a slightly more abstract presentation of the 'statistical model' (Kool, 1989, pp. 94–5). The probability model for the observation process can be written as:

$$(y_{t+1}|\zeta_{t+1}) \sim N(\zeta_{t+1}x'_{t+1}, \sigma^2_t h) \tag{2.19}$$

This equation is equivalent to the measurement equation (2.17). The state equation (2.18) can be replaced by the following three equations.

$$(\zeta_t|I_t) \sim N(z_t, \sigma^2 R_t) \tag{2.20}$$

$$(\zeta_{t+1}|I_t) \sim N(\Gamma_t z_t, \sigma^2 R_{t+1|t}) \tag{2.21}$$

$$R_{t+1|t} = A^{-0.5} \Gamma R_t \Gamma' A^{-0.5} \tag{2.22}$$

It is assumed that the posterior normal distribution for the parameter vector ζ_t is captured in (2.20), where I_t is the available information set up to and including observation y_t and R_t is the covariance matrix of ζ. z_t is the estimate of ζ_t, which has come about by using all information up to and including period t. The prior normal distribution of next period's parameter vector ζ_{t+1}, conditional on information up to and including period t, equals expression (2.21). The term $R_{t+1|t}$ is the conditional covariance matrix of ζ. This covariance matrix is derived from a transformation of the covariance matrix in period t (R_t). The character of this transformation process is determined by two factors. The first element is the transition matrix Γ mentioned earlier. The second factor is diagonal matrix A with elements smaller than or equal to one and larger than zero. This matrix is called the discount matrix. It enables the user to regulate the speed and magnitude with which the regression parameters change over time. The situation in which matrix A is identical to a unit matrix, corresponds to the case of deterministic parameters. The smaller a diagonal element of A, the larger the variability of the corresponding element of vector ζ. Summarizing, the time-dependency of ζ_t is incorporated by discounting the relative weight of old data (that is, values of x in the past) in the parameters of the normal distributions (see equations (2.19) to (2.22)). The rationale behind the inclusion of discount factors is treated below.

In practice, the Kalman filter offers the opportunity to adjust the estimates of ζ over time by employing a two-stage procedure. The first step boils down to generating an optimal forecast of y in period $t + 1$ ($\tilde{y}_{t+1}$) with the help of the prediction equation, given the available information up to and including period t. When in period $t + 1$ the true value of y becomes available, it is known to what extent $\tilde{y}$ differs from y. Subsequently, by means of the updating equation, which is used as soon as new information in the form of next period's prediction error, that is, the recursive residual, is established, it is checked whether the state parameters require some adjustment.

However, one might have much more confidence in the constancy of some coefficients than in the constancy of other parameters. This provides an argument for a different treatment of new information in updating all parameters, which can be regulated in the MSKF algorithm by choosing different discount factors in one regression (by means of matrix A). For example, assume for a moment that y is the demand for a consumer good depending on only two exogenous variables: income (x_{1t}) and taste (x_{2t}). A priori, one expects the impact of income on y to be more or less stable throughout the years. Taste on the other hand may well change rather quickly through time possibly due to the influence of mass media on people. In other words, short-run movements in the parameter on taste seem more plausible than short-run fluctuations in the coefficient on income. Hence, the informational content of old observations concerning taste must diminish more rapidly than that with regard to income.

From the above, it is clear that in empirical work the implementation of the MSKF method requires prior knowledge of the economic relation in question. The user must have some idea of the transition matrix (Γ), the variance factor of the observation equation ($\sigma^2 h_t$) and either the covariance matrix of the transition error factor ($\sigma^2 M_t$) or the discount factors attached to the individual elements of vector x (matrix A). If one assumes that all these unknown parameters can be stacked in a vector θ (Kool, 1989, p. 80), the general state space model in equations (2.17) and (2.18) may be rewritten as:

$$y_t = \zeta_t x'_{t-1} + \varepsilon_t \tag{2.23}$$

$$\zeta_t = \Gamma_t(\theta_t)\zeta_{t-1} + v_t \tag{2.24}$$

As exact modelling of the above transition equation (2.24) is rather troublesome because of insufficient knowledge of vector θ, the MSKF method has the built-in capacity to implement several models with different values for the elements of this parameter vector simultaneously. The economic interpretation of this feature is quite simple. People are continuously exposed to new information. Since the possible responses to new facts are countless, the use of just one model (with fixed characteristics) would by no means be a reflection of reality. Besides, no single model holds for all times. The MSKF algorithm applied accounts for this aspect. In other words, it belongs to the class of 'Parallel Filtering' models. Kool (1989) puts the features of these models in a nutshell:

> The basic idea of parallel filtering methods in general is that a parameter vector θ with unknown and potentially time-dependent value is squeezed into a finite set, roughly spanning the space of values θ may take. A set of parallel models is simultaneously estimated in a recursive manner, where each model corresponds with one given parameter vector θ from the discrete set. The individual model's forecasts are combined into a single weighted forecast of the process under consideration, with the relative weights attached to each model depending on its relative success in forecasting in the recent past. (p. 91)

A (complicated) non-linear interaction exists between the various parallel models, which enables the MSKF method to deal with both gradual and abrupt changes in θ. This feature is extremely attractive since it facilitates a clear distinction between 'normal' and extraordinary large prediction errors. The latter type of forecast errors is normally classified as outlier shocks. The German unification mentioned earlier is an example of a very large shock.

When implementing the MSKF method the first n models are always describing situations in which normal-sized errors occur, while the remaining models describe the behaviour of an economic variable in case of excessive large shocks. The former models are always used simultaneously by the MSKF method. The nature of new information and the prior probability distributions on the different models determine to what extent the MSKF method updates the parameter estimates. By contrast, the outlier models are used parallel to the normal-sized error models only if the MSKF method detects on the basis of a so-called tracking signal that the forecasting performance of the standard-sized error models is extremely bad. Another signal indicates when the adjustment has been completed and the outlier models may be ignored again until the next break signal. The combined prior probability on outlier models must be much smaller than the total prior probability on 'standard-sized' models of course (otherwise each prediction error could be labeled an outlier). Therefore, in the empirical work, I shall set the total prior probability on the first n models at 95 percent, while the prior probability on the 'large error' models then will be the remaining 5 percent.

The degree to which outliers influence the next period's parameter estimates depends on the extent to which the outlier is related to structural shifts in the economic relation under review. If a substantial prediction error emerges, because a permanent change in the relation has taken place, this shock should have a significant impact on these estimates. On the other hand, if an outlier is totally unrelated to structural changes, it ought not affect the estimates a great deal. In order to increase the robustness of the MSKF method to outlier shocks, a correction mechanism is incorporated to reflect the fact that in some circumstances it is preferable to let an outlier influence the parameter estimates quickly and in other situations to ignore an outlier almost completely. The initial estimate of the effects an outlier could have is based on the perceived character of former outliers.

Apart from the obvious advantages of the MSKF method over the ex-post approaches, it also has its drawbacks as successful implementation of this method demands a sensible choice of the number of models to use and the specification of each model. This aspect mirrors both the potential strength and the major weakness of the method (Kool, 1989, pp. 119–23). The free choice of the number of models to be used and their specification enables the modeller to tackle almost every possible forecasting problem, but enhances the number of conceivable misspecifications explosively. For instance, the reduction of the informational value of past observations heavily relies on the discount factors chosen by the user. When the discount factor on a parameter is unity, the weight of observations in the past in the current parameter estimate is not reduced. A discount factor well below unity, will generally increase the parameter's speed of adjustment after a shock. Such an increased parameter sensitivity may be undesirable when in reality the parameter only changes gradually and smoothly (or very rarely). In conclusion: too much discounting may lead to too much parameter adjustment. Therefore, the method's flexibility requires the user to have a marked amount of knowledge of its characteristics.

After this brief survey of the technical and methodological aspects of the MSKF method, I now move on to the clarification of the use of this technique in the context of the P^*-framework. In subsequent chapters, I shall employ the MSKF algorithm to track movements in velocity (V) and real output (Q) in several European countries in a univariate regression framework. Suppose that variable y in equation (2.23) stands for velocity (V) or output (Q), respectively. The explanatory variables are an intercept and a linear time trend.[28] In the empirical analysis, six alternative parallel models are formulated. The first three models are continuously used in forecasting V or Q, while the remaining models are used only in the case of an outlier. Model 1 is treated as a benchmark model. The other models are specified in terms of their difference with model 1. Model 1 is used as the model representing mostly temporary shocks with discount factors close to one. In this model, forecasts errors are assumed to be predominantly incidental with little impact on the parameter estimates. Unlike model 1, model 2 supposes that prediction errors arise generally due to unexpected permanent shifts in the intercept (that is, the level of the endogenous variable; this is approximately an IMA(1,1)-process). In this case, the forecast error is almost completely reflected in the new estimate of the constant term. Model 3 accounts for the occurrence of unexpected permanent changes in intercept and trend at the same time and represents the case of permanent growth rate shifts in V or Q (which closely corresponds to an IMA(2,2)-process). The remaining models have corresponding characteristics with respect to large outliers.

Let us now suppose that economic actors form a forecast of, for instance, velocity in period $t + 1$ based on all available and relevant knowledge up to and including period t. This prediction reflects the expected actual velocity in period $t + 1$. Hence, it contains information about the anticipated future course of velocity. Viewed in this light, the forecast can serve as a proxy for trend velocity (V^*).[29] In the same way, an empirically meaningful measure for potential real output (Q^*) will be derived. Combining the estimates of V^* and Q^* and using the actual money supply (M), I finally obtain a proxy for P^* as well.[30]

APPENDIX 2A UNIT ROOTS: THEORY AND TESTING STRATEGY

During the last decade, the issue of stationarity of time series has attracted much attention. Economists became aware of a new set of econometric difficulties that arise when one or more variables of interest have unit roots in their time series representations. Standard asymptotic distribution theory often does not apply to regressions involving such variables, and inference can go seriously astray if this is ignored. A lengthy paper by Campbell and Perron (1991) surveys unit root econometrics. As the starting point for the explanation of unit roots, it is often useful to think of a macroeconomic time series w_t as the sum of several components with different properties.

$$w_t = TD_t + Z_t \qquad (A2.1)$$

Here TD is a deterministic trend and Z denotes the noise function or stochastic component of w. The unit root hypothesis concerns the behaviour of the noise function, but the specification of the deterministic part is crucial in testing this hypothesis. Although TD_t can be specified in many ways, the leading postulate is that TD is linear in time t, that is:

$$TD_t = \kappa + \delta t \qquad (A2.2)$$

κ is a constant and t represents a linear time trend. In my empirical research, I also assume that this is the correct representation of the deterministic component of the time series under consideration.[31]

Following Campbell and Perron (1991), the noise function Z_t can be described by an autoregressive-moving average process:

$$A(L)\, Z_t = B(L)\, e_t \qquad\qquad (A2.3)$$

where $A(L)$ $\{= 1 - \zeta_1 L - \zeta_2 L^2 \ldots - \zeta_c L^c\}$ and $B(L)$ are polynomials in the lag operator L of order c and d, respectively, and e_t is a sequence of independently and identically distributed innovations. The noise function Z_t is assumed to have mean zero, as the deterministic trend includes the mean of w_t. Furthermore, it is hypothesized that the moving average polynomial $B(L)$ has roots strictly outside the unit circle. Thus, equation (A2.3) summarizes the univariate dynamics of the process Z_t.

One can now distinguish two alternative models for w_t. In the trend-stationary model, the roots of $A(L)$, the autoregressive polynomial, are strictly outside the unit circle (that is, greater than one in absolute value) so that Z_t is a stationary process and w_t is stationary around a trend. In the difference-stationary model, Z_t has one unit autoregressive root and all other roots strictly outside the unit circle (that is, $\zeta_1 = 1$ and $\zeta_2 = \zeta_3 = \ldots = \zeta_c < 1$). In this case, $\Delta Z_t = (1 - L)Z_t = Z_t - Z_{t-1}$ is a stationary process and Δw_t is stationary around a fixed mean. The unit root hypothesis is that w_t is difference-stationary or that random disturbances permanently alter the level of the series. The trend-stationary and the difference-stationary models are generally referred to as I(0) and I(1) models, respectively.

In practice, the testing strategy of the unit root hypothesis begins by considering the simplest case where the noise component Z_t (the series w_t less its deterministic trend) is an AR(1) process with no moving average component:

$$(1-\zeta L)\, Z_t = e_t \qquad or \qquad Z_t = \zeta Z_{t-1} + e_t \qquad\qquad (A2.4)$$

Here Z_t has a unit root if ζ has the value one. In this case, Z_t can also be written as the value at some reference point in the past plus all subsequent changes:

$$Z_t = Z_0 + \sum_{j=0}^{t-1} e_{t-j} \qquad\qquad (A2.5)$$

Clearly, all past disturbances have an enduring effect on the future trajectory of the noise component: the process is non-stationary. It is not difficult to see that long-term forecasts of economic variables with a stochastic trend will depend on all past shocks and the variance of the forecast error will increase without bound. The process in expression (A2.4) can also be rewritten as

$$\Delta Z_t = \rho Z_{t-1} + e_t \qquad or \qquad \Delta Z_t = \rho w_{t-1} - \rho TD_{t-1} + e_t \qquad (A2.6)$$

where $\rho = \zeta - 1$. Here the null hypothesis of a unit root is given by $\rho = 0$, while trend-stationarity implies that $\rho < 0$.[32] Later, I discuss how the procedures are modified if allowance is made for additional serial correlation.

Since I am interested in the properties of the stochastic component of w_t (Z_t), a common strategy is first to 'detrend' the series and analyse the time series behaviour of the estimated residuals. Under the above premise, the unit root hypothesis can be tested by estimating the following regression:

$$\Delta w_t = \tau TD_t^* + \rho w_{t-1} + e_t \qquad (A2.7)$$

and using the t-statistic for testing $\rho = 0$, denoted t_ρ.[33] Under the null hypothesis of a unit root, the asymptotic distribution of t_ρ is non-normal and varies with the trend specification. For (i) $TD_t = 0$; (ii) $TD_t = \kappa$; or (iii) $TD_t = \kappa + \delta t$, critical values for the asymptotic distribution of t_ρ can be found in Fuller (1976, p. 373). As it is unknown a priori which set of deterministic regressors to include,[34] I apply the sequential testing strategy introduced by Perron (1988), which starts from the most general trend specification (an intercept and a first-order trend polynomial) and tests down to more restricted specifications (see below).

I now consider the case where the noise function Z_t obeys an ARMA(c,d) process (expression (A2.3)), rather than the AR(1) model (equation (A2.6)). In other words, there is serial correlation in the stochastic component (Z_t). Here a new issue arises, namely that the asymptotic distribution of the statistic t_ρ in first order autoregressions such as (A2.7) depends on the correlation structure of the data. Hence, modifications are necessary to overcome this dependency on nuisance parameters. I have opted for the parametric correction advocated by Dickey and Fuller (1979) among others. This correction is motivated by the case of a pure AR(c) process, that is, $A(L)Z_t = e_t$. In this case, we can write:

$$\Delta Z_t = \rho Z_{t-1} + \sum_{i=1}^{c-1} \gamma_i \Delta Z_{t-i} \qquad (A2.8)$$

with $\rho = \{(\Sigma_{j=1}^c \alpha_j) - 1\}$ and $\gamma_i = -\Sigma_{j=i+1}^c \alpha_j$.[35] As before, the noise component Z_t has a unit root if $\rho = 0$. The regression equation then takes the form:

$$\Delta w_t = \tau TD_t^* + \rho w_{t-1} + \sum_{i=1}^{k} \gamma_i \Delta w_{t-i} + e_t \qquad (A2.9)$$

with $\kappa = \rho - 1$. In the case of a pure AR(c) process, the asymptotic distribution of t_ρ obtained from (A2.9) is the same as the asymptotic distribution of t_p obtained using a first-order autoregression (equation (A2.7)). In practice, it is often quite difficult to choose the correct truncation lag parameter k, because the order c is usually unknown.[36] In order to determine the value of k, I follow a data-dependent procedure suggested by Campbell and Perron (1991), which is easy to implement and is likely to yield tests with better size and power properties. I start with some upper bound on k, say k_{max}, chosen a priori. If the last lag included is significant (using the standard asymptotic distribution), I select $k = k_{max}$. If this is not the case, I decrease the order of the estimated autoregression by one until the coefficient on the last lag included is significant. However, if none is significant, I select $k = 0$ and expression (A2.9) collapses into equation (A2.7).

So far I have focused on the case of I(0) versus I(1) variables (which is, in fact, the main case of interest to macroeconomists). This excludes the possibility of multiple unit roots. Dickey and Pantula (1987) have formulated a general testing procedure allowing an arbitrary number of unit roots. The core of this method is that before the presence of just one unit root can be tested, the possibility of multiple unit roots has to be investigated. The procedure tests the null hypothesis of n unit roots against the alternative of $n - 1$ unit roots. Since most of the economic time series appear to have one or two unit roots, I shall restrict myself to the examination of a situation in which a time series has three unit roots at the most. The first step involves estimation of equation (A2.10):

$$\Delta^3 w_t = \mu TD_t + \beta \Delta^2 w_{t-1} + \sum_{i=1}^{k} \theta_i \Delta^3 w_{t-i} \qquad \text{(A2.10)}$$

When the null hypothesis of three unit roots ($\beta = 0$) has to be rejected, it must be checked if w_t has exactly two unit roots. Hence, I proceed by estimating relation

$$\Delta^2 w_t = \omega TD_t + \lambda \Delta w_{t-1} + \sum_{i=1}^{k} \xi_i \Delta^2 w_{t-i} \qquad \text{(A2.11)}$$

When this hypothesis is also rejected (that is, λ is significantly different from zero), the next and last step involves a test on precisely one unit root ($\rho = 0$).

$$\Delta w_t = \tau TD_t^* + \rho w_{t-1} + \sum_{i=1}^{k} \gamma_i \Delta w_{t-i} \qquad \text{(A2.12)}$$

Substitution of equation (A2.2) in expression (A2.12) gives

$$\Delta w_t = \kappa^* + \delta^* t + \rho w_{t-1} + \sum_{i=1}^{k} \gamma_i \Delta w_{t-i} \qquad \text{(A2.13)}$$

If $\delta^* = 0$, there is no time trend; if $\rho = 0$, the series has a unit root (that is, it is non-stationary). If the series has a unit root, κ^* is interpreted as its drift.

Expression (A2.13) acts as a starting point for my testing strategy for one unit root. This procedure implies a sequence of tests that runs from general to restricted alternative hypotheses. By means of likelihood ratio statistics constructed by and tabulated in Dickey and Fuller (1981), it is possible to test for the simultaneous occurrence of a unit root, a constant and/or a time trend in expression (A2.13). The test statistic is a conventional t-test, which, however, does not follow the standard t-distribution.

NOTES

1. In an edited version of the article, Hallman et al. (1991) have investigated the forecasting quality of a number of alternative inflation models. These models include an output and velocity gap model, an ARIMA (0, 2, 1)-model and a Treasury-bill model, where the price gap is replaced by the lagged quarterly change in the yield of 90-day Treasury bills. The Root Mean Squared Forecast Error appeared to be lowest in the P^*-model. Therefore, the authors concluded on page 853 that: 'the P^*-forecasts are superior to the alternatives'. It also turned out that the forecast errors of some models could be partly explained by the differential between the inflation forecasts from the respective alternative models and the P^*-model.
2. For an in-depth discussion of the technical and algebraic features of the Kalman filter method the reader is referred to Harvey (1991) and Kool (1989).
3. If the lagged price gap influences both P and P^*, the regression outcomes of the traditional P^*-model are difficult to interpret. I return to this issue in Section 2.2.2.
4. For example, an ad hoc assumption that seems to conform reasonably well with annual US data over the 1955–88 period is to use the previous year's inflation rate as the lagged information.
5. In Appendix 2A, I briefly discuss the (econometric) techniques that are generally applied to uncover these empirical properties as well as the testing strategy of the unit root hypothesis.
6. The distribution of the t-statistic for this coefficient is nonstandard. Dickey and Fuller (1979) derived representations for the limiting distribution of the estimator γ that holds when $\gamma = 0$. Notice that, if the price gap is dropped from the equation, this t-statistic is precisely the Augmented Dickey-Fuller test statistic (ADF) for testing the hypothesis of a unit root in inflation.
7. On the basis of formal tests, HPS (1989) reject the hypothesis of a unit root in the price gap — that is, the price gap series appears to be stationary in logarithms — but the same test does not reject a unit root in inflation. These results support a model specification in accordance with equation (2.5). A simple way to test whether the first difference of $p - p^*$ should have been included is to ask whether equation (2.5) improperly omitted the second lag of the price gap $(p_{t-2} - p_{t-2}^*)$. The Lagrange multiplier test indicates that the latter variable does not belong in expression (2.5) (HPS, 1989, Table 2, p. 11). Moreover, in the period 1954–88, parameter γ was not significantly different from zero.
8. As HPS (1989, p. 12) rightly state, money may well influence nominal GNP. Thus, in neo-Keynesian models, inflation is also to a great extent determined by monetary phenomena.
9. A formal proof can be found in HPS (1989, p. 26).
10. Earlier research by Rasche (1987) reveals that the estimated lag coefficients found in HPS (1989) are quite similar to the first four lag parameters ensuing from an autoregressive representation of an ARIMA(0, 2, 1) process where the estimated value of the single moving average parameter is about −0.65 (see PR, 1990, p. 6). To put it differently, the fourth order autoregressive structure assumed in HPS's expression (2.5) is a close approximation to the infinite order AR structure of an ARIMA(0, 2, 1) model of the logarithm of the GNP

deflator, since 88 percent of the coefficient weights in an infinite geometric distributed lag with an estimated moving average coefficient of −0.65 is achieved by lag four. Rasche's model looks like:

$$\Sigma_{i=0}^{\infty} (0.65)^i \, \Delta\pi_{t-i} = \mu_t$$

or equivalently

$$\Delta\pi_t = -\,0.65 \, \Delta\pi_{t-1} - 0.42 \, \Delta\pi_{t-2} - 0.27 \, \Delta\pi_{t-3} - 0.18 \, \Delta\pi_{t-4} - \Sigma_{i=5}^{\infty} \Delta\pi_{t-i} + \mu_t$$

The only difference between equation (2.5) and the latter expression is the inclusion of the price gap in the former. However, this term is an appropriate addition to the time series model in the latter, if p and p^* meet the principles of cointegrated variables (and are I(2)). Under these conditions deviations of p from p^* are not only transitory, but the time series p can also be described by an ECM (as argued in the main text).

11. EF (1991) determine the most appropriate specification of the inflation equation on the basis of the J-test and JA-test from Davidson and MacKinnon (1981) and Fisher and McAleer (1981), respectively. These tests examine whether there is information in a rival expression not contained in the model under investigation by adding the predicted values of the rival equation as regressors. If the estimated coefficients are significant, the model is said not to reject the rival equation.

12. In an unpublished version of their paper, Reimers and Tödter (1992) also included changes in the costs of production factors labour and capital in the equation.

13. In most Western European countries, the monetary authorities have adopted the latter policy, i.e. they seek to achieve price stability in terms of a constant inflation rate.

14. Note that equation (2.1) holds true by identity and can be consistent with an entirely different causal ordering: inflation could originate from a different process and money could adjust subsequently to accommodate a higher price level (IMF, 1994).

15. This means that the monetary authorities in both the UK and the US have not tried to fix monetary conditions but have consistently followed an accommodating monetary policy (Funke and Hall, 1994). Hence, the response to an increase in prices has been to let the money supply rise.

16. To address the issue of causation, I have performed simple Granger causality tests on inflation and monetary expansion for the countries under consideration in the next three chapters. In all instances, I find evidence that money influences prices and vice versa.

17. Laxton and Tetlow (1992) have shown that the history of measuring potential output mirrors economic thought regarding the importance of the supply side of the economy and economists' understanding of it.

18. Interestingly, in a revised version of the original P^*-model, Orphanides and Porter (1996) show that assuming a constant equilibrium velocity of M2 for the US over the period 1959.2—1996.1 is not an accurate representation. Therefore, they examine the comovements of velocity and the opportunity cost of money suggested from traditional money demand formulations as alternative source of information regarding potential changes in equilibrium velocity and compute the change in V^* implied by that relationship.

19. It is easy to show that HPS must assume that future income velocity of money remains constant and is equal to one.

20. Hoeller and Poret (1991) conclude that a unit root in velocity in the United States is present when semi-annual data in the time span 1960—90 are submitted to (Augmented) Dickey-Fuller tests. This implies that velocity did not tend to revert to some mean value or deterministic time trend in the long run.

21. Okun's law states that the ratio of the percentage shortfall in output during a recession to the percentage point increase in the unemployment rate is roughly equal to three. According to Adams and Coe (1990), Braun's approach has, however, a number of drawbacks. The most

important is that his estimates of potential output depend entirely on the estimates of the natural rate of unemployment and embody no further information on the structural determinants of potential output.

22. Recently, Mayer (1995) and Tewes (1995) have criticized RT's model. Their main objection is that wealth effects should have been explicitly incorporated in RT's long-run velocity equation used to compute V.

23. Harvey (1991) has demonstrated that the HP filter actually uses an ARIMA(0, 2, 1) structure in this decomposition of time series.

24. See Kool (1989, Chapter 1) for an extensive exposition of the ideas underlying the use of the Kalman filter.

25. Actually, a good understanding of the functioning of the sophisticated Kalman filter technique can only be achieved by studying its technical features in detail. However, such a technical explanation is beyond the scope of this book. Therefore, the discussion below will be in rather informal terms and will chiefly focus on aspects that are of interest as part of the ultimate goal, namely the construction of Q^* and V.

26. To be precise, σ_t is modelled as a stochastic variable following an inverse gamma-distribution. Its time dependency is caused by the application of a discount factor, equal to 0.975 in empirical research (Kool, 1989, p. 153).

27. In fact, it must be assumed that the covariance matrix of the transition error vector v_t is zero $(\sigma^2 M_t = 0)$.

28. Although this approach differs to a certain extent from conventional empirical research where economic variables are added as regressors in the estimation equation, it expresses my view that an intercept and a time-dependent trend will cover many economic influences on a variable which are difficult to specify and sometimes have a flimsy theoretical underpinning. In addition, these effects may change considerably over time. Moreover, the above objection is for the greater part met by the fact that the parameter on both the intercept and time trend is 'automatically' adjusted if necessary. Hence, the constructed equilibrium variables can be regarded as a sophisticated extrapolation of the actual time series.

29. Bomhoff (1991), Dueker (1993a) and Hein and Veugelers (1983) use a (different) Kalman filter technique to forecast velocity in a multivariate framework.

30. In the empirical implementation of the P^*-concept, I have not constructed proxies for P^* based on the actual time series of P. In this 'direct' approach, one cannot distinguish between the impact of real and monetary disturbances on the inflation process anymore. Note that the latter feature is in fact the novelty of the P^*-model.

31. In practice, TD_t can be far more complicated of course.

32. Diebold and Rudebusch (1989) have rightly stressed that much of the empirical literature relevant to the persistence debate examines the existence of a permanent component, but that this only provides a first step to the more interesting question of the importance of the permanent component. I shall, however, not dwell on this subject.

33. Differencing equation (2A.1) gives:

$$\Delta w_t = \Delta TD_t + \Delta Z_t \qquad \text{(i)}$$

Substitution of expression (2A.6) in equation (i) results in

$$\Delta w_t = \Delta TD_t + \rho w_{t-1} - \rho TD_{t-1} + e_t \qquad \text{(ii)}$$

Recall that $TD_t = \kappa + \delta t$, so that after rearranging several terms we finally obtain:

$$\Delta w_t = TD^* + \rho w_{t-1} + e_t \qquad \text{(iii)}$$

where: $TD^* = \delta^* t + \kappa^*$, $\delta^* = -\rho\delta$ and $\kappa^* = -\delta + \rho\delta - \rho\kappa$

Thus the trend t must be included to make sure that regression equation (A2.7) in the main text nests both the null hypothesis of a unit root and the alternative hypothesis that w_t is stationary.

34. Serious problems arise when the set of deterministic variables TD_t employed to construct Z_t differ from the true deterministic influences present in time series w. For example, suppose no deterministic regressors are included but w has in fact a nonzero mean. Hence, the intercept is wrongfully omitted when constructing the stochastic component Z_t in time series w. In this case, the power of the test will decrease to zero as the mean increases in absolute value (see the 'rules' 4 and 5 in Campbell and Perron 1991, p. 151).

35. ρ is the difference between the sum of the autoregressive coefficients and one. Notice that virtually the same method is applied by Hallman, Porter and Small (1989; see Section 2.1).

36. The outcome of unit root tests is sensitive to the particular choice of this truncation lag parameter. Several factors may explain this. For instance, too few lags may adversely affect the size of the test. Furthermore, the introduction of too many lags may reduce power (see Campbell and Perron, 1991, pp. 154–5).

3. Testing the P^*-Model for Four Initial ERM Members

Inflation targets are a central ingredient in the Bundesbank's monetary strategy, serving as a basis to derive the monetary target. The Bundesbank's commitment to the latter is a mere strategic one; in contrast, the inflation target is the Bank's overriding long-run concern.

von Hagen (1995), p. 119

1 INTRODUCTION

In this chapter, I apply the P^*-concept for four founding members of the European Exchange Rate Mechanism (ERM), namely Belgium, France, Germany and the Netherlands. These countries have participated in the ERM from the creation of the European Monetary System (EMS) in March 1979. That is, I investigate whether their equilibrium price levels are tied to domestic money stocks. Contrary to most previous P^*-articles, both a narrow and a broad monetary aggregate (*M1* and *M3*, respectively) will be used in the analysis. Apart from theoretical arguments to consider both monetary aggregates, this choice is consistent with the evolution of the central monetary target in many Western countries. Indeed, throughout the decades, monetary policy makers have focused on different central monetary variables in reaction to erratic developments of particular monetary aggregates.

This chapter is not confined to a mere description and presentation of the econometric results ensuing from testing the P^*-model for these countries. Various related issues, such as the evolution of the actual key economic variables incorporated in the P^*-framework (for example, inflation, velocity and output), will be discussed in the context of relevant recent economic literature. For example, many empirical and theoretical studies are devoted to the possible impact of the ERM on inflation convergence across its members or to long-term trends in the velocity of narrow and broad monetary aggregates (or, equivalently, the stability of national money demand functions). Moreover, the P^*-framework is connected with a particular monetary strategy, namely monetary targeting. Many economists commonly associate the Bundesbank with this concept. In fact, the Bundesbank was the first central bank to announce and pursue monetary goals after the breakdown of the Bretton Woods System, and has been one of the few central banks commited to such a strategy in the past decade (von Hagen, 1995). By contrast, Belgium and the Netherlands have always joined various exchange rate arrangements to stabilize their currencies against the German mark since the collapse of this System.[1] This policy choice was motivated by the fact that Germany is the most important trading partner of both countries and that Germany's reputation as a country pursuing consistent counter-inflationary policies is undisputed. By pegging to the German mark, one actually expects that German monetary policy and, in the longer run, the level of German inflation are imported by the Netherlands and Belgium. In order to assess the policy relevance of the price gap model, the recent history of monetary policy in these countries will be dealt with as well.

The plan of this chapter is as follows. In Section 2, I take a preliminary look at the actual economic variables featuring in the P^*-framework. Here, I also examine their time series properties using the unit root testing procedure outlined in Appendix 2A. Section 3 presents the results of the multi-state Kalman filter (MSKF) estimations of potential real output (Q^*) and equilibrium velocity (V^*).[2] Subsequently, I determine long-run or equilibrium price levels (P^*) and the components of the price gaps. The appropriateness and applicability of the P^*-framework is empirically investigated in Part 4. With respect to the choice of the dynamic inflation specifications for individual countries, I refer to Section 2.2.3 of Chapter 2, where a reasonable case for variations in these expressions among countries is made. In addition, the recent history of monetary policy in individual countries will be sketched to see whether the regression results may have contained useful information for monetary policy makers. Section 5 concludes.

2 A PRELIMINARY LOOK AT THE ACTUAL DATA

In this chapter, I use seasonally adjusted quarterly data. Apart from the data on *M1* and *M3* which are obtained from the respective national central banks, all figures have been taken from the *BIS*-databank.[3] The income variables are, depending on the availability, GNP or GDP. The real income data are in 1985 prices. Only for Belgium, the real and nominal income figures are interpolated according to the quarterly pattern of industrial production. Table 3.1 contains information about inflation, real GDP/GNP growth and the velocity of *M1* and *M3* over different subsamples covering the period 1970.1—1992.4. Here, inflation is defined as the change in the GDP/GNP deflator $(\pi_t = \ln P_t - \ln P_{t-1})$.[4] The entire sample is broken down into several subperiods. I distinguish a pre-ERM and ERM period, whereby the latter is again divided into two subperiods.

Table 3.1 Inflation, economic growth and velocity of M1 *and* M3[a]

	INFLATION (in percentages)							
Sample	1970.1—1992.4		1970.1—1978.4		1979.2—1984.4		1985.1—1992.4	
	M	SD	M	SD	M	SD	M	SD
Belgium	1.3	0.8	1.7	0.9	1.3	0.6	0.8	0.4
France	1.8	0.9	2.1	0.8	2.3	0.8	0.8	0.4
Germany[b]	1.0	0.8	1.4	1.0	0.9	0.4	0.8	0.5
Netherlands	1.2	1.3	1.9	1.2	1.0	1.2	0.4	0.5
	GROWTH RATES OF REAL GDP (in percentage points)							
Sample	1970.1—1992.4		1970.1—1978.4		1979.1—1984.4		1985.1—1992.4	
	M	SD	M	SD	M	SD	M	SD
Belgium	0.7	2.2	1.0	2.1	0.2	2.6	0.8	1.9
France	0.8	0.7	0.9	0.7	0.4	0.7	0.7	0.5
Germany[b]	0.7	1.4	0.8	1.6	0.3	1.1	0.8	0.9
Netherlands	0.6	1.7	0.9	1.7	0.2	2.0	0.7	1.2
	VELOCITY OF *M1* (in levels)[c]							
Sample	1970.1—1992.4		1970.1—1978.4		1979.1—1984.4		1985.1—1992.4	
	M	SD	M	SD	M	SD	M	SD
Belgium	1.1	0.2	0.9	0.1	1.1	0.1	1.3	0.1
France	0.9	0.1	0.8	0.1	1.0	0.0	1.0	0.1
Germany[b]	1.5	0.1	1.6	0.1	1.6	0.0	1.4	0.1
Netherlands	1.2	0.1	1.2	0.1	1.2	0.1	1.1	0.0
	VELOCITY OF *M3* (in levels)[c]							
Sample	1970.1—1992.4		1970.1—1978.4		1979.1—1984.4		1985.1—1992.4	
	M	SD	M	SD	M	SD	M	SD
Belgium	0.4	0.0	0.4	0.0	0.4	0.0	0.3	0.0
France	0.4	0.0	0.4	0.0	0.4	0.0	0.4	0.0
Germany[b]	0.5	0.1	0.6	0.0	0.5	0.0	0.5	0.0
Netherlands	0.4	0.1	0.5	0.0	0.4	0.0	0.4	0.0

Notes:
a. M denotes the mean and SD stands for the standard deviation of the series multiplied by 100. The data are quarterly and seasonally adjusted.
b. The German figures are multiplicatively corrected for the breaks in the time series due to German unification in 1990.3.
c. Velocity is defined as nominal GDP divided by the respective money definition.

2.1   Inflation

The upper part of Table 3.1 shows that inflation differs markedly across the four countries in the whole sample. The average inflation rate was the highest in France, followed by Belgium, the Netherlands and Germany, respectively. The underlying figures also demonstrate that the Netherlands and Belgium, and to a lesser extent Germany, are sometimes confronted with a negative rate of inflation, while France never experienced a considerable deflation. Turning to the different subsamples, one can observe a clear convergence towards low inflation. The variability of inflation has also dropped to a considerable extent with the passage of time. France stands apart, with a slight increase in inflation in the period from the outset of the EMS in March 1979 until the mid-1980s.

On the basis of these figures, some economists conclude that the ERM has been successful in bringing inflation under control after 1983 (Bini Smaghi, 1994). Caporale and Pittis (1993) argue that the stronger exchange rate commitment, or equivalently the time required for inflation-prone countries to acquire the anti-inflationary reputation of the Bundesbank, has induced convergence in economic variables closely connected to monetary policy. They believe that the channel through which the ERM has influenced the rate of inflation is via its impact on expectations (see also Giavazzi and Giovannini, 1989). This has resulted in a marked reduction in inflation differentials vis-à-vis Germany in the last subperiod.[5] In their perception, France in particular provides a good illustration of a country with a past record of relatively high inflation, that has switched from inflation discipline 'at home' to external discipline and is now 'toeing the line' (see Argy, 1992). Theoretically, these studies seem to favour the instrumentalist view of the EMS. In this view, the fact that the exchange rates are not allowed to float freely implies the synchronization of monetary behaviour among the member countries and, therefore, the convergence of the inflation rates. However, for this mechanism to work, two conditions must be satisfied. First, the authorities must pursue monetary and fiscal policies that are compatible with the rigidity of the exchange rate. Second, the public must be convinced that such policies will really be followed (see, for example, Loureiro, 1992b).

According to the literature just cited, the exchange rate constraint has thus ultimately functioned as an instrument for achieving internal objectives (that is, a reasonble degree of price stability). A large number of empirical studies on the contribution of the ERM on inflation convergence among its members oppose this view, though.[6] In a nutshell, the pattern of inflation since the late 1970s is not EMS specific (see also Loureiro, 1992a). The same path of inflation is discernible in all present member states of the European Union. This suggests that common factors have been at work. Here, one can for example think of the increased commitment to price stability by the monetary

Table 3.2   ADF unit root tests[a,b]

Log levels (H_0 = time series have one unit root (I(1), m = 1)

Variable	GDP deflator	Real GDP	$M1$-velocity	$M3$-velocity
	A	B	C	D
Belgium	−1.3 (t, 5)	−2.4 (t, 4)	−1.3 (t, 2)	−3.2 (t, 3)
France	−2.6 (t, 3)	−2.7 (t, 2)	−1.7 (t, 2)	−2.3 (t, 5)
Germany	−2.2 (t, 1)	−2.2 (t, 4)	−2.4 (t, 3)	−4.6' (t, 2)
Netherlands	−3.1 (t, 3)	−2.9 (t, 0)	−3.3 (t, 4)	−2.3 (t, 2)

Growth rates (H_0 = time series contain two unit roots (I(2), m = 2)

Variable	GDP deflator	Real GDP	$M1$-velocity	$M3$-velocity
Belgium	−1.7 (c, 5)	−3.4' (c, 5)	−4.2' (c, 3)	−3.6' (c, 2)
France	−2.8 (t, 4)	−3.2' (c, 3)	−5.2' (n, 4)	−2.9' (c, 4)
Germany	−2.2 (c, 3)	−3.2' (c, 3)	−3.1' (c, 1)	−3.3' (c, 0)
Netherlands	−3.0 (t, 4)	−3.5' (c, 7)	−3.8' (c, 5)	−2.9' (c, 2)

Notes:

a. The testing equation looks like: $\Delta^m x_t = \tau\, TD + \rho\, \Delta^{m-1} x_{t-1} + \Sigma_{j=1}^{8} \gamma_j \Delta^m x_{t-j}$. Here, x is the dependent variable, m denotes the order of integration (m = 1 or 2) and TD stands for the deterministic variables (intercept and/or time trend). The t-statistic of ρ on the lagged level of the dependent variable is used to determine whether the endogenous variable is stationary or not.

b. The entries show the relevant test statistic. The information in parentheses indicates the use of a constant only, c, or a constant and a trend, t. A specification without an intercept and time trend is indicated as (n, ...). The figure in parentheses shows the number of lagged dependent variables included (j). The symbol ' means that the statistic differs significantly from zero at the five percent level.

authorities (which was facilitated by the process of granting central banks greater independence[7]) and changing public attitudes towards inflation (Collins, 1988).

I now turn to the question whether inflation in the selected countries is stationary. To put it another way, I want to know whether or not the underlying stochastic process that generated the series can be assumed to be invariant with respect to time. Column A of Table 3.2 tells us that the GDP deflator has to be differenced twice to obtain stationarity in all cases (that is, ln P is integrated of order two, I(2)). The presence of two unit roots implies that the change in the inflation rate ($\Delta\pi$) tends to revert to some mean value or deterministic time trend over the sample periods. Therefore, I take this variable as the dependent term in the estimation equations in Part 4.

2.2   Economic Growth

Unlike the inflation rates, the average growth rates of real GNP/GDP differ only slightly in the four countries. On balance, France beats every other country with a real economic growth rate of almost 0.8 percent on a quarterly basis. This was mainly due to its favourable economic growth figures in the 1970s and early 1980s (see Table 3.1). The nearly identical expansion rates of real output in the Netherlands and Germany (of about 0.65 percent) is a sign that these countries are economically closely linked. Another interesting aspect is the relatively low standard deviation of the French growth rate.[8]

In the first two subsamples, the differences in economic growth are considerably more pronounced; the dispersion between the worst and best performing economies amounted to about 0.2 percentage points. In the beginning of the 1980s, all countries experienced a substantial deceleration in expansion rates. In relation to the 1970s, the unweighted average growth rate fell from 0.9 to a mere 0.3 percent. The Dutch and Belgian economies in particular were seriously hit by the worldwide economic downswing. Thereafter, a recovery of the world economy presented itself. The countries benefitted from this upsurge roughly to the same extent. Just as in the pre-EMS period, Germany occupied an extreme position, but this time in a positive sense. Interestingly, the variability of the growth figures has displayed a weak downward trend in the course of time. This may hint at changes in the characteristics, that is, the amplitude and intensity, of business cycles.

Formal stationarity tests strongly point to the presence of one root unit in real GNP/GDP (see column B of Table 3.2). These findings are consistent with the results of other studies (for example, Christiano and Eichenbaum, 1989). In other words, real GNP/GDP does not tend to revert to some long-run trend. Only first-differencing will yield stationary series of this variable. In economic terms, this implies that the effects of some shocks will not dissipate after several years, but will be permanent instead.[9] The presence of a permanent component would thus mean that some macroeconomic distortions would have a long-lasting effect on the economy. This conflicts with traditional formulations of both Keynesian and classical macroeconomic theories, where output fluctuations, for a variety of reasons, are mostly temporary deviations from a deterministic growth path of natural or equilibrium output. A considerable permanent component implies instead that fluctuations in output in essence mirror permanent shifts in the level of output.

2.3   Velocity of *M1* and *M3*

In Section 4, the P^*-model will be estimated with velocity gaps based on a narrow and broad monetary aggregate (*M1* and *M3*, respectively). These different measures of money correspond to the two main approaches of the theory of money demand, i.e. transactions theories, and asset or portfolio theories.[10] Generally speaking, *M1* is defined as the sum of currency in circulation and demand deposits of non-banks. Although the *M3* concept does not comprise the same components in the selected countries, it is in any case composed of *M1* plus time deposits (with up to 2 or 4 years maturity) plus short-term savings deposits.[11] The lower part of Table 3.1 presents a picture of the mean and standard deviation of *M1* and *M3* velocity.

Germany has the highest velocity of money, followed by the Netherlands, irrespective of the definition of the money supply and the subperiod under consideration. Another remarkable feature is that *M1*-velocity is more volatile than *M3*-velocity. Presumably, this stems from the fact that the private sector tries to economize on holdings of *M1*, because its components bear little or no interest.[12] As a consequence, non-banks frequently substitute interest-bearing assets belonging to *M3* for currency or demand deposits or vice versa. Obviously, these portfolio shifts do not affect the (standard deviation of the) broad monetary aggregate, but lead to considerable fluctuations in *M1*. A common characteristic of both concepts of money is that the variability of their respective velocities has diminished in the early 1980s but has again increased somewhat more in recent years (due to the greater variability of nominal output).

Table 3.1 also reveals that *M1*-velocity did not move in the same direction in the four countries. While *M1*-velocity in the Netherlands and Germany declined marginally, France and particularly Belgium encountered an increase. This probably points to differences in the magnitude and impact of financial innovations. In addressing how financial innovation might have affected the demand for narrow money, most studies take the transactions theory of money demand as a starting point (Judd and Scadding, 1982). In general, two features of this theory suggest ways of modelling the impact of financial innovation on the demand for money. The first factor is the role of transactions costs in determining the demand for money. Lower costs of converting other assets into money allow money holders to keep smaller money balances. The second aspect is that innovations in cash management techniques generally mitigate the variance of cash flows, thereby allowing economic agents to reduce their precautionary balances.[13] Both elements have presumably attributed to the substantial decline in *M1*, or equivalently the rise in velocity of *M1*, in Belgium and France.[14] In Figure 3.1, these developments are visualized. On the other hand, the steadily increasing use of German marks for transaction purposes in Eastern Europe in particular has probably largely compensated for factors exerting a downward impact on the demand for banknotes and coin inside Germany (see Seitz, 1995).

As far as *M3*-velocity is concerned, the maximum values were reached without exception in the pre-EMS period. During the entire period, however, the expansion of the *M3* money stock surpassed the growth in nominal output. Consequently, the unweighted average velocity of *M3* came down from approximately 0.5 to 0.4 in the last subperiod. In the economic literature on velocity of (broadly defined) money balances, several explanations are put forward for this phenomenon. In addition to financial innovations and regime shifts, Boughton (1992) lists four other general factors that may have been important determinants of the falling trend in *M3*-velocity: (1) shifts in inflationary expectations; (2) open-economy considerations such as expected exchange rate changes; (3) the effect of non-unitary real income elasticities on velocity; and (4) shifts in the term structure of interest rates.[15]

At this point the question arises whether velocity is stationary or not. If not, one cannot use the HPS 'method' to generate equilibrium velocity (V^*), which simply comes down to computing the average velocity in the sample period. In case of nonstationarity, I have to construct trend velocity in another way. For *M1*-velocity, the ADF tests do not reject the null hypothesis of one unit root in *M1*-velocity in all countries (see column C of Table 3.2). By contrast, the findings with respect to the velocity of *M3* are mixed; the velocity of *M3* in Germany turns out to be stationary, whereas this variable contains a unit root in the other countries. The interpretation of this outcome is that after monetary or real disturbances have taken place, German *M3*-velocity returns to its equilibrium value over time, which is not true for the other countries. This feature is closely linked with the often observed relatively stable demand for broad money in Germany (which is extremely relevant for its monetary policy).[16] These results are corroborated by numerous other studies. Fase and Winder (1993) find that the stability of the demand for money not only seems to increase for broader definitions of monetary aggregates but that it also shows to some extent a remarkable pattern suggesting less stability for smaller countries.

A possible explanation for the stationarity of *M3*-velocity in Germany is that since the breakdown of the Bretton Woods System in the early 1970s the Bundesbank has adopted a (single) monetary policy regime: monetary targeting. By contrast, the other countries switched from some form of monetary targeting to exchange rate targeting in the past decades. Nowadays, they give priority to the exchange rate objective which makes it, *de facto*, impossible to follow an independent domestic money supply policy at the same time, because the interest rate instrument must be reserved for the exchange rate target. As pointed out in Section 3 of Chapter 2, regime shifts can be a prominent source of instability in macroeconomic time series. Von Hagen (1993) mentions another plausible explanation for the relative stability

Figure 3.1 Velocity of money (in levels)

Belgium

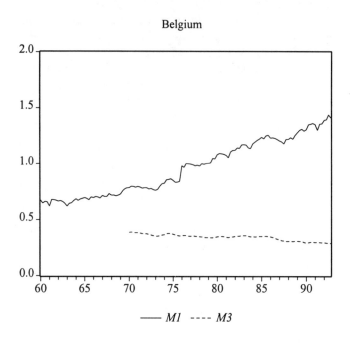

France

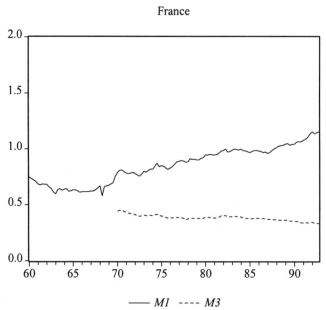

Figure 3.1 Velocity of money (in levels; continued)

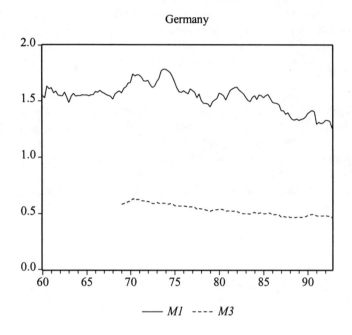

Germany

——— *M1*   ---- *M3*

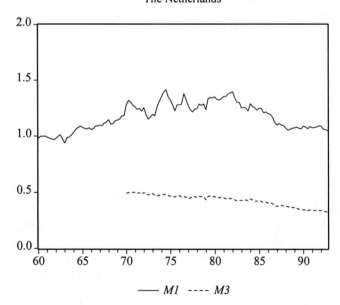

The Netherlands

——— *M1*   ---- *M3*

of German money demand. He states that it should not be very surprising that the German velocity of money passes a large number of tests addressing various alternative forms of instability since the early 1960s. This feature can be predominantly attributed to the minor extent of financial innovations in Germany over the past three decades compared to, say, the United States, where financial innovation was widespread (see also Goodhart, 1989, especially Section II).[17]

Non-stationary velocity can have important practical implications for monetary policymakers. The existence of a permanent component (that is, a unit root) in velocity implies that some monetary of real shocks persist through time. As a consequence, some fluctuations in velocity represent permanent movements in trend velocity (V^*). For monetary authorities, this persistence is rather unsettling. Persistence would call into question, at a fundamental level, the appropriateness of any monetary action aimed at controlling inflation through monetary targeting. For if the stochastic component in velocity is significant and there is no steady trend to which velocity returns, attempts at influencing velocity and thereby inflation are at best misguided. In addition, when each movement in velocity is largely permanent, the costs and benefits of monetary actions are very different from those in a situation where movements are transitory. In other words, the 'price' of higher or lower velocity over the whole future path must be weighed in the policy calculus. Analytically, the central issues for monetary authorities with money supply targets are to identify the factors that are driving changes in velocity and to determine whether these factors are permanent or temporary. In Section 3.3, I try to tackle this issue with the help of the Kalman filter technique, which offers the opportunity to disentangle structural shifts from transitory factors in time series.

3 THE DETERMINATION OF THE PRICE GAPS

This section follows the sequence of steps to be taken to construct price gaps that satisfy the assumptions of the P^*-approach. To start with, the equilibrium levels of real output and velocity (in logarithms) will be proxied with the multi-state Kalman filter (MSKF) technique as outlined in Section 3.2 of Chapter 2. This algorithm is implemented with six parallel models, including three outlier models. The first three models represent the underlying data generating process in case normal-sized prediction errors occur. Model 1 treats forecast errors as largely transitory. Model 2 accounts for permanent shifts in the level of the actual series, which implies that the coefficient on the intercept is allowed to change over time. Model 3 is designed to deal with permanent shocks in the growth rate of the series. In this case, the parameter on the linear time trend may exhibit fluctuations. Models 4, 5 and 6 are the outlier models and have similar characteristics as models 1, 2 and 3, respectively. To distinguish the normal-sized error systems from the outlier models, I have assumed that the conditional forecast variance of outlier models must be 16 times as high as the conditional forecast variance of normal-sized error models. Finally, the MSKF technique is implemented with uniform initializations for all other input parameters, so as to enhance the comparability of the final results across countries.

Table 3.3 records some summary statistics about the predictive power of sets of models. The statistics considered are the mean absolute error (*mae*), the root mean squared error (*rmse*) and the first order autocorrelation of the forecast error (*foc*) and the Durbin Watson statistic (*DW*). These statistics again confirm that V_{m1}^* is much more volatile than V_{m3}^*. From an economic viewpoint, this could be interpreted to mean that it takes economic agents more thought predicting V_{m1} than V_{m3}; without exception the *mae* and *rmse* of the former are higher. Finally, the Durbin Watson statistic does not indicate autocorrelation problems.

Table 3.3 Summary statistics of the forecast errors in Q* *and* V*

	Trend velocity of *M1*				Trend velocity of *M3*				Potential real output			
	mae	*rmse*	*foc*	*DW*	*mae*	*rmse*	*foc*	*DW*	*mae*	*rmse*	*foc*	*DW*
Belgium	0.033	0.043	−0.160	2.32	0.021	0.026	0.079	1.84	0.016	0.020	−0.051	2.10
France	0.026	0.037	0.001	2.00	0.012	0.017	0.015	1.97	0.007	0.013	−0.130	2.26
Germany	0.029	0.036	0.024	1.95	0.015	0.019	0.089	1.82	0.011	0.014	0.077	1.85
Netherlands	0.035	0.045	0.028	1.99	0.021	0.025	0.006	2.00	0.013	0.017	−0.041	2.08

Notes: *mae* is the mean absolute error, *rmse* is the root mean squared error, *foc* denoted the first order autocorrelation and *DW* is the Durbin Watson statistic ($\approx 2 - 2\,foc$).

Section 3.1 first dwells upon the question which models the MSKF has actually picked in generating the equilibrium variables over time and pays attention to the development of the parameters on both explanatory variables (that is, the intercept and time trend) over the years. In Section 3.2, I take a preliminary look at the — components of the — price gaps and their relation with inflation. Since the gaps and the coefficients on the exogenous variables in the output and velocity estimations appear to move more or less in the same direction in all countries, I shall primarily concentrate on the empirical results for Germany and the Netherlands. This choice is prompted by the proclaimed tight economic links between these countries.

Figure 3.2 Prior probabilities on models for Q*

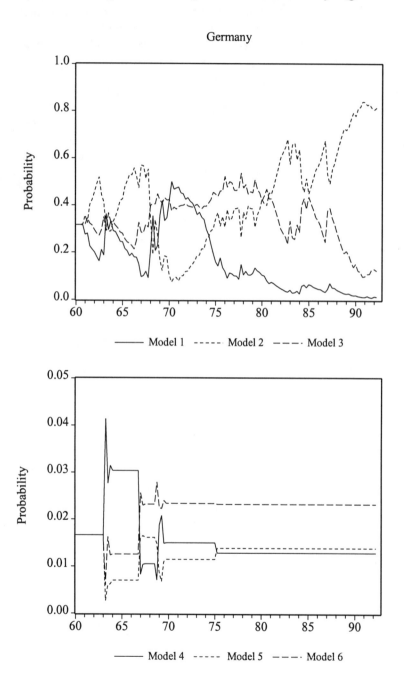

Figure 3.2 Prior probabilities on models for Q* (continued)

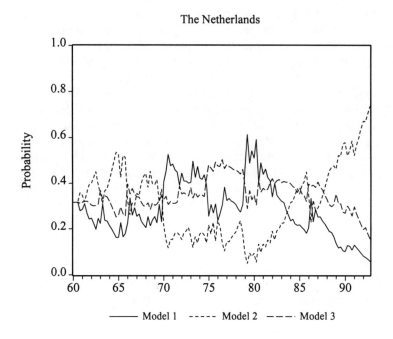

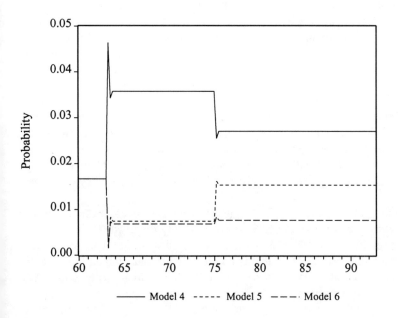

3.1   The Construction of Potential Real Output and Trend Velocity

Figure 3.2 provides a picture of the prior probabilities on the six models used to produce potential real output in both countries. When starting the algorithm, the method does not favour one particular model by assumption. The prior probability on each normal-sized error model is initialized at 31.3 percent (that is, 95 percent divided by 3), whereas each outlier model has a prior probability of 1.67 percent (that is, 5 percent divided by 3). Despite the fact that the specification of the models is identical for both countries, some interesting differences catch the eye. In the case of Germany, the MSKF method regulary switches from one model to another in forecasting real output until the end of the 1960s. From about 1975 onwards, preference for models allowing for permanent changes in coefficients, stands out. Especially from the early 1980s, the prediction errors (or, alternatively, distortions) are mainly interpreted as permanent shifts in the level of Q. Nowadays, transitory shocks are rarely found. Apparently, the nature of the statistical process generating real output has altered remarkably. It has developed from a mixture of different processes into an over-riding preference for the process represented by model 2.

Conversely, for the Netherlands a distinct preference for model 2 originated not long ago. Until the mid-1980s, the method on average assigned an equal weight to the separate models. This stems from the fact that the speed of adjustment of prior probabilities ultimately depends on the information content of each new realization compared to the prediction. An observation that could equally well be generated by every individual model contains little information about the relative attractiveness of each model. In this case, learning is limited and the prior probabilities remain approximately constant, which seemingly happened to be the case in the period up to about 1985. On the other hand, from the mid-1980s onwards, individual observations appear to have the characteristics of one particular model. Thus, 'the degree of learning' increased and the prior probabilities changed substantially resulting in a sharp decline in the prior probability of model 1. As a consequence, the pattern of probability distributions on the normal-sized errors models has recently become quite similar to that in Germany. This could perhaps partly reflect the increased economic linkage between these countries.

Looking at the lower panel of Figure 3.2, one can conclude that the large prediction error models 4, 5 and 6 are not used very frequently in conjunction with the normal-sized error models, indicating that the tracking signal has been chosen properly. For Germany and the Netherlands, the outlier models participated four and two times, respectively, in the estimation procedure. All large shocks in Germany and the Netherlands are located in the first half of the sample period. The large prediction errors in Germany were by turns transitory or permanent, while, by the method's judgement, the breaks in the

Table 3.4   Outlier occurrences in the estimation of Q^*

	Belgium	France	Germany	Netherlands
1 Indication of break at date	74.3	68.1	63.1	63.1
Return to normal estimation in	75.1	69.1	64.1	63.4
2 Indication of break at date		74.4	66.4	75.1
Return to normal estimation in		75.3	67.3	75.3
3 Indication of break at date		80.4	68.3	
Return to normal estimation in		81.4	69.4	
4 Indication of break at date			75.1	
Return to normal estimation in			75.2	

Dutch series have predominantly temporary implications for the parameter estimates.

As additional information, Table 3.4 reports the quarters in which the signal indicated a break and the quarters in which the method returned to normal estimation again. For the sake of completeness, I have also shown the outlier occurrences for Belgium and France. Some of the breakpoints can be perfectly coupled with extraordinary economic and historical events. The first outlier discovered in Germany and the Netherlands can presumably be attributed to bad weather conditions in 1963.1. This quarter was characterized by a large number of lost working days (which led to a reduction of German construction investment of about 25 percent). Since both countries were at that time still rebuilding their countries after World War II, the influence of this contraction was clearly visible in total real output.[18] The second German outlier is not attributable to a specific event. The third break in German real output is probably partly associated with the introduction of a value added tax in January 1968. When the authorities announced this measure, private households decided in large numbers to advance their planned expenditures for 1968. The subsequent drop in consumer spending in the first quarters of 1968 is to a certain extent the mirror image of the upsurge in 1967.4. In the case of France, the first shock is undoubtedly related to the students' protests in May 1968. This social unrest nearly brought the French economy to a standstill.

Not surprisingly, some distortions hit national economies in a similar way and at the same time (for example, the oil crisis in 1973), so that the dates of large prediction errors in individual countries sometimes coincided. It may seem a little bit odd that the large error models are only activated eighteen months after the first energy crisis presented itself. This lagged reaction is quite understandable, however. The tracking signal also triggers the use of the

Inflation Patterns and Monetary Policy

Figure 3.3 Coefficients on intercept and time trend for Q*

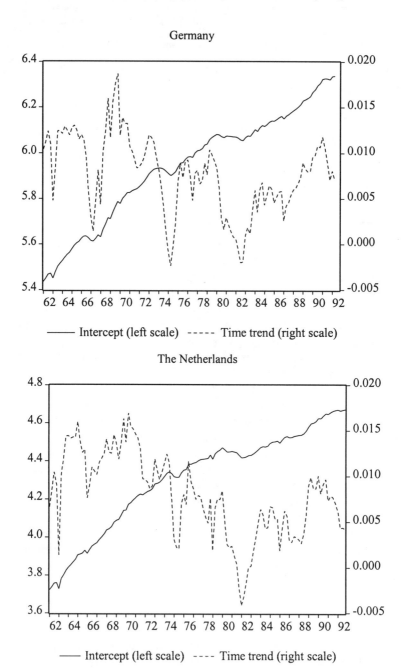

outlier models in the estimation procedure when it detects systematically biased forecast errors. Around 1973, a number of negative residuals emerged in a row indicating that the method systematically overestimated real output. Thus, the method seems quite capable of tracing (well-known) breaks in real output.

Some breaks in the parameters on both explanatory variables can also be discovered by examining the development of these coefficients over time. For this, Figure 3.3 offers a lead. In addition, the first shock can indeed be classified as largely temporary, as the accompanying movements in the coefficient on the linear trend are almost completely neutralized within one or two years. The economic downswing after the oil crisis of 1973 is noticeable in the course of the parameters as well. Owing to the (economic agents') learning process incorporated in the MSKF method, the prior probabilities on the separate outlier models are adjusted in such a way that the likelihood of permanent effects of future disturbances on real output increased: the probability distribution on model 4 (accounting for transitory outliers) dropped — slightly — in favour of the combined prior probabilities on models 5 and 6.

The forecasting accuracy of the individual models used to create V_{m1}^* is depicted in Figure 3.4. Almost from the beginning of the 1960s, the MSKF method does not esteem the appropriateness of model 2 very high, but mainly deploys model 1 and 3 to forecast next period's $M1$-velocity for Germany. The probability that model 2 is the correct model for predicting $M1$-velocity for the Netherlands dropped quickly in the early 1970s. Afterwards, the prior probability on model 2 stabilized around a low level of 5 percent. The interpretation is that this model's predictions of V_{m1} based on all available and relevant information up to and including period t are mostly too far away from the realizations in period $t + 1$. The outlier models are activated once and twice for Germany and the Netherlands, respectively. For Germany, the shock of the unification is clearly noticeable. After analysing the nature of subsequent forecast errors, the MSKF method eventually regards this distortion as a permanent shift in the level of $M1$-velocity.

The movements in the coefficients on the exogenous variables are plotted in Figure 3.5. The parameters on the intercepts exhibited roughly the same pattern. Around 1980, they reached their highest levels in the entire sample. Thereafter, a sharp fall was evident. During the greater part of the sample, the trend coefficients have been negatively signed and displayed rather erratic fluctuations, thus mirroring the volatility of V_{m1}.

Inspection of the statistical aspects of the models applied to create V_{m3}^* reveals considerable differences compared to those used to construct V_{m1}^*. To begin with, the (development of the) prior probabilities are not identical (Figure 3.6). The relevance of model 1 and 3 for calculating the German trend velocity of $M3$ diminishes almost immediately and is practically reduced to nil in the 1980s. Hence, there is strong evidence that model 2 outperforms the

Figure 3.4 Prior probabilities on models for V* with M1

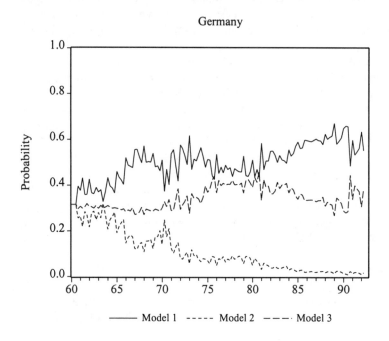

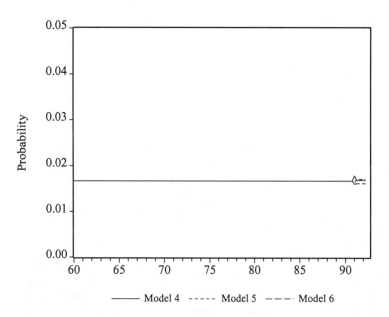

Figure 3.4 Prior probabilities on models for V* with M1 (continued)

The Netherlands

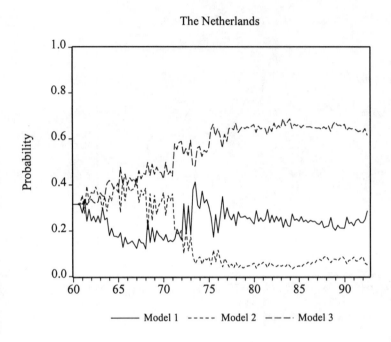

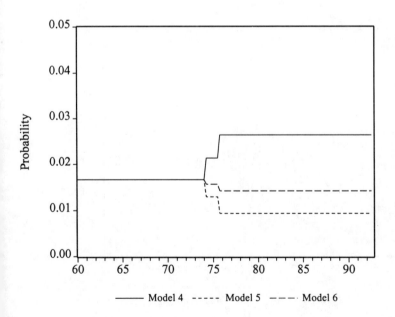

Figure 3.5 Coefficients on intercept and time trend for V* with M1

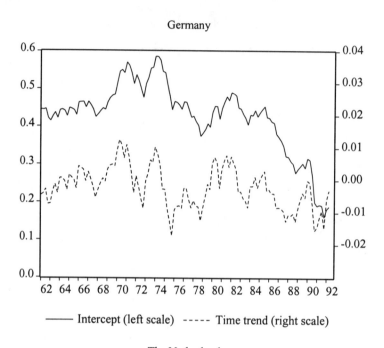

Germany

——— Intercept (left scale) - - - - - Time trend (right scale)

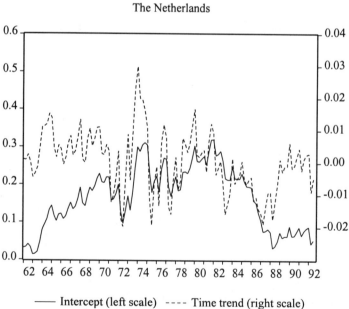

The Netherlands

——— Intercept (left scale) - - - - Time trend (right scale)

other models. This means that most forecast errors are viewed as permanent changes in the level of V_{m3}. Besides, the statistical process of this series does not appear to have changed much in the period under review.[19] In case of the Netherlands, the prior probabilities do not diverge much from their initial value of 31.3 percent, as the availability of new information does not lead to major shifts in the relative weights of the individual models. At the same time, this underscores the ambiguous nature of the statistical process generating Dutch V_{m3}. Finally, the outlier models are only deployed once in case of Germany.

Figure 3.7 plots the behaviour of the coefficients on the intercept and time trend for *M3*-velocity. Obviously, these lines reflect the picture ensuing from the path of the prior probabilities on the various models. For Germany, one can observe a fairly constant (negative) coefficient on the linear trend, which agrees with the low prior probability on model 3. By contrast, the parameter on the intercept is frequently adjusted downward which is logical if we look at Figure 3.6. The Dutch results point to the same steady and smooth decline of the parameter on the intercept.

Table 3.5 ADF unit root tests for the gaps (in levels)

	Price gap		Velocity gap		Output gap
	M1	*M3*	*M1*	*M3*	
Belgium	−5.4′ (*n*, 3)	−6.6′ (*n*, 0)	−6.0′ (*n*, 3)	−7.6′ (*n*, 2)	−6.5′ (*n*, 2)
France	−8.2′ (*n*, 0)	−6.3′ (*n*, 3)	−4.1′ (*n*, 1)	−6.3′ (*n*, 1)	−5.3′ (*n*, 1)
Germany	−6.5′ (*n*, 2)	−7.1′ (*n*, 0)	−5.5′ (*n*, 2)	−4.1′ (*n*, 0)	−7.5′ (*n*, 1)
Netherlands	−7.3′ (*n*, 2)	−4.3′ (*n*, 4)	−5.9′ (*n*, 0)	−7.2′ (*n*, 1)	−8.3′ (*n*, 0)

Notes: The entries show the relevant test statistic. The *n* in parentheses indicates that a specification without an intercept and time trend is used. The figure in parentheses shows the number of lagged dependent variables included. The symbol ′ means that the statistic differs significantly from zero at the five percent level.

3.2 The Construction of P^* and the Price Gaps

The next step involves the investigation of the statistical properties of trend velocity and potential real output on the one hand and the relationship between these equilibrium variables and their actual counterparts on the other. Following the testing procedure described in appendix 2A, the equilibrium variables prove to be integrated of the same order as the original variables. On the basis of the estimates of Q^* and V^* and the actual money supply, I obtain a proxy for P^*. Subsequently, augmented Dickey-Fuller tests are conducted to verify whether the gaps between the equilibrium and actual variables are stationary. Table 3.5 shows that the equilibrium and actual variables meet the

Figure 3.6 Prior probabilities on models for V* with M3

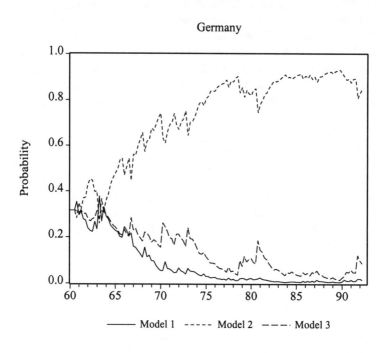

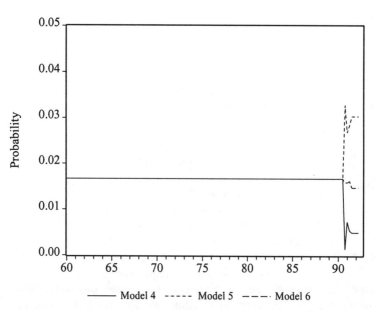

Figure 3.6 Prior probabilities on models for V* with M3 (continued)

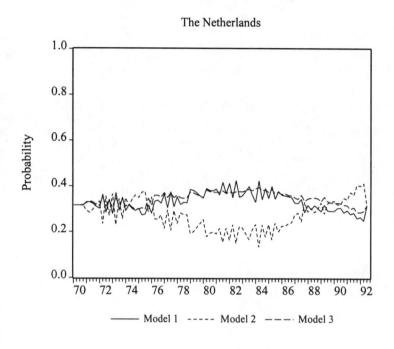

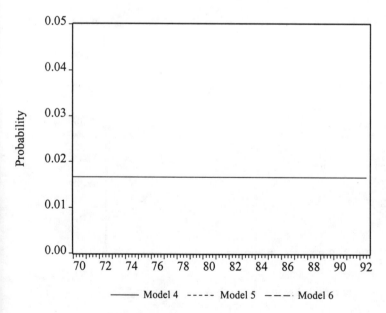

Figure 3.7 Coefficients on intercept and time trend for V* with M3

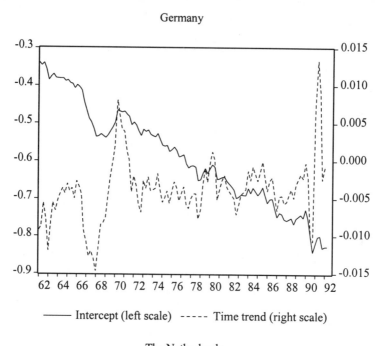

Germany

Intercept (left scale) ----- Time trend (right scale)

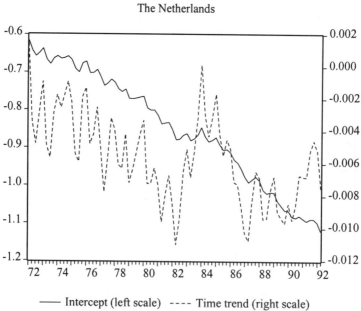

The Netherlands

Intercept (left scale) ---- Time trend (right scale)

criteria of cointegration (including p^* and p). Hence, the estimated gaps satisfy the crucial condition of the P^*-model that deviations of p from p^* are only transitory.

The stationarity of the components of the price gaps is also visible in Figure 3.8: the gaps fluctuate around zero. However, for P^* to be useful as an inflation indicator, the price gap $(p - p^*)$, should vary inversely with the actual inflation rate. When the price gap decreases, the model predicts that prices will tend to rise faster or fall slower toward equilibrium. When the price gap increases, prices should tend to rise slower or fall faster. Upon close visual inspection of Figure 3.8, one can discern certain periods where positive price gaps seems to precede a period of some disinflation. This is most evident in Germany in the time span 1963–67, when the price gap was almost permanently positive and the rate of inflation fell from about 3.75 percent in the first quarter of 1966 to a mere 0.3 percent in the second quarter of 1967. Subsequently, the price gap turned negative for more than one year while inflation rose again to almost 3.75 percent. This figure also allows for detecting large economic disturbances throughout the decades. For instance, relatively large disruptions have occurred in the beginning of the 1970s. These distortions possibly reflect the collapse of the Bretton Woods System in the early 1970s and pertubations ensuing from supply side shocks (notably the first oil crisis). This resulted in negative price gaps around 1975. According to the P^*-model (and other standard economic theories), this should have an upward pressure on inflation. In the case of Germany, an obvious negative peak in the velocity gap of *M3* arose around 1991. This was due to the monetary union formed between East and West Germany on July 1, 1990, which made the Deutsche mark (DM) the only legal tender and the German Bundesbank the sole monetary authority in the unified currency area. On this date, bank deposits of East German residents were made eligible for conversion into DM. Immediately after conversion, East German *M3* amounted to approximately 15 percent of West German *M3*. In contrast, monetary union added an estimated 8.8 percent real output to the currency area (von Hagen, 1993). In view of this discrepancy, actual velocity V suddenly fell (also in relation to the expected or equilibrium velocity V^* based on all relevant and available information up to July 1990) and the Bundesbank repeatedly argued that the excess supply of money created by the monetary union implied a potential for a price-level increase. This reasoning illustrates the Bundesbank's conviction of the price soaring effects of a negative velocity gap (that is, $v - v^* < 0$).

As a preliminary exercise, I plotted the lagged price gap (PG_{-1}) and a change in the inflation rate $(\Delta\pi)$ in a scatter diagram. Figure 3.9 shows a cloud of points through which an estimated 'regression' line is depicted. A negative correlation seems to exits between these variables. Naturally, this partial analysis does not permit strong conclusions about the significance of this relationship. This has to be explored in a richer model. Another issue

Figure 3.8 Inflation and components of price gaps

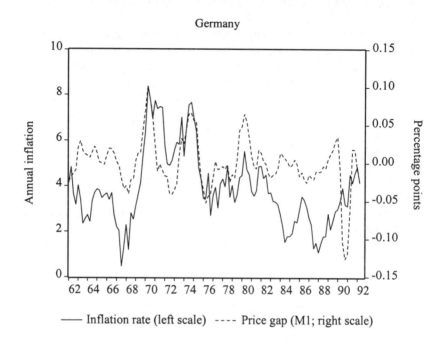

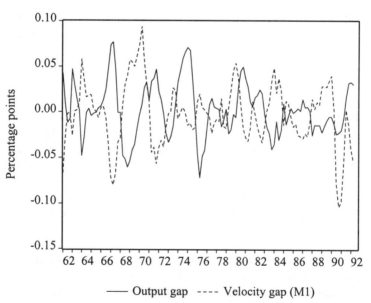

Figure 3.8 Inflation and components of price gaps (continued)

The Netherlands

—— Inflation rate (left scale)   ---- Price gap (M1; right scale)

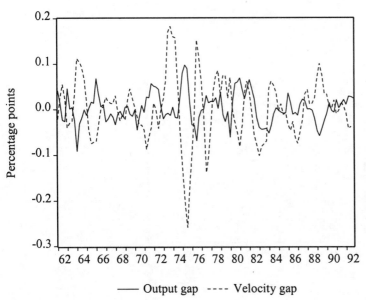

—— Output gap   ---- Velocity gap

Figure 3.9 Scatter diagram of inflation and lagged price gaps

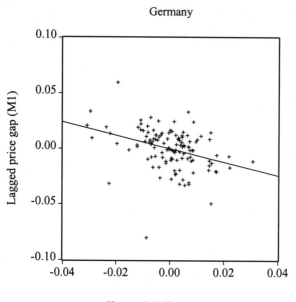

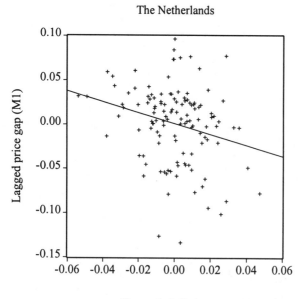

concerns the lag with which the inflation rate responds to a disturbance. It is quite conceivable that the restoration of equilibrium ($p = p^*$) does not take place in one quarter. Consequently, the effect of a shock may be reflected significantly in the inflation rate with a certain lag (not necessarily equal to one period). This underscores the importance of some inquiry of appropriate lag structures in the price gap models to be estimated in the next section.[20]

4 REGRESSION RESULTS

As explained in Section 2.2.3 of Chapter 2, two price gap specifications will be estimated. The benchmark equations have the following format:

$$\Delta \pi_t = \alpha_0 + \alpha_1 PG_{t-n}^{mq} + \sum_{j=1}^{4} \beta_j \Delta \pi_{t-j} + \tau \Delta p_{t-m}^{en} \qquad \alpha_1 < 0 \qquad (3.1)$$

$$\Delta \pi_t = \zeta_0 + \zeta_1 VG_{t-n}^{mq} + \zeta_2 OG_{t-n} + \sum_{j=1}^{4} \beta_j \Delta \pi_{t-j} + \tau \Delta p_{t-m}^{en} \qquad (3.2)$$

$$\zeta_1, \zeta_2 < 0$$

$$\Delta \Delta_4 P_t = \alpha_0 + \alpha_1 \sum_{i=1}^{4} PG_{t-i}^{mq} + \sum_{i=1}^{4} \beta_i \Delta \Delta_4 P_{t-i} + \tau \Delta_4 p_{t-m}^{en} \qquad (3.3)$$

$$\alpha_1 < 0$$

$$\Delta \Delta_4 P_t = \zeta_0 + \zeta_1 \sum_{i=1}^{4} VG_{t-i}^{mq} + \zeta_2 \sum_{i=1}^{4} OG_{t-i} + \sum_{i=1}^{4} \beta_i \Delta \Delta_4 P_{t-i}$$
$$+ \tau \Delta_4 p_{t-m}^{en} \qquad \zeta_1, \zeta_2 < 0 \qquad (3.4)$$

PG, *VG* and *OG* denote the price, velocity and output gap, respectively. The superscript *mq* represents the definition of money used to construct the gaps; PG^{m1} and VG^{m1} are gaps based on *M1*, while PG^{m3} and VG^{m3} are computed with *M3*. The P^*-model assumes the signs of the parameters for the gaps to be negative. p^{en} is the log of energy prices which is hypothesized to pick up the effects of 'imported' price shocks. In equations (3.1) and (3.2), I let the data decide with which lags the gaps enter the expressions. Having established that the log of the GDP deflators are I(2), I have omitted π_{t-1} and $\Delta_4 p_{t-1}$ from the estimation equations. Moreover, insignificant lags of the dependent variable will be deleted from all baseline models.

For each country, the regression results are presented in separate tables with a similar lay out. The upper part reports the outcomes of the specifications with *M1*, whereas the lower half presents the estimations with *M3*.[21] The length of the sample period is dictated by the availability of the data and differs therefore across countries. The empirical outcomes are checked for autocorrelation, heteroskedasticity and nonnormality of the residuals. I also conduct stability tests and test hypotheses involving restrictions on the coefficients of the velocity and output gaps in particular. After having discussed the technical features of the estimations, I focus on the economic interpretation of the results.

4.1   Belgium

4.1.1   Econometric analysis of the estimation results

The estimated expressions for Belgium and their corresponding statistical properties are shown in Table 3.6. The statistical characteristics of the models are quite satisfactory. All coefficients of the gaps have the expected negative signs as predicted by the P^*-model. For model I, a simple specification search indicates that PG^{ml} significantly affects inflation rate after just one quarter. On the other hand, it takes three quarters before a negative price gap based on $M3$ shows up in an increase in the inflation rate. This is quite understandable from an economic viewpoint. Indeed, the transaction motive for holding money is presumably better reflected in $M1$, of which the components bear little or no interest. Discrepancies of actual and equilibrium velocity of $M1$ are thus more likely to influence the inflation rate in the short run than velocity gaps based on $M3$. The latter distortions can also result from portfolio considerations which are not necessarily directly related to economic agents' spending behaviour and inflation.

Another noteworthy aspect of model I is the divergent magnitude of the parameters of the price and velocity gaps when $M1$ or $M3$ is employed to assemble p^*. Estimations with $M1$ lead to a smaller absolute coefficient of the price gap (0.05) than with $M3$ (0.13).[22] For this, the greater fluctuations of the velocity gap based on $M1$ (VG^{ml}) are responsible. By contrast, the coefficient of the output gap is more or less the same in model I_{ml} and model I_{m3} with an absolute value of about 0.15. Although the coefficients of the velocity gaps differs from those of the output gaps, formal Wald tests do not reject the hypothesis of equality of the parameters of both gaps.

Turning to the examination of model II, where the dependent variable is the annual growth rate of quarterly data ($\Delta\Delta_4\,p$), one can conclude that the specification with $M3$ yields more favourable outcomes. All gaps in model II_{m3} contribute significantly to the explanation of inflation, whereas only the output gap possesses informative value in model II_{ml}. Perhaps partly because of the shorter sample period, model II_{m3} scores better with respect to robustness and stability as well. When the complete data set is split into two subsets — before and after the establishment of the European exchange rate mechanism in 1979.1 — the Chow test indicates a break point (BP) in model II_{ml}. Thus, the coefficient vector may not be regarded as constant over the

Table 3.6 Regression results for Belgium (model with M1: sample 1965.1–1992.4; model with M3: sample 1973.1–1992.4)

Model	DV	α_0	GAP	ΔDV_{-1}	ΔDV_{-2}	ΔDV_{-3}	ΔDV_{-4}	$\Delta p_n^{e_n}$	R² (SE)	WALD (Q(8))	FOR (BP)	NORM (ARCH)
I$^a_{m1}$	$\Delta\pi$	0.0 (0.2)	$-0.046\ PG_{-1}$ (2.1')	-0.43 (4.4")	-0.35 (3.2")	-0.25 (2.4)	-0.25 (2.6")	0.016 (2.3')	0.47 (0.57)	(3.2)	0.6[1] (0.8)[2]	5.8 (4.1)
I$^b_{m1}$	$\Delta\pi$	0.0 (0.1)	$-0.047\ VG_{-1}$ (2.2') $-0.13\ OG_{-1}$ (2.4)	-0.42 (4.4")	-0.40 (3.7")	-0.25 (2.2)	-0.24 (2.5)	0.017 (2.5)	0.48 (0.57)	2.9 (3.3)	0.7[1] (0.7)[2]	11.0" (7.3)
II$^a_{m1}$	$\Delta\Delta_{dp}$	0.0 (0.5)	$-0.015\ \sum_{i=1}^{4} PG_{-i}$ (1.2)	1.33 (14.4")	-0.34 (2.9")	-0.34 (3.0")	0.33 (4.0")	0.010 (3.6")	0.74 (0.65)	(11.1)	0.9[1] (3.3")[2]	12.4 (4.6)
II$^b_{m1}$	$\Delta\Delta_{dp}$	0.1 (0.4)	$-0.017\ \sum_{i=1}^{4} VG_{-i}$ (1.4) $-0.051\ \sum_{i=1}^{4} OG_{-i}$ (2.1')	1.33 (14.5")	-0.34 (2.9")	-0.29 (2.5)	0.29 (3.4")	0.009 (3.5")	0.73 (0.64)	3.0 (12.4)	0.9[1] (3.3")[2]	0.4 (4.7)
I$^a_{m3}$	$\Delta\pi$	0.0 (0.4)	$-0.129\ PG_{-3}$ (2.4)	-0.35 (3.0")	-0.25 (1.9')	-0.28 (2.4)	-0.27 (2.2)	0.012 (1.7')	0.53 (0.59)	(1.2)	0.6[3] (0.4)[4]	4.6 (2.8)
I$^b_{m3}$	$\Delta\pi$	0.0 (0.5)	$-0.122\ VG_{-3}$ (2.4) $-0.167\ OG_{-3}$ (2.4)	-0.36 (3.0")	-0.26 (1.9')	-0.28 (2.4)	-0.28 (2.2)	0.012 (1.7')	0.53 (0.61)	1.4 (1.3)	0.5[3] (0.3)[4]	4.8 (2.4)
II$^a_{m3}$	$\Delta\Delta_{dp}$	0.0 (0.3)	$-0.070\ \sum_{i=1}^{4} PG_{-i}$ (3.2")	1.44 (12.9")	-0.50 (4.8")			0.049 (4.1")	0.65 (0.64)	(9.6)	0.7[3] (1.7)[4]	0.4 (0.5)
II$^b_{m3}$	$\Delta\Delta_{dp}$	0.0 (0.2)	$-0.064\ \sum_{i=1}^{4} VG_{-i}$ (2.7) $-0.080\ \sum_{i=1}^{4} OG_{-i}$ (3.1")	1.43 (12.7")	-0.44 (4.6")			0.047 (3.8")	0.65 (0.64)	0.6 (11.4)	0.6[3] (1.4)[4]	0.3 (0.9)

Notes: DV denotes the dependent variable; α_0 is the intercept; *GAP* stands for the price, velocity and output gap, respectively (*PG, VG* and *OG*); $\Delta p_n^{e_n}$ is the change in energy prices. The heteroskedasticity consistent t-values are recorded below the estimated coefficients in parentheses. SE is the standard error of the regression. WALD denotes Wald's statistic (distributed as $\chi^2(1)$) for testing the hypothesis that the parameters on the velocity and output are equal. Q(8) is the Box–Pierce statistic for testing serial correlation. FOR is an out-of-sample prediction (F-statistic) test to examine the stability of the equation ([1]FOR = 85.1; [3]FOR = 88.1). BP is Chow's breakpoint test ([2]BP = 1979.1; [4]BP = 1982.1). NORM is the Jarque-Bera statistic for testing the normality of the residuals. ARCH is a test for fourth order Auto Regressive Conditional Heteroskedasticity with an asymptotic χ^2 distribution. The symbols °, ' and " represent significance at the 10, 5 and 0 percent level, respectively.

Figure 3.10 Recursive estimates of parameters of the gaps and energy prices (model II with M1)

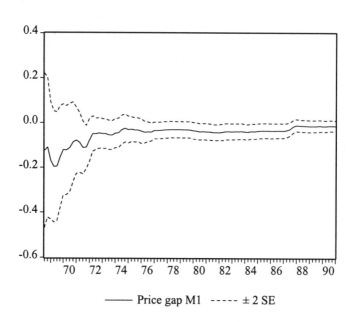

Price gap M1   ----- ± 2 SE

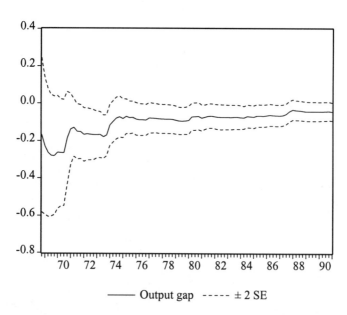

Output gap   ----- ± 2 SE

Figure 3.10 Recursive estimates of parameters of the gaps and energy prices (continued; model II with M1)

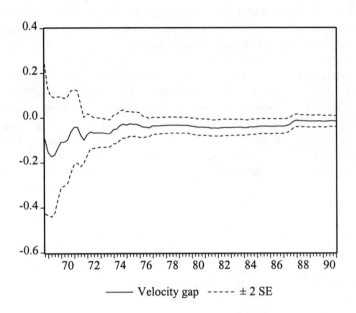

——— Velocity gap ----- ± 2 SE

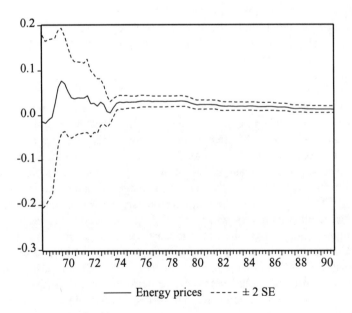

——— Energy prices ----- ± 2 SE

subsets. However, this result just lends weak support for the view that the switch from floating to fixed exchange rates has — slightly — changed the inflationary process in Belgium. I find significant breaks in this model from approximately 1975 up to about 1983 at the beginning of each individual year. So, the observed break in 1979 cannot be fully attributed to the monetary regime switch, suggesting that other factors play a role as well. Judged by a more conventional method to trace the evolution of coefficients, that is, recursive estimation, it is much more likely that from approximately 1974 until about 1983 a gradual instead of a sudden change in (some) coefficients has taken place. The output produced by recursive estimation demonstrate that no parameter in model II_{m1} displays significant variation during this time span (Figure 3.10). However, the recursive coefficient estimates do show jumps around 1970 as the postulated equation tries to digest structural breaks. These relative fierce fluctuations probably mirror the monetary regime shift in 1971 associated with the collapse of the Bretton Woods System.[23] This event seems to have had some repercussions on the dynamics of inflation. The cumulative sum (of squares) test developed in Brown et al. (1975) reveals, however, that the constancy of all parameters over time is beyond question. This finding is buttressed by the ARCH test statistics reported in Table 3.6.

4.1.2 Economic analysis of the estimation results and implications for monetary policy

At this point, one might ask if this framework has any relevance for monetary policy purposes. Before one can answer this question, the function that monetary aggregates perform in the monetary decision making process must be clear. In fact, before 1975, Belgian monetary policy centred on both internal and external goals (to govern business cycle fluctuations and to combat inflation on the one hand and to maintain a fixed exchange rate on the other). Since 1975, only the exchange rate target plays a role in the implementation of monetary policy in Belgium.[24] Hence, Belgian monetary policy has never focused on monetary targeting.[25] Even before several (large) countries had begun to doubt the stability of money demand, the Belgian monetary authorities felt that in a small and open economy the relationship between the exchange rate and inflation was by far more reliable as a guidance for the monetary policy actions than changes in the money supply (Eizenga, 1994). In this respect, the Belgian monetary philosophy has differed from that in the other countries, which in the past have opted or currently opt for the money supply as the intermediary target (see the following subsections). It also explains why the Belgian franc has never floated after the breakdown of Bretton Woods, but joined (together with the Dutch guilder) the mostly short-lived fixed exchange rate experiments of the 1970s (the snake and the snake in the tunnel) and entered the ERM in 1979. In view of this, the P^*-results cannot be translated into policy recommendations.

Table 3.7 *Regression results for France (model with M1: sample 1964.1–1992.4; model with M3: sample 1973.1–1992.4)*

Model	DV	α_0	GAP	ΔDV_{-1}	ΔDV_{-2}	ΔDV_{-3}	ΔDV_{-4}	Δp_n^{en}	R^2 (SE)	WALD (Q(8))	FOR (BP)	NORM (ARCH)
I_{m1}^{a}	$\Delta\pi$	0.0 (0.6)	$-0.048\ PG_{-1}$ (2.2)	-0.74 (8.9")	-0.43 (4.1")	-0.39 (4.0")	-0.30 (3.4")	0.016 (2.6")	0.42 (0.77)	11.8	0.3[1] (0.6[2])	31.4" (0.8)
I_{m1}^{b}	$\Delta\pi$	0.0 (0.0)	$-0.047\ VG_{-1}$ (2.3) $0.10\ OG_{-1}$ (1.5)	-0.67 (7.2")	-0.41 (4.0")	-0.37 (3.9")	-0.29 (3.3")	0.013 (2.2")	0.45 (0.75)	5.8'	0.4[1] (0.9[2])	18.8" (13.4")
II_{m1}^{a}	$\Delta\Delta_q p$	0.0 (0.5)	$-0.014\ \sum_{i=1}^{4} PG_{-i}$ (1.2)				-0.53 (8.3")	0.010 (3.6")	0.41 (0.90)	10.2	0.3[1] (0.1[2])	42.1" (9.6")
II_{m1}^{b}	$\Delta\Delta_q p$	0.1 (0.4)	$-0.016\ \sum_{i=1}^{4} VG_{-i}$ (1.5) $0.046\ \sum_{i=1}^{4} OG_{-i}$ (1.3)				-0.53 (8.3")	0.009 (3.3")	0.43 (0.89)	3.4	0.3[1] (0.5[2])	23.7" (11.1")
I_{m3}^{a}	$\Delta\pi$	0.0 (0.7)	$-0.087\ PG_{-3}$ (2.0)	-0.73 (7.5")	-0.45 (4.1")	-0.38 (3.5")	-0.26 (2.8")	0.012 (2.9")	0.47 (0.52)	2.1	0.7[3] (0.8[4])	1.5 (2.9)
I_{m3}^{b}	$\Delta\pi$	0.0 (0.8)	$-0.080\ VG_{-3}$ (1.8°) $-0.127\ OG_{-3}$ (1.7)	-0.74 (7.5")	-0.47 (4.1")	-0.38 (3.6")	-0.26 (2.8")	0.013 (2.9")	0.47 (0.52)	0.4	0.7[3] (0.7[4])	1.7 (4.5)
II_{m3}^{a}	$\Delta\Delta_q p$	0.0 (0.3)	$-0.035\ \sum_{i=1}^{4} PG_{-i}$ (1.2)	0.26 (2.4)			0.38 (3.6")	0.015 (2.1")	0.35 (0.69)	6.6	0.6[3] (1.8[4])	11.2" (1.7)
II_{m3}^{b}	$\Delta\Delta_q p$	0.0 (0.2)	$-0.025\ \sum_{i=1}^{4} VG_{-i}$ (0.7) $-0.048\ \sum_{i=1}^{4} OG_{-i}$ (1.3)	0.25 (2.2)			0.39 (3.6")	0.015 (2.1")	0.34 (0.69)	0.4	0.6[3] (1.4[4])	14.6" (1.7)

Notes: DV denotes the dependent variable; α_0 is the intercept; GAP stands for the price, velocity and output gap, respectively (PG, VG and OG); Δp_n^{en} is the change in energy prices. The heteroskedasticity consistent t–values are recorded below the estimated coefficients in parentheses. SE is the standard error of the regression. WALD denotes Wald's statistic (distributed as $\chi^2(1)$) for testing the hypothesis that the parameters on the velocity and output are equal. Q(8) is the Box–Pierce statistic for testing serial correlation. FOR is an out-of-sample prediction (F–statistic) test to examine the stability of the equation ([1]FOR = 85.1; [2]FOR = 88.1). BP is Chow's breakpoint test ([3]BP = 1979.1; [4]BP = 1982.1). NORM is the Jarque–Bera statistic for testing the normality of the residuals. ARCH is a test for fourth order Auto Regressive Conditional Heteroskedasticity with an asymptotic χ^2 distribution. The symbols °, ' and " represent significance at the 10, 5 and 0 percent level, respectively.

4.1.3 Recapitulation

Although no policy implications can be extracted from the P^*-framework, it does contain information for future inflationary tendencies in Belgium. Moreover, from a statistical viewpoint the findings are very satisfactory too, since most specifications pass many of the diagnostic checks. However, a slight preference for the models with $M3$ exists, because these prove to be — somewhat — more robust and stable.

4.2   France

4.2.1 Econometric analysis of the estimation results

The regression results for France are tabulated in Table 3.7. A quick glance conveys that the P^*-concept could serve as an useful tool for predicting inflationary tendencies in the French economy in the short run. The price gaps in model I have explanatory power, irrespective of the definition of the money stock. The estimations with the output and velocity gap separately give peculiar results. It appears that the coefficient of the output gap is never significant. Besides, this parameter does not carry the expected negative sign in model I_{m1}. Conversely, the velocity gap either with $M1$ or $M3$ always has a statistically significant negative impact on the dependent variable, with the exception of model II. Hence, the negative correlation between the endogenous variable and the price gap in model I predominantly stems from the significance of the velocity gap. This explains why the coefficients of the price and velocity gaps in the latter specifications are nearly identical.

The statistical properties of the models with $M3$ are obviously better than those with $M1$. This is to a certain extent related to the different sample periods. The late 1960s are characterized by several tumultuous events. This also explains why the residuals of the models with $M1$ are nonnormally distributed. Further, the results of ARCH test for heteroskedasticity in the residuals are sometimes unsatisfactory. As for the stability of the estimated equations, Chow tests do not point to structural breaks at the dates recorded in the tables. In order to verify whether the specifications are stable throughout the entire sample, I have tested for the occurrence of shifts in the relationships at the beginning of each year. This exercise reveals significant breaks in the models with $M1$ from the beginning the 1970s until the late 1970s. The estimated dynamic link between inflation (or its change) and the explanatory variables has apparently been prone to alterations in the course of time. To locate the dates at which the inflationary process underwent major changes more precisely, the equations are re-estimated with recursive least squares (RLS). In the upper half of Figure 3.11, the squared recursive residuals (CUSUMQ) of model II_{m1}^a generated by RLS and some other lines are depicted. The significance of the departure of the solid line representing the test statistic from its expected value, derived under the assumption of parameter constancy, is assessed by reference to a pair of parallel straight

Figure 3.11 CUSUMQ statistic and French inflation

CUSUMQ of model IIa with M1

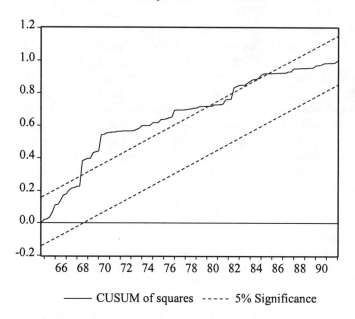

—— CUSUM of squares   ----- 5% Significance

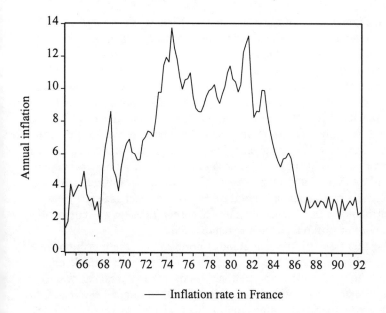

—— Inflation rate in France

lines around the expected value. The mean value line rises from zero at the starting date to one at the end of the sample. When the test statistic does not move parallel to the band spanned by the critical lines, this suggests parameter instability.

Obviously, instabilities come to the fore around 1970–71 and in the beginning of 1980s.[26] Thus, different inflation dynamics are in operation in different episodes. The implications for the coefficients stand out when the regressions are rerun with OLS for the subsamples where the CUSUMQ statistics does not display remarkable jumps (or, equivalently, where the pattern of actual inflation does not exhibit a considerable change). In this case, the regression results nearly always change dramatically, necessitating a reformulation of the conclusions drawn in the above paragraphs. For example in model II_{m3}, none of the gaps significantly contributes to the explanation of the dependent variable over the complete sample. However, the coefficients of the gaps are substantially higher in the period 1973.1–1983.4 than in the entire sample. In addition, they are equal in magnitude (-0.12) with absolute t-ratios ranging from 2.2 to 2.5. The parameters of the lagged dependent variables and their t-values are on the other hand virtually the same as in the benchmark equations. The statistical properties also improve remarkably. In conclusion, the P^*-framework seems to be more valid for France from the beginning of the 1970s until the early 1980s.

4.2.2 Economic analysis of the estimation results and implications for monetary policy

Judged by Figure 3.11, one can argue that periods of instability in the inflation equations appear to be in one way or another related to changes in monetary regimes. Actually, the acceleration of inflation in the beginning of the 1970s concurs with the breakdown of the Bretton Woods System,[27] while the drop in inflation in the early 1980s coincides with an increasing emphasis on nominal convergence and coordination of monetary policies to underpin exchange-rate stability within the European Monetary System. However, even today there is little consensus in economic literature as to the exact consequences of the regime changes.[28] The familiar problem is that observed differences across exchange rate regimes in the behaviour of macroeconomic variables like inflation and output may reflect differences in the economic and/or political environment and not the effects of the exchange rate *per se*.[29] Another difficulty is that our set of empirical observations may be compatible with a number of different economic interpretations.

Keeping these qualifications in mind, I do think that the transition from fixed to flexible exchange rates has to some extent left its mark on the regression results.[30] Under the Bretton Woods regime, France was to a considerable extent constrained in the policies that might be pursued to cushion domestic (demand and/or supply) shocks. Under more flexible rates, in contrast, France had more freedom to conduct policies directed at stabilizing its economic growth (vis-à-vis other countries), but at the cost of stronger fluctuations in inflation rates. Hence, apart from the tensions in the exchange markets due to persistent current-account deficits in the United States and the so-called dollar overhang, inflation accelerated sharply in France as a result of rather ambitious demand management policies and wage indexation in response to rising import prices (Gros and Thygesen, 1992, p. 25). Consequently the development of inflation in the period starting around 1973 and ending at approximately 1983 depends more heavily on local disturbances, which accords with our empirical observation that the coefficient of the output gap is in some cases strongly significant in this sample. This could also be one of the explanations why the P^*-concept is more valid for France in the time span 1973—83.

The deceleration of inflation in the early 1980s, coinciding with the second period of severe parameter instability (Figure 3.11), went hand in hand with a gradual turnaround in monetary and fiscal policy in France.[31] The French authorities became more and more convinced that relying on market adjustment rather than devaluation to improve productivity and achieve competitiveness would lead to a leaner, more efficient economy. To this end, France increasingly committed itself to fight inflation by pegging the franc to the Deutsche mark and giving fiscal consolidation priority (so as to promote exchange rate stability in the European Monetary System).[32] In fact, French macroeconomic policy shifted from 'competitiveness through devaluation' to 'competitiveness through disinflation' (Trichet, 1992). The underlying philosophy was a simple one: getting inflation down was just the first phase. By continuing to have low inflation, lower than its neighbours, France could become more competitive, improve its current account and return to full employment with low inflation. Furthermore, this 'new' strategy was accompanied by structural policies aimed at improving market mechanisms, from the liberalization of prices to the lifting of restrictions on foreign exchange transactions (Blanchard and Muet, 1993; Icard, 1991).

By tying its currency to the Deutsche mark, France has theoretically become unable to determine its own long-run price level.[33] As a result, in the last decade French inflation has (again) become to a greater degree sensitive to foreign (German) monetary developments, diminishing the informative value of the domestic price gaps for inflation. Further research is however needed to test whether the impact of foreign price gaps on French inflation is more important than the 'domestic' gaps under the prevailing system of fixed exchange rates.[34] Here, we also touch upon the issue of (a)symmetry in the European Community examined in numerous studies.[35]

From the above, it implicitly follows that the relevance of the P^*-concept for French monetary policymakers is limited nowadays. However, the Banque de France has a somewhat different opinion on this matter (Icard, 1994). It is repeatedly argued that since the late 1970s the Banque de France successfully relies on two intermediate objectives to achieve its ultimate goal, that is, price stability, one of which is external and the other internal.[36] The external one stems from strict compliance with the rules of the ERM. The internal medium-term objective is aimed at controlling money supply growth.[37] This practice is seen as a way to reinforce the credibility of the anti-inflationary commitment and to influence the formation of inflationary expectations. For a justification of this strategy, Icard (1993) refers to Svensson (1992), whose theory seems to reconcile the French exchange rate policy with the perceived room for monetary autonomy.[38] Just like Jozzo (1993) and Quintyn (1993), I am, however, rather sceptical about the true capability of the French authorities to run an autonomous monetary policy given the fact that the defence of the parity against the Deutsche mark has become the top priority for monetary policy.

4.2.3 Recapitulation

At first sight, the results for France are somewhat disappointing in some respects. The parameters of the price and velocity gap are indeed significant and correctly signed in model I, but the same conclusion cannot be drawn for the output gap. Deepening of the analysis by estimating the models with recursive least squares sheds some light on this issue. Several specifications appear to display instabilities in some periods. I think that these instabilities, at least partly, originated from shifts in monetary policy regimes and changing attitudes towards inflation in the past three decades. This view is confirmed by re-estimating the expressions for the time span starting around the downfall of the Bretton Woods System and ending approximately five years after the establishment of the European Exchange rate mechanism. During this period, the P^*-concept is quite capable of predicting the direction of price developments in the short-run. In this time frame, the output gap term is significant as well. This could be a reflection of the incentives and constraints imposed by fixed and flexible exchange rates.

4.3   Germany

4.3.1 Econometric analysis of the estimation results

Before discussing the empirical evidence for Germany, it must be stressed that the German unification has caused major breaks in the time series used in the P^*-framework. To check whether the results are unduly influenced by German unification, I have included both a dummy that is one in 1991.1 and zero elsewhere, and a dummy that is one in 1991.2 and zero elsewhere in the German inflation regressions. Under the assumption that the unification caused a long-run price level shift without influencing long-run inflation, I hypothesize an initial rise in inflation with an identical decline afterwards. If true, this would lead to a significant positive coefficient on the 1991.1 dummy and a significant negative coefficient of similar magnitude on the 1991.2 dummy. The empirical results appear to support this hypothesis. Generally

Table 3.8 Regression results for Germany (sample 1965.1–1992.4)

Model	DV	α_0	GAP	ΔDV_{-1}	ΔDV_{-2}	ΔDV_{-3}	ΔDV_{-4}	$\Delta p_n^{e_n}$	R^2 (SE)	WALD (Q(8))	FOR (BP)	NORM (ARCH)
I_{m1}^{a}	$\Delta\pi$	0.0	$-0.004\ PG_{-1}$	-0.98	-0.79	-0.59		0.011	0.63		0.3[1]	0.6
		(0.1)	(0.2)	(11.9″)	(7.8″)	(7.1″)		(2.1′)	(0.66)	(6.7)	(0.6)[2]	(14.6″)
I_{m1}^{b}	$\Delta\pi$	0.0	$0.004\ VG_{-1}$ $-0.138\ OG_{-1}$	-0.94	-0.75	-0.55		0.012	0.65	9.0″	0.4[1]	0.7
		(0.0)	(0.2) (2.9″)	(11.5″)	(7.6″)	(6.9″)		(2.4′)	(0.64)	(9.8)	(0.7)[2]	(9.6″)
II_{m1}^{a}	$\Delta\Delta_4 p$	0.0	$-0.023\ \Sigma_{i=1}^{4}\ PG_{-i}$	0.85	0.36		-0.26	0.040	0.84		0.4[1]	0.6
		(0.5)	(1.9°)	(9.2″)	(3.1″)		(5.4″)	(3.1″)	(0.70)	(6.3)	(0.1)[2]	(5.5)
II_{m1}^{b}	$\Delta\Delta_4 p$	0.1	$-0.009\ \Sigma_{i=1}^{4}\ VG_{-i}$ $-0.094\ \Sigma_{i=1}^{4}\ OG_{-i}$	0.77	0.41		-0.22	0.036	0.85	14.0″	0.4[1]	1.6
		(0.4)	(0.6) (4.2″)	(8.7″)	(3.8″)		(3.1″)	(2.9″)	(0.66)	(8.6)	(0.3)[2]	(1.9)
I_{m3}^{a}	$\Delta\pi$	0.0	$-0.102\ PG_{-3}$	-0.90	-0.72	-0.54		0.015	0.64		0.3[3]	0.4
		(0.0)	(2.3′)	(10.7″)	(7.3″)	(6.8″)		(2.7′)	(0.65)	(9.1)	(0.6)[4]	(13.3′)
I_{m3}^{b}	$\Delta\pi$	0.0	$-0.069\ VG_{-3}$ $-0.190\ OG_{-3}$	-0.88	-0.69	-0.52		0.015	0.66	6.1′	0.4[3]	0.7
		(0.8)	(1.7°) (3.3″)	(10.5″)	(7.2″)	(6.8″)		(2.8″)	(0.63)	(11.0)	(0.5)[4]	(9.0)
II_{m3}^{a}	$\Delta\Delta_4 p$	0.0	$-0.113\ \Sigma_{i=1}^{4}\ PG_{-i}$	0.85	0.44		-0.34	0.048	0.86		0.4[3]	4.2
		(0.3)	(4.9″)	(10.2″)	(4.2″)		(4.9″)	(4.2″)	(0.64)	(9.7)	(0.2)[4]	(0.4)
II_{m3}^{b}	$\Delta\Delta_4 p$	0.0	$-0.084\ \Sigma_{i=1}^{4}\ VG_{-i}$ $-0.131\ \Sigma_{i=1}^{4}\ OG_{-i}$	0.81	0.45		-0.30	0.044	0.86	3.4	0.4[3]	5.6
		(0.2)	(3.1″) (5.3″)	(9.5″)	(4.3″)		(4.3″)	(3.9″)	(0.63)	(9.6)	(0.1)[4]	(0.3)

Notes: DV denotes the dependent variable; α_0 is the intercept; *GAP* stands for the price, velocity and output gap, respectively (*PG, VG* and *OG*); $\Delta p_n^{e_n}$ is the change in energy prices. The heteroskedasticity consistent t-values are recorded below the estimated coefficients in parentheses. SE is the standard error of the regression. WALD denotes Wald's statistic (distributed as $\chi^2(1)$) for testing the hypothesis that the parameters on the velocity and output are equal. Q(8) is the Box–Pierce statistic for testing serial correlation. FOR is an out-of sample prediction (F–statistic) test to examine the stability of the equation ([1]FOR = 85.1; [3]FOR = 85.1). BP is Chow's breakpoint test ([2]BP = 1979.1; [4]BP = 1979.1). NORM is the Jarque–Bera statistic for testing the normality of the residuals. ARCH is a test for fourth order Auto Regressive Conditional Heteroskedasticity with an asymptotic χ^2 distribution. The symbols °, ′ and ″ represent significance at the 10, 5 and 0 percent level, respectively.

speaking, the 1991.1 dummy has a parameter equal to 0.0075 with a t-value of 6.0, and the coefficient on the 1991.2 dummy is −0.0062 with a t-value of 5.7. Their sum differs insignificantly from zero. The German regression results in Table 3.8 are for the specification including the dummy variables. The impact of the inclusion of the dummies on the gap coefficients and their significance turns out to be marginal. Moreover, the econometric results also hardly change when I abstract from the entire post-unification period 1991.1−1992.4 in the estimation sample.[39]

From Table 3.8, it can be inferred that the gap models with $M3$-velocity are more appropriate for forecasting purposes than those with $M1$-velocity. Only in model II_{m1}, the price gap term exerts a negative impact on inflation. The poor performance of the $M1$-models stems from insignificance of the velocity gaps. The parameters of the output gaps have the correct signs and differ significantly from zero. In all models with $M1$, an increase in the output gap of one percentage point shows up in a fall of inflation of about −0.1 percentage point. In the specifications with $M3$, the gaps are significantly negatively correlated with the dependent variable. The coefficients of these gaps amount to about −0.10. Hence, there is a statistical significant long-run relation between $M3$ (through P^*) and the price level. Model II_{m3} delivers the best estimation results.[40] Observe that the equality restriction of the parameters on the velocity and output gap could not be rejected for the latter model, suggesting that both gaps affect inflation in a similar way. Just like in the other countries, changes in energy prices translate into price movements. This factor may even occasionally dominate the fluctuations in inflation. However, when energy price changes are not accommodated by monetary policy, their effects on the equilibrium price level are only transitory.

Concerning the statistical properties, it may be noted that the residuals do not always meet the condition of homoskedasticity. Heteroskedasticity of the disturbance terms is particularly apparent in model I. Since this could signal instabilities in the equations as well, I have iteratively searched for breakpoints at the beginning of each year. Chow tests indeed detect breakpoints in model I, which are mainly concentrated in the period 1971 up to approximately 1975. No significant breaks are found in specification II, again confirming the relative robustness and stability of this model.

Subsequently, I have recursively estimated the equations. The cumulative sum of squares (CUSUMQ) generated by this method is plotted in Figure 3.12. for model I. The graph shows two distinct periods of parameter instability. The first lies around 1973, whereas the second is discernible in the early 1980s. In order to get an overall impression of the consequences of instability, model I is re-estimated with the OLS technique for two sample periods. As a dividing line between these periods we have roughly taken the dates at which the CUSUMQ statistic moves out of and into, respectively, the five percent significance boundaries. Table 3.9 contains the coefficient estimates for Δp^{en} and the gaps for specification I in these subsamples.

Figure 3.12 CUSUMQ statistic

Model Ia with M1

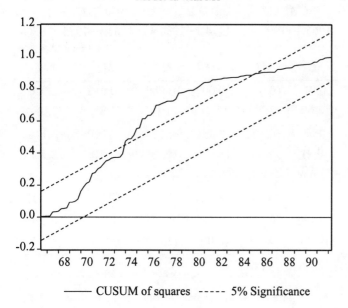

—— CUSUM of squares ----- 5% Significance

Model Ia with M3

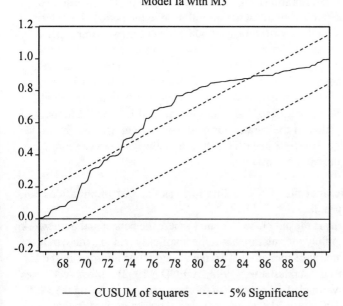

—— CUSUM of squares ----- 5% Significance

Table 3.9 Parameter estimates for the gaps and Δp^{en} in model I over different samples (absolute t-values in parentheses)

Period	A[a] 1965.1–1992.4		B 1974.1–1983.4		C 1965.1–1973.4 and 1984.1–1992.4	
	M1	*M3*	*M1*	*M3*	*M1*	*M3*
Δp^{en}	0.011	0.015	−0.007	0.009	0.015	0.020
	(2.6′)	(2.7″)	(1.3)	(1.1)	(1.9°)	(3.0″)
price gap	−0.004	−0.102	0.051	−0.054	−0.060	−0.148
	(0.2)	(2.3′)	(1.8°)	(0.7)	(2.5′)	(2.9″)
velocity gap	0.004	−0.069	0.059	−0.018	−0.053	−0.122
	(0.2)	(1.5)	(2.3′)	(0.2)	(2.2′)	(2.5′)
output gap	−0.138	−0.190	−0.155	−0.185	−0.155	−0.259
	(2.9′)	(3.3″)	(2.0′)	(2.2′)	(2.7′)	(4.2″)

Notes: a. These figures are taken from Table 3.8.

The instability of the parameters clearly stands out. In the time span with relatively higher, but stable inflation, Δp^{en} can be deleted from the equations without a serious deterioration of the overall statistical fit. On the other hand, this term exerts a significant influence on inflation in the period characterized by comparatively moderate inflation (period C). Over the two sample periods, the values of the gap parameters also show variation. So far the story is analogous to that of France. However, the results for Germany are rather different from those for France in the sense that the P^*-framework seems to be more applicable for Germany in period C owing to the higher t-ratio of the coefficients of the velocity gap.[41] By contrast, formal tests indicate that the hypothesis of equality of the parameters of the output gap in the subsamples cannot be rejected. Hence, a negative output gap always exercises a roughly similar upward pressure on inflation.[42]

4.3.2 Economic analysis of the estimation results and implications for monetary policy

Actually, Germany is the only major country where the conceptual framework for its monetary policy formulation has rather explicitly lain in a modern form of the quantity theory of money, that is, the P^*-model of inflation in the last decades (Deutsche Bundesbank, 1992; OECD, 1993). Most countries abandoned or downgraded the practice of monetary targeting during the 1980s as regulatory and institutional changes in financial markets raised doubts about the stability of the underlying money-income relationships which underpins the approach. Germany seems to have been less affected by the forces that have undermined the role of monetary aggregates elsewhere. The stability of the long-run relation of the money stock to prices may be due in part to the historical pattern of financial change in Germany. In contrast to other countries, domestic financial liberalization was well advanced in Germany by 1970 and has progressed relatively slowly since then. In addition, financial change in the form of the development of new financial instruments has been relatively slow to evolve as a result of the early removal of controls on exchange rates and interest rates.[43]

Since 1974, the German pursuit of the price stability objective has been through the setting of and subsequent adherence to quantitative targets for the expansion of the money stock derived from estimates of the growth rate of potential output (Q^*), 'inevitable' or normative inflation, and the trend change of the income velocity of money (V^*).[44] These targets provide a reference point for decision making. The key feature is that these targets offer a benchmark policy rule that is intended to meet a clearly articulated long-term inflation goal (see, for example, Clarida and Gertler, 1996). So far, the Bundesbank has hit the targets as often as it has missed them.[45] This monetary philosophy presupposes that the theoretical basis, in other words the link between monetary expansion and price trends, is maintained in practice, which implies that inflation is negatively correlated with the price gaps. From this perspective, the empirical findings must be rather comforting for the German monetary authorities. The estimations suggest that the equilibrium price level calculated with *M3* significantly influences prices and transforms the development of the current intermediate target variable of the Deutsche Bundesbank into price level coordinates. This empirically significant transmission reveals the potential risks for price stability of an excessive growth of *M3*. This offers some justification for, or is consistent with, the medium-term orientation of the Bundesbank's policy of monetary targeting since the mid-1970s.

The estimations also hint that German unification has hardly destabilized the inflationary process and the link between monetary aggregates and inflation. Of course, this is a tentative outcome because of the scarcity of observations after the unification. However, with hindsight, higher inflation did not (instantaneously) materialize in the aftermath of unification, which led to exceptionally large price gaps. Kröger and Teuteman (1992) list several factors why inflationary implications were initially much less significant than had been feared, despite the large demand surplus. For instance, the excess demand was mainly for consumer durables, which have a high price elasticity and a large import component. In addition, imports to Germany were made easier as the demand profiles were asymmetric, that is, excess demand in (East) Germany and excess supply in some partner countries. Regarding the stable link between *M* and prices after unification, my findings are corroborated by other recent work. By estimating the German money demand function recursively, Mayer and Fels (1994) conclude that the change in the long-run velocity of money has remained remarkably stable in the wake of unification. Moreover, Gerlach (1994) and Falk and Funke (1995) find that the unification has at most only temporarily worsened the stability of the German money demand equation. Recent statistical evidence is thus supportive for the view that there has been no discernible break in the long-run demand for money as a result of monetary unification.

Like inflation behaviour in other countries, various stability tests do indicate that both the transition from fixed to more flexible exchange rates around 1971 and the supply side shocks associated with sky-rocketing energy prices in 1973—74 provoked an alteration in the dynamics of inflation in Germany, too. However, the German rate of inflation has never surpassed the French inflation rate after the breakdown of Bretton Woods System. As opposed to France, Germany has not shifted the emphasis to the objective of output stabilization rather than price stability after the transition to flexible exchange rates in monetary and fiscal policies. This can be largely explained by the deep-rooted and historically motivated aversion to inflation in Germany.[46] Consequently, the French inflation underwent an additional upward impulse in the early 1970s, owing to a less anti-inflationary attitude in macroeconomic policies (that is, even before the energy crisis took place).

Aside from these different macroeconomic policy preferences, the divergent degrees of monetary autonomy in Germany and France are visible in the regression outcomes. Together with the longstanding tradition of minimizing domestic inflationary pressures, Germany has never really pegged the Deutsche mark to any other currency (during almost the entire sample it was, in fact, the other way round). Furthermore, Germany has always set its monetary policy to achieve its own long-term inflation objectives rather independently from the goals of other countries. The German (equilibrium) price level is thus more insulated from monetary developments in other (European) countries, for example, France. Theoretically, this implies that inflation in Germany has always been more sensitive to national disturbances, which are of course indirectly connected with international shocks. The empirical findings suggest that both the strong negative attitude toward inflation and the circumstance that Germany has de facto been the anchor for other European countries since the late 1960s has accounted for the negative impact of most individual gaps on inflation in the entire sample and in period C in particular (see Table 3.9).

4.3.3 Recapitulation

Over the entire sample, the gaps computed with *M3* are more reliable as predictors of potential inflationary pressures in Germany than those based on *M1*. The superiority of the former specifications results from the higher t-ratios of the parameters of the velocity gaps. From the perspective of the Bundesbank, this must be reassuring since *M3* has been its intermediate target for more than ten years now. As with France, it is likely that the instabilities in model I are in a way associated with either shifts in the prevailing exchange rate regimes and/or fierce fluctuations in energy prices.

4.4   The Netherlands

4.4.1   Econometric analysis of the estimation results
Generally speaking, the informative value of the P^*-framework for modelling inflationary trends in the Netherlands is quite satisfactory. Apart from model II_{m1}, inflation is significantly negatively linked with individual gaps (Table 3.10).[47] Moreover, imposing the restriction of equality on the coefficients of the output and velocity gaps cannot be rejected (except for specification II_{m1}). Hence, the impact of divergences between actual and equilibrium values of output and velocity, respectively, on the dependent variable is roughly similar.

Like in the other countries, the empirics indicate that disequilibria in the real and monetary side, mirrored in price gaps, do not affect the dependent variable directly, that is, after one quarter, but with some lag. This sluggishness of price adjustment is caused by well-known factors (for example, wage contracts). Another similarity with the other countries is that the smallest and largest values of the gap parameters are found in specifications with *M1* and *M3*, respectively. As expected, the estimated parameters for the output gaps vary to lesser extent across specifications with either *M1* or *M3* and over time. Hence, the sensitivity of the dependent variable to discrepancies in the real sphere has not greatly altered since the early 1960s. In case actual output exceeds potential by 1 percentage point, inflation accelerates by about 0.2 percentage point in model I. In model II, a positive output gap of 1 percentage point will result in a fall of the endogenous variable of approximately 0.12 percentage point.

When examining the statistical features of the models, one can observe that most specifications pass all diagnostic tests. Only in model I_{m1} and II_{m3}, there are weak signs of heteroskedastic error terms. As for the stability of the equations, the empirical results have acceptable properties in all instances. In episodes where the benchmark inflation expressions in the other countries exhibit structural breaks, no significant instabilities in the Dutch relationships are found. Throughout the 1970s, the relevant Chow tests fail to detect break points at the beginning of every single year. The robustness of the regressions is also confirmed by the Chow forecast tests. The constancy of the parameters over the whole time interval is also beyond dispute. The cumulative sum of squares obtained from recursive least squares point to overall stability of the expressions. During the entire sample, this statistic neatly moves parallel to the 'critical five percent' lines. To illustrate the stable nature of the equations, Figure 3.13 depicts the course of the recursively estimated parameters of the price gaps for specification I.

Table 3.10 Regression results for the Netherlands (model with M1: sample 1963.1–1992.4; model with M3: sample 1973.1–1992.4)

Model	DV	α_0	GAP		ΔDV_{-1}	ΔDV_{-2}	ΔDV_{-3}	ΔDV_{-4}	Δp_n^e	R^2 (SE)	WALD Q(8)	FOR (BP)	NORM (ARCH)
I_{m1}^a	$\Delta\pi$	0.0 (0.2)	$-0.089\ PG_{-2}$ (2.3')		-1.00 (11.3")	-0.79 (6.8")	-0.66 (5.2")	-0.47 (3.9")	0.027 (2.8")	0.55 (1.18)	(3.1)	0.8[1] (1.3)[2]	1.1 (13.0')
I_{m1}^b	$\Delta\pi$	0.0 (0.1)	$-0.091\ VG_{-2}$ (2.4')	$-0.196\ OG_{-2}$ (2.0')	-1.02 (11.4")	-0.81 (6.9")	-0.64 (5.0")	-0.46 (3.9")	0.027 (2.8")	0.55 (1.18)	1.4 (2.5)	0.8[1] (1.3)[2]	1.3 (14.3')
II_{m1}^a	$\Delta\Delta_4 p$	0.0 (0.5)	$-0.030\ \Sigma_{i=1}^4\ PG_{-i}$ (1.4)				-0.41 (5.2")	0.21 (2.7')	0.013 (2.8")	0.29 (1.37)	(13.1)	0.7[1] (0.4)[2]	0.8 (7.7)
II_{m1}^b	$\Delta\Delta_4 p$	0.1 (0.4)	$-0.034\ \Sigma_{i=1}^4\ VG_{-i}$ (1.6°)	$-0.147\ \Sigma_{i=1}^4\ OG_{-i}$ (3.3")			-0.35 (4.5")	0.22 (2.9")	0.014 (3.1")	0.33 (1.32)	8.8" (11.1)	0.8[1] (1.3)[2]	0.5 (7.7)
I_{m3}^a	$\Delta\pi$	0.0 (0.9)	$-0.255\ PG_{-3}$ (3.2")		-0.99 (9.5")	-0.79 (7.2")	-0.51 (4.4")	-0.33 (3.4")	0.026 (3.1")	0.53 (1.05)	(3.1)	1.1[3] (1.0)[4]	0.5 (3.0)
I_{m3}^b	$\Delta\pi$	0.0 (0.8)	$-0.253\ VG_{-3}$ (3.0")	$-0.266\ OG_{-3}$ (2.3')	-0.99 (9.5")	-0.79 (7.1")	-0.52 (4.4")	-0.33 (3.4")	0.027 (3.0")	0.52 (1.05)	0.0 (3.1)	1.1[3] (1.0)[4]	0.5 (3.1)
II_{m3}^a	$\Delta\Delta_4 p$	0.0 (0.3)	$-0.104\ \Sigma_{i=1}^4\ PG_{-i}$ (2.3')				-0.41 (4.2")	0.15 (1.5°)	0.040 (2.4')	0.32 (1.25)	(6.2)	1.1[3] (0.5)[4]	0.2 (11.2')
II_{m3}^b	$\Delta\Delta_4 p$	0.0 (0.2)	$-0.105\ \Sigma_{i=1}^4\ VG_{-i}$ (1.9°)	$-0.103\ \Sigma_{i=1}^4\ OG_{-i}$ (2.0')			-0.41 (4.0")	0.15 (1.5°)	0.040 (2.4')	0.31 (1.26)	0.0 (6.3)	1.3[3] (0.9)[4]	0.2 (11.5')

Notes: DV denotes the dependent variable; α_0 is the intercept; *GAP* stands for the price, velocity and output gap, respectively (*PG, VG* and *OG*); Δp_n^e is the change in energy prices. The heteroskedasticity consistent t–values are recorded below the estimated coefficients in parentheses. SE is the standard error of the regression. WALD denotes Wald's statistic (distributed as $\chi^2(1)$) for testing the hypothesis that the parameters on the velocity and output are equal. Q(8) is the Box–Pierce statistic for testing serial correlation. FOR is an out–of sample prediction (F–statistic) test to examine the stability of the equation ([1]FOR = 85.1; [3]FOR = 88.1). BP is Chow's breakpoint test ([2]BP = 1979.1; [4]BP = 1982.1). NORM is the Jarque–Bera statistic for testing the normality of the residuals. ARCH is a test for fourth order Auto Regressive Conditional Heteroskedasticity with an asymptotic χ^2 distribution. The symbols °, ' and " represent significance at the 10, 5 and 0 percent level, respectively.

Figure 3.13 Recursive estimates of coefficients on price gaps

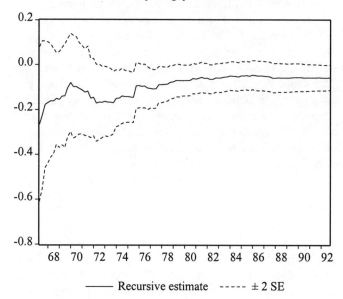

Parameter of price gap in model Ia with M1

―――― Recursive estimate   ----- ± 2 SE

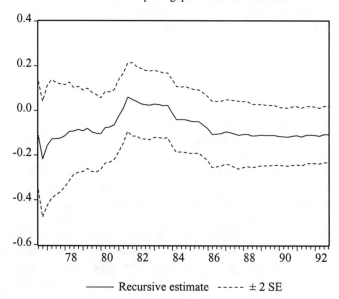

Parameter of price gap in model Ia with M3

―――― Recursive estimate   ----- ± 2 SE

4.4.2 Economic analysis of the estimation results and implications for monetary policy

For Dutch monetary policy makers, the significant and more or less stable correlation between the gaps and inflation may be somewhat puzzling. To understand why, it is instructive to sketch the history of monetary policy in the Netherlands since the early 1970s. In the 1970s and the early 1980s, Dutch monetary policy was directed towards a stable exchange rate of the guilder and control of the liquidity ratio, that is, the inverse of velocity.[48] Although a conflict could theoretically arise between both objectives, the Dutch central bank (henceforth DNB) argued that the exchange rate could be stabilized by manipulating the short-term interest rate, while direct and indirect credit controls, in combination with restrictions on international capital movements, could be used to regulate the overall growth rate of the monetary aggregate.[49]

However, in the early 1980s the exchange rate goal gained increasingly more weight in Dutch monetary policy making relative to the liquidity ratio. This ratio has gradually become less informative because of financial innovations and the liberalization of international capital flows. These developments had actually made the overall money growth largely endogenous, neccesitating a reformulation of DNB's policy strategy. As a result of this changing financial environment, DNB started to monitor and target only the domestic component of money creation in order to support the exchange rate objective. Indeed, the informal restrictions on the credit supply by the banking sector which were in force in the 1980s were only motivated by exchange rate considerations. At that time, excessive domestic money creation was supposed to deteriorate the exchange rate of the guilder (De Haan and Hoogduin, 1987).

In the beginning of the 1990s, DNB left the latter strategy for several (mutually dependent) reasons (see DNB, 1991, pp. 25–6). First, doubts had arisen about the validity of an important assumption underlying the Dutch monetary philosophy: the stability of the money demand function (e.g. Cesar et al., 1990; van Ees et al., 1989).[50] Second, the constantly swelling international capital flows were increasingly complicating a policy aimed at monetary targeting. Finally, the sharp deceleration of inflation after 1983 was irreconcilable with the persistent fast growth of the money supply. These factors prompted DNB to focus its attention solely on the exchange rate objective, that is, maintaining a stable exchange rate of the guilder against the D-mark.

Having said all this, one can understand why the empirical results are probably somewhat confusing for DNB. Despite the downgrading of monetary variables in the monetary policy process, I find a rather stable significant relation between the price level and the money supply. This obviously contradicts the (theoretical) notion that the domestic price gap loses its impact on inflation if the exchange rate is fixed.[51] However, the results should not be interpreted to mean that DNB is — still — in a position to influence the price level via the money supply.[52] For this conclusion to hold, DNB should have been able and willing to control the money stock with the available instruments. Given the priority attached to the exchange rate objective, this is highly unlikely. Besides, I believe that monetary authorities cannot strive for both an exchange rate objective and a monetary target at the same time.

4.4.3 Recapitulation

The empirical findings cannot be translated into monetary policy recommendations for the Dutch monetary authorities. However, one should not go as far as to say that the P^*-framework has no value at all. Its usefulness lies in the analytical field. The estimations suggest that the gaps matter for the future course of inflation, which is important to recognize.

5 CONCLUDING REMARKS

Testing the validity of the P^*-concept for four EMS-members has offered interesting insights. In most regressions, national price movements are significantly correlated with domestic monetary and real disturbances so that the P^*-framework has predictive and analytical relevance. Another feature is that estimations with gaps based on *M1* yield smaller gap coefficients than regressions with *M3*. The greater volatility of *M1* is largely responsible for this. The overall statistical properties of the former models are generally also somewhat worse than those of the latter. Contrary to previous P^*-studies, the flexible model specifications explicitly allow for the possibility that price gaps show up in inflation rates with variable lags. In this regard, I find that velocity gaps with *M1* usually affect inflation with a shorter time lag. A plausible explanation is that this money concept is mostly used for transactions purposes.

However, the extent to which these empirical findings can be useful in formulating recommendations for appropriate monetary policy actions in individual countries hings basically on three factors. The first factor has to do with the intermediate goals to which the monetary authorities have committed themselves. In fact, domestic money growth targets have been fully subordinated to exchange rate goals in Belgium, France and the Netherlands for many years now. These countries attempt to maintain a fixed value of their respective currencies vis-à-vis the Deutsche mark. Under these circumstances, internal monetary developments become theoretically highly endogenous and, as a consequence, almost unmanageable for the monetary authorities.

The second crucial factor is the ability of monetary authorities to influence the domestic money supply. All things considered, this comes down to the question as to whether the Bundesbank has had effective policy instruments at its disposal to steer the development of the German money supply in the desired direction, which in turn affects the price level in the long run. Should this be the case, the findings suggest that the Bundesbank has pursued the right monetary policy philosophy of monetary targeting, as movements in *M3* — and to a somewhat lesser extent *M1* — seem to have had a significant impact on inflation through the price and velocity gaps (and play an important role in the determination of the price level).

A related third issue concerns the nature of the transmission of shocks from other countries when the exchange rate is fixed — or is limited in its fluctuation as is the case for the countries participating in the EMS — and the relevance of the analysis in the light of the Economic and Monetary Union. The significant strides toward both economic and monetary integration within the European Union seen in the last few years may make it more useful to include gaps that account for monetary and real distortions in other countries rather than purely domestic gaps in the inflation relationships for the separate countries.[53] This is especially relevant for the countries under study. Introducing EU-wide real and monetary discrepancies instead of domestic gaps in the expressions not only offer an opportunity to investigate the current state of integration between the countries and the degree of (a)symmetry in the EMS, but could also add valuable information about the most appropriate (future) common monetary policy to be conducted in the EMU by the European Central Bank. In Chapter 4, I turn to this subject in detail.

NOTES

1. However, it should be noted that Belgium in 1990 publicly declared its intention to aim at a very narrow range of fluctuation of its currency against the Deutsche mark. In the 1980s, the aim had been to maintain a stable relationship between the Belgian franc and the ECU (Eizenga, 1994).
2. The MSKF technique is explained in detail in Section 2.3.2.
3. Since seasonally adjusted data are used it is not necessary to test for the time series properties of the variables by taking into account the possibility that they have a 'seasonal' unit root, which facilitates the analysis to some extent.
4. From this point onwards, I use the term inflation for the quarterly change in the natural logarithm of the GDP/GNP price deflator.
5. However, the significance of this partial convergence is difficult to assess as other important economic variables continued to diverge during this period.
6. I return to this issue in Chapter 7.
7. For a investigation of the relationship between central bank independence and inflation, see Alesina (1988) and Grilli et al. (1991).
8. Perhaps, this can partly be explained by the structure of the French economy, which differs to a certain extent from that of the other countries in the sense that the influence of the goverment on the economy is more noticeable. Hence, the sensitivity of the French economy to shocks might probably be somewhat more mitigated. This could be a reason why the fluctuations in its real GDP-growth are fairly moderate compared to those in the other countries.

9. Beaudry and Koop (1993) point to the possibility of asymmetric persistence in GNP. The results of their paper suggest that describing all output fluctuations as highly persistent may be incorrect (and thereby may contribute to the reappraisal of some macroeconomic theories). In particular, they find the effects of negative shocks to be mainly temporary and the consequences of positive shocks to be very persistent. Business cycle asymmetries are also studied in Hamilton (1989) and Diebold and Rudebusch (1989), among others.

10. The transactions theories, epitomized in the inventory theoretic models of Baumol (1952) and Tobin (1956), emphasized money's role as a medium of exchange. In this theory, a narrowly defined money stock (*M1*) is at the centre. Asset theories of money demand consider the demand for money more broadly as part of a problem of allocating wealth among a portfolio of assets which include money as just one component (Friedman, 1956; Tobin, 1958). Here, the definition of money should be broadened to include liquid substitutes like savings deposits (for example, *M3*).

11. It should be pointed out that the European central banks have worked hard on the harmonization of the broad monetary aggregates as part of the process towards the Economic and Monetary Union in Europe.

12. A survey conducted by the Dutch central bank among 1828 firms in the period June–September 1991 reveals that this remark is not entirely valid for Dutch enterprises. A finding of the interview study is that almost 65 per cent of these firms receives interest on demand deposits held at banks (de Haan et al., 1992).

13. Both theory and empirical evidence indicate that these developments ensue from the effects of economic growth on the demand for currency and other assets (see Ireland, 1994, for a brief overview of this literature in the past decades). Bordo and Jonung (1987, Chapter 6) use postwar data from 84 countries to document that the level of a broad monetary aggregate rises relative to the level of a narrower aggregate both within and across economies as income per capita increases.

14. Icard (1991) asserts that: 'it can be often noticed, as is the case in France, that financial innovation exerts a powerful influence on the velocity of monetary aggregates, particularly for narrow aggregates'.

15. Santoni (1987) comes up with another explanation for the permanent fall in velocity based on portfolio considerations, which suggest that velocity is more closely related to wealth than to current income. The theory implies that, when wealth increases relative to current income, velocity decreases, ceteris paribus. Therefore, if the theory is valid, an increase in wealth could be an additional determinant of the constant fall in *M3*-velocity. Recent empirical work by Fase and Winder (1997) confirms this hypothesis for various countries.

16. Multicountry studies of money demand mostly find that Germany has the most stable money demand compared to other (large) EU countries. For Germany, Fase (1994) also concludes that the demand for broad money is generally more stable than the demand for narrow money.

17. The term financial innovation tends to make most people think of exotic new instruments, for example, swaps, options, forward rate agreements, and so on, but it comprises just as well the lifting of controls imposed by the authorities, both 'prudential' and (in)direct credit restrictions.

18. Nowadays, the impact of fluctuations in construction activities on the whole economy is considerably less than in the 1960s due to the diminished relative economic importance of the construction sector.

19. Seen from the Bundesbank's perspective, it is reassuring to ascertain that the German monetary unification has not as yet altered this process.

20. A modest exploration of economically sensible lag structures does not make the analysis very vulnerable to the well-known objections regarding the practice of selective reporting of the results of a specification search (Cooley and LeRoy, 1981). If a reader knows that an intensive search could underly the reported tests, he, of course, discounts heavily or completely the researcher's claims for validation of a theory for which the author is

obviously acting as an advocate. In this situation, the reader naturally mostly adopts a low or zero signal-to-noise ratio to the presented findings.

21. The t-ratios reported below the estimated coefficients are computed with heteroskedasticity-consistent standard errors.

22. The parameter on PG^{m3} in model I is somewhat smaller to that estimated by Hoeller and Poret (1991, p. 18), who employed the Hodrick—Prescott filter technique to generate p^* and used a slightly different model specification.

23. A detailed consideration of the history and historiography of Bretton Woods is presented in Eichengreen (1993).

24. See the Belgische Vereniging der Banken (1988) for an assessment of the instruments and conduct of monetary policy in Belgium in the 1970s—80s.

25. See the Belgian central bank (1981) for an explanation of this policy strategy.

26. These findings are exemplary for the other models.

27. Under this regime attempts were made to ensure a degree of exchange rate stability by fixing bilateral fluctuation bands by law and by a widespread use of capital controls (Giovannini, 1993).

28. Bordo (1993) compares the economic performance of different international monetary regimes. In addition, the question why some monetary regimes have been more successful than others is addressed.

29. For instance, the evidence of a high degree of price stability in the convertible phase of Bretton Woods (1959—70) is indeed consistent with the traditional view that fixed rate regimes provide a stable nominal anchor, but could also reflect the absence of major shocks (Bordo, 1993, p. 133). Moreover, it is not clear whether the disinflation in the early 1980s in the EMS was totally a consequence of the EMS since this deceleration was broadly in line with that observable elsewhere in industrial countries (see Section 2.1).

30. A similar opinion is taken by Bayoumi and Eichengreen (1994a).

31. Bruneel (1992) offers a detailed treatment of the analytical backgrounds and operating procedures of monetary policy in France since the early 1970s.

32. According to Icard (1993), the French government formally reasserted its commitment to pegging the exchange rate of the franc and also switched back onto the path of sound macroeconomic conditions and a balanced policy mix in 1983. This implied that the French government deficit was gradually trimmed and that the index-linking procedures for wage settlements were abandoned. The determined efforts made on these two important macroeconomic fronts played a crucial role in bringing down inflation. Hence, the weight of inflation in the policy decision-making process has just firmly increased in the early 1980s.

33. According to Biltoft and Boersch (1992), the willingness of France to accept German leadership in the ERM has been justified on the grounds that this was an effective way of bringing down domestic inflation. By maintaining the nominal tie to the Deutsche mark, France has imported the Bundesbank's credibility in controlling inflation and thereby gained anti-inflation credibility more effectively than otherwise. This policy is believed to have worked particularly well for France, a country with historically relatively high rates of inflation and a central bank that has not enjoyed the same degree of independence as the Bundesbank for a long time (for instance, Alesina, 1988 and Grilli et al., 1991). In fact, the Banque de France has just recently obtained a more independent status. The new statute provides the Banque de France with independence in determining Central Bank rates and in deciding monetary policy objectives and enhances its automony. With regard to exchange rate policy, the Government determines the exchange rate regime and the parity of the French franc, whereas the French central bank is responsible for achieving this parity (OECD Economic Survey: France, 1994, esp. pp. 35—43).

34. Kool and Tatom (1994) investigate the importance of exchange rate regimes for the determinants of prices and inflation in five small European countries: Austria, Belgium, Denmark, the Netherlands and Switzerland. They develop a generalized P^*-model that accounts for the effect of German gaps on domestic inflation in these countries. The main

finding is that the estimations of the inflation equations significantly improve when allowance is made for the German influence on their equilibrium domestic price levels during fixed exchange rate periods. Hence, the long-run equilibrium price level toward which domestic prices adjust in these countries is (to a large extent) determined by German monetary policy.

35. See Artus et al. (1991), Galy (1992), Herz and Röger (1992), Gardner and Perraudin (1993), among others.

36. Even in the last few years before EMU, the Banque de France (1996) has stated its monetary philosophy in these words.

37. The French authorities have set a target for monetary growth since 1977; in the last few years the targeted aggregate has been either *M2* (from 1988 to 1990) or *M3* (since 1991). In 1979, France became one of the few industrial countries explicitly pursuing an exchange rate and monetary target. During the first EMS years (1979–82), the French commitment to a stable exchange rate was not very firm. However, in 1983 the French economic policy stance changed dramatically and the anti-inflationary policy got the highest priority, as described in the main text. Against this background Quintyn (1993, p. 289) states that: 'the authorities' focus gradually shifted from control of the quantity of money to interest rate control to achieve the exchange rate target.'

38. Svensson (1992) showed that, in theory, when an exchange rate target is credible, keeping it within the bounds of a fluctuation band is compatible with relative monetary independence. This would seem to demonstrate that maintaining a domestic target is justified.

39. This suggests that the monetary union has not disrupted the German inflationary process to a considerable extent (see also Mayer and Fels, 1994; Gerlach, 1994).

40. Actually, this specification is also preferred by the two researchers of the Bundesbank mentioned in Section 2.2.2 of Chapter 2. Reimers and Tödter (1994) find a parameter of the price gap of -0.08, while we estimate a coefficient of -0.11. The difference can be explained by several factors, among them the use of another approach to calculate p^* and a different estimation period.

41. Recall that for France the P^*-concept appears to be less useful in period C due to the low explanatory power of the output gap.

42. Besides a substantial rise of the explanatory power of the gaps, the statistical features of model I are definitely better in period **C** than in the whole sample (not reported here).

43. Kole and Meade (1995) sketch a brief history of monetary targeting in the G-7 countries and describe the German experience with monetary targeting in detail.

44. For practical reasons, the concept of money has been altered several times (for example, in 1988 from the central bank money stock to the broad monetary aggregate, *M3*) and the specification of targets has varied, but the policy strategy has remained the same for almost twenty years (see Schächter and Stokman, 1992).

45. Several empirical studies conclude that the Bundesbank seems to be better characterized as an inflation targeter (see Chapter 6) than a money targeter. Bernanke and Mihov (1996) assert that the Bundesbank only uses money growth as an important informational variable and operational guide. Von Hagen (1995) even claims that from the inception of the current regime the Bundesbank has actually 'backed out' its money growth targets from a quantity equation which uses as an input an inflation projection for the next year. Thus, it might be alternatively argued that inflation objectives, rather than monetary targets, are the driving force behind German monetary policy.

46. This remark is supported by Schächter and Stokman (1992). They find that the Bundesbank followed the same strict course of anti-inflationary policy in several subperiods.

47. Hoeller and Poret (1991, p. 16) find that none of the separate gaps — calculated with the Hodrick–Prescott filter — has significant explanatory power for inflation in the Netherlands. Besides, they use other data.

48. Using the liquidity ratio as an intermediate target constituted a framework quite similar to that in Germany. Within this framework, a desired growth rate of money supply was formulated, taking into account (unavoidable) price increases, the expected growth in real

income and cyclical fluctuations in the demand for liquidity.

49. Dutch monetary policy has been characterized by Zijlstra (1985) as a moderately monetarist policy. For further discussions of this policy, reference is made to den Dunnen (1979) and Fase (1985). In addition, appendix A in van Straaten (1989) contains an overview of the instruments designed and applied since 1952 to influence the growth rate of the domestic money supply.

50. See Goodhart (1989) for a review of the wide literature that tries to address the question why the relationship between money and income may become unstable.

51. The underlying reasoning is straightforward. Suppose that current domestic prices are consistent with the foreign equilibrium price level, which implies that the foreign price gap equals zero, whereas the domestic gap is positive at the same time. Then, the domestic-determined gap is expected to narrow by an adjustment of the money stock, not by an adjustment of domestic prices and inflation. The extent to and the speed with which this equilibration takes place heavily depend on the degree of international capital mobility (Kool and Tatom, 1994).

52. Roubini (1988) argues that in case capital market imperfections exist, monetary authorities in small open countries with fixed exchange rates can in principle still steer the development of the domestic money supply in the short and medium term. A survey of bank behaviour in the Netherlands shows that international capital mobility in loan and deposit markets is still very modest (Swank, 1994). This suggests that attempts to control the lending and funding activities of Dutch banks generally hardly motivate borrowers and depositors to switch to foreign intermediaries. Furthermore, van Ees et al. (1993) demonstrate that even small countries with fixed exchange rates may have some room for an autonomous monetary policy due to imperfect international capital mobility resulting from asymmetric information.

53. Empirical work along the same lines is recently conducted by Bayoumi and Kenen (1993) and Monticelli (1993a), among others.

4.   Money and Prices in a Small EMU

A favourite cliché among central bankers is that monetary targeting is as much an art as a science. Yet, to the extent it is a science, it is more econometrics than economics. Undoubtedly, this conventional wisdom reflects the fact that the eternal trial-and-error process associated with monetary targeting, can be best perceived as being in the intersection of these concepts.

Sardelis (1993), p. 43

1   INTRODUCTION

The creators of the EMS considered the establishment of 'a zone of monetary stability in Europe', comprising 'greater stability at home and abroad', as their main objective. It is undoubtedly true that the hopes of the optimists have been realized only in part, because the EMS experienced several realignments, notably in the first years of its existence, and faced heavy storms in 1992–93. However, the initial widespread expectations that a system of fixed, though adjustable, exchange rates would not hold together for long, or, conversely, would degenerate into a system of frequent small exchange rate adjustments, akin to a crawling peg, have definitely not materialized.[1] In fact, the countries participating in the EMS have shown more and more political determination to keep the system in operation throughout the years.

In the late 1980s, the drive towards monetary integration in Europe gained new momentum with the adoption of the so-called Delors Report at the European Council of Madrid in June 1989. This report finally led to the signature in February 1992 of the Maastricht Treaty on European Union, which was ratified — although not without some difficulties — by Member States in the following months and became effective on 1 November 1993. A challenging and complex issue to be dealt with is the preparation of the future single monetary policy in the third and final stage of the Economic and Monetary Union (EMU).[2] The responsibility for preparing this policy and for reinforcing the coordination of national monetary policies in the European Union has been entrusted to the European Monetary Institute (EMI), which succeeded the Committee of Governors of European Central Banks on 1 January 1994.

In building an adequate monetary framework for the European System of Central Banks (ESCB), numerous concerns can be distinguished (Giovannini, 1990; Monticelli and Viñals, 1993; among others). One of these is to investigate which targets can be useful in the conduct of the future monetary policy as well as exploring which variable is most suited to play that role.[3] It is possible that national central banks will ultimately settle for the use of intermediate monetary targets.[4] In this respect, it is sometimes argued that since the Bundesbank (Buba) relies rather successfully on monetary targeting since 1975, the continuation of this strategy in Stage Three could allow the transfer of some degree of anti-inflationary credibility to the ESCB as well (Issing, 1994).[5] Hypothetically, a means of smoothing the transition to Stage Three could have been that the anchor country (Germany) has gradually placed more weight on monetary conditions in other ERM countries in the formulation and execution of its monetary policy in the course of the 1990s.[6]

To gain empirical insights into these issues, I extend the traditional P^*-model in Section 2. This new version allows for the possibility that the domestic equilibrium price level in Belgium, France, Germany and the Netherlands (henceforth the core group) is determined by a European monetary aggregate through the exchange rate constraint. Before one can explore the possible existence of such a relationship, an aggregation method for adding national variables has to be selected. This subject is dealt with in Section 3. Section 4 first pays attention to the statistical properties of the 'European' variables. The equilibrium values of the European variables needed for the construction of European price gaps are proxied with the multi-state Kalman filter technique (see Section 3.2 of Chapter 2). Section 5 briefly focuses on some technical outcomes of the Kalman filter computations. Subsequently, I place these calculations in the context of recent studies on European integration bearing resemblance with the optimum currency area literature. Section 7 presents empirical evidence of the validity of the extended P^*-concept for the four countries. In addition, I examine whether the impact of an ERM-wide money supply on domestic inflation rates is separate from, and more powerful than that of the countries' own national monetary aggregates. The applicability of the P^*-framework for the core group as a whole is tested in the last subsection of Part 7. The concluding section summarizes the main policy implications.

2 THE EXTENDED P^*-MODEL

The view underlying the traditional P^*-framework that purely domestic monetary aggregates eventually determine the equilibrium price level in individual countries had already implicitly been challenged by McKinnon in 1982, though in a completely different context. He found empirical evidence that the national (convertible) monies of an inner group of industrial countries were highly substitutable in demand according to anticipated exchange rate movements. This international currency substitution destabilized national money demands, which in turn led to a breakdown of the relationship between national inflation rates and the growth rates of national money supplies. However, national price movements appeared to be satisfactorily explicable by considering the growth of a crude index of a global monetary aggregate (comprising the money stocks for countries with convertible currencies in the 1970s).

The currencies of the core ERM countries may, however, have become even closer substitutes for one another in the course of time than those of the group of industrial countries in which McKinnon was interested more than a decade ago (Bayoumi and Kenen, 1993).[7] This could stem from closer adherence to the 'rules' of the ERM causing convergence of national monetary policies (Haldane, 1991) and the liberalization and deregulation of international capital flows in the 1980s. Lane and Poloz (1992) have empirically shown that currency substitution may indeed play a role in money demand in countries currently participating in the ERM.[8] Apart from currency substitution, an increased sensitivity of national inflation rates to monetary developments in other European countries could also ensue from the Single Market project (Cassard et al., 1994). This process has stimulated trade between European countries (Sapir et al., 1994; Sapir and Sekkat, 1995), thus potentially increasing the degree of economic integration in Europe.

To cope with the above considerations, I extend the closed economy version of the P^*-concept discussed in Section 2.1 of Chapter 2 to a similar monetary framework that is empirically applicable in a situation where symmetric monetary spillover effects between ERM countries exist. More precisely, I assume that European equivalents of equations (2.1) to (2.5) can be formulated.[9] Note that this strategy presupposes the existence of a stable demand for an ERM-wide monetary aggregate.[10] In this case, the following equations result:

$$P_{eur} = M_{eur}(V_{eur}/Q_{eur}) \tag{4.1}$$

$$P_{eur}^* = M_{eur}(V_{eur}^*/Q_{eur}^*) \tag{4.2}$$

$$GAP_{eur} = (p_{eur} - p_{eur}^*) = (q_{eur} - q_{eur}^*) + (v_{eur} - v_{eur}^*) \tag{4.3}$$

$$\pi^{eur} = \alpha(p_{eur} - p_{eur}^*)_{t-n} + \sum_{j=1}^{5} \delta_j \pi_{t-j}^{eur} \qquad \alpha < 0 \tag{4.4}$$

$$\Delta\pi^{eur} = \alpha(p_{eur} - p_{eur}^*)_{t-n} + \gamma \pi_{t-1}^{eur} + \sum_{j=1}^{4} \beta_j \Delta\pi_{t-j}^{eur} \qquad \alpha < 0 \tag{4.5}$$

Theoretically, the ERM-wide money supply does not only determine the equilibrium European price level, but also pins down the equilibrium price level in each of the core countries through the exchange rate constraint, or in symbols:

$$P_i^{d*} = E_i \, P_{eur}^* \, / \, ER_i^* \qquad (4.6)$$

where P_i^{d*} equilibrium domestic price level of country i

E_i nominal exchange rate of country i, equal to the number of equilibrium domestic currency units per unit of foreign currency in which the European aggregates are expressed

P_{eur}^* equilibrium European price level

ER_i^* equilibrium real exchange rate of country i

The extended model has important theoretical implications for the short-run price dynamics in each country. First, p_i^* from equation (2.3) must be replaced by p_i^{d*} as defined in expression (4.6), yielding a European or foreign price gap (GAP^{f_1}).

$$GAP_i^d = (\, p_i - p_i^* \,) \qquad (2.3)$$

$$GAP_i^{f_1} = (\, p_i - p_i^{d*} \,) = [\, p_i - (\, p_{eur}^* + e_i - er_i^* \,) \,] \qquad (4.7)$$

where GAP_i^d and GAP_i^{fj} are the domestic and European price gap, respectively. The lower case symbols denote logarithmic levels. The foreign price gap (GAP_i^{fj}) is now expected to influence the future path of inflation in each country.[11] When the domestic price level exceeds the European equilibrium price level (adjusted for changes in nominal and equilibrium real exchange rates), I hypothesize that downward pressure on domestic inflation results. The amount of pressure this gap actually exerts on inflation in the core countries and the speed of adjustment toward equilibrium depend on the extent of arbitrage in goods and capital markets, and the degree to which the economies are integrated (Kool and Tatom, 1994).

The second implication of the extended model is that the effect of the domestic price gap on domestic inflation developments is expected to decrease with higher economic and financial integration in Europe. Since the degree of monetary integration in Europe has presumably increased over time, it seems recommendable to examine the relative impact of purely domestic and European price gaps on domestic inflation over time.

Both theoretical considerations are tested in Section 7. In a first test, I simply replace the domestic gap by the foreign gap. In a second test, I insert both gaps simultaneously in the inflation equation, or formally:

$$\Delta \pi_t^i = \alpha_1 GAP_{i,t-n}^d + \alpha_2 GAP_{i,t-n}^{f_2} + \gamma \pi_{t-1}^i + \sum_{j=1}^{4} \beta_j \Delta \pi_{t-j}^i \qquad (4.8)$$

$$\alpha_1 \, , \, \alpha_2 < 0$$

It should be pointed out that there is a subtle, yet important difference between GAP_i^{f2} and GAP_i^{f1} from equation (4.7). The European variables used to construct GAP_i^{f2} do not comprise national data for the country in question. For the Netherlands, for example, European aggregates are constructed using data for Belgium, France and Germany only. This way, potential multicollinearity problems due to the existence of correlation between GAP_i^d and GAP_i^{f1}, which also encompasses national data of country i, are avoided. This is especially relevant for Germany and to a lesser extent France which have a relatively large weight in a European aggregate for all countries together. Moreover, equation (4.8) enables us to explore whether the impact of a European money supply on domestic inflation is separate from, and more powerful than that of the countries' own national monetary aggregates. Here, the domestic price gap and the European price gap compete for the influence on actual domestic inflation dynamics. One extreme would be a total crowding out of the domestic price gap by the European one. Obviously, this is most likely to occur in the case of small open economies with perfect capital mobility, where domestic monetary policy is almost completely ineffective. In the other extreme situation, only the domestic gap would drive actual inflation. Then, the country is totally independent of ERM-wide monetary developments. Germany appears the most likely candidate for this scenario. Of course, intermediate positions are possible as well when both gaps prove to have a significant impact on price developments.

An important element in constructing the European price gaps concerns the computation of variables on a European scale. In the next section, I turn to this issue.

3 AGGREGATION ISSUES

The issues involved in adding national variables can basically be divided into two. The first question is whether the data measure the same concept. This aspect plays in particular for monetary aggregates in individual countries. Indeed, if these money stocks do not comprise the same elements, no sum of the national monetary aggregates will be an accurate gauge of countries' contributions to the aggregate money supply. A rough comparison of national definitions has, however, revealed that the aggregates are reasonably similar in terms of the types of assets they include (Economic Unit, 1991).[12]

The absence of major inconsistencies in the asset composition of aggregates does not simply guarantee the avoidance of omissions or duplications in the area-wide monetary measures, which result from adding up national aggregates. More precisely, in the empirical analysis the ERM-wide money stock is underestimated. This stems from the exclusion of so-called cross-border holdings (CBHs) in monetary assets of the private non-financial sector.[13] At present, money stock statistics compiled by almost all EU central banks exclude deposits held by residents in banks located in foreign countries. However, recent studies by the Economic Unit (1993) and Monticelli (1993a) reach the conclusion that so far no EU-wide definition of broad money extended to include CBHs outperforms the traditional EU-wide measure of money obtained from simple aggregation of national definitions regarding its relevance for monetary analysis and policy making. Put differently, the conventional EU-wide broad money (still) helps to predict developments in both nominal and real income. This suggests that movements in CBHs are apparently not clearly linked with spending decisions but are instead presumably more motivated by portfolio considerations. Consequently, changes in CBHs convey — as yet — little information for future developments in aggregate income and prices. Partly for this reason, I also concentrate on the traditional definition of EU-wide money, that is, excluding CBHs. A practical argument to ignore CBHs is that the incompleteness and unreliability of the existing data and the short period for which they are available impair any attempt to construct area-wide aggregates including CBHs since 1960.[14] However, CBHs are likely to increase further in the near future if the progress of financial and economic integration continues to be attended (as it has in recent years) by significant shifts of money holdings across EU countries (Economic Unit, 1993). Consequently, the coverage of the aggregated money supplies will presumably decrease and these developments may ultimately undermine the significance of these aggregates as indicators of policy.

The second issue is already implicitly touched upon in the previous paragraph. It concerns the conversion method to be applied for the aggregation of the countries' data on the money stock and nominal and real GNP/GDP. Earlier studies on European money demand have used different methods of aggregation, immediately indicating that the method to convert quantity variables into a common currency is at least somewhat controversial. The first method makes use of actual exchange rates. An example of this approach can be found in Monticelli and Strauss-Kahn (1991) and Monticelli (1993a), who opt for the exchange rate vis-à-vis the ECU. The second alternative, employed by Bekx and Tullio (1989) and Artis et al. (1993), takes base-period exchange rates in aggregation. A third method is to use data on levels of the variables adjusted by purchasing-power-parity (PPP) exchange rates (Kremers and Lane, 1990).[15] Instead of forming a weighted sum of the levels of the individual money supplies, Bayoumi and Kenen (1993) sum the weighted rates of change (calculated as the changes in the logarithms of the money stock).

All the methods have conceptual drawbacks. For instance, PPP weights are to some extent endogenous, as monetary policy will generally influence the path for prices and exchange rates. Conversely, base-period exchange rates are not obviously relevant for other periods. Market exchange rates, on the other hand, may be distorted by speculative bubbles, exchange rate intervention, asymmetric speed of adjustment in goods and asset markets or macroeconomic shocks (see Annex IV, IMF, *World Economic Outlook*, 1992). The latter observation argues in favour of the use of PPP equivalents.[16]

Taking the above into consideration, I add the national variables with two different conversion methods; I use base-period and current exchange rates against the German mark in aggregation.[17] For money, real and nominal output respectively, the European aggregates may be expressed as:

$$M_{eur} = \sum_i M_i E_i \qquad (4.9)$$

$$Q^r_{eur} = \sum_i Q^r_i E_i \qquad (4.10)$$

$$Q^n_{eur} = \sum_i Q^n_i E_i \qquad (4.11)$$

where all exchange rates (E) are defined as the number of units of marks per unit of the domestic currency. From these expressions, a European aggregate price level can be derived:

$$P_{eur} = \frac{Q^n_{eur}}{Q^r_{eur}} = \sum_i \frac{(Q^n_i E_i)}{\sum_i (Q^r_i E_i)} = \sum_i \frac{(Q^r_i E_i)P_i}{\sum_i (Q^r_i E_i)} \qquad (4.12)$$

Thus, the European price level is a weighted average of national price indices (P_i). The weights are the shares of real output in individual countries in the ERM aggregate computed either with base-period or current nominal exchange rates.[18]

To get an impression of the development of the conversion factors over time, I have plotted the nominal exchange rates of the Belgian franc (BFR), French franc (FF) and guilder against the Deutsche mark in the top panel of Figure 4.1. The real exchange rates, that is, the nominal exchange rate per unit of Deutsche marks multiplied by the German price deflator relative to each country's price level, are depicted in the lower panel of Figure 4.1.

Until the late 1960s, no spectacular movements in nominal exchange rates are noticeable. These years were in fact the heyday of the Bretton Woods System (although Germany and the Netherlands revalued their currencies by 5 percent in 1961). The fairly tranquil environment of the 1960s was, however punctuated by a number of crises, starting with the devaluation of the pound sterling in 1967 by nearly 15 percent. At the beginning of 1968, the FF came under speculative pressures. After an aborted effort to agree on a realignment in October 1968, the FF was ultimately sharply devalued by 11.1 percent in August 1969.[19] After the collapse of Bretton Woods, the value of the FF steadily declined due to persistent positive inflation differences with Germany.

Figure 4.1 Nominal and real exchange rate against the German mark

Nominal exchange rate (1960 = 1)

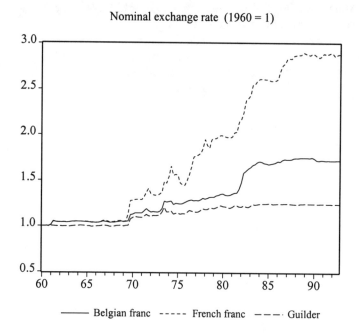

———— Belgian franc   - - - - - French franc   — — — Guilder

Real exchange rate (1960 = 1)

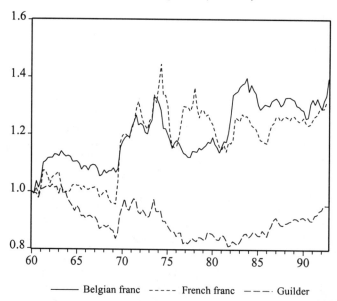

———— Belgian franc   - - - - - French franc   — — — Guilder

The other currencies also lost ground against the German mark, albeit to a much lesser extent than the FF. This reflects the determination of Belgium and the Netherlands in particular to seek stable exchange rates with Germany, which was exemplified by the creation of 'the Snake' in 1972.[20] Around the mid-1980s, the depreciation of the FF came to an end as a consequence of radical changes in French macroeconomic and monetary policies.[21] All in all, the FF depreciated by about 300 percent in the whole time span, whereas the devaluation of the BFR and the guilder amounted to approximately 170 and 25 percent, respectively. As Figure 4.1 illustrates, the fall in nominal exchange rates was almost entirely realized before 1985, the date at which the ERM started to 'harden'.[22]

Real exchange rate movements have on balance been much smaller. Both the FF and BFR have undergone a real depreciation of about 35 percent over the entire sample. Conversely, the guilder has appreciated about 5 percent in real terms against the German mark. However, since the mid-1980s the real exchange rates stabilized as convergence in inflation rates increased.[23]

4 THE ACTUAL AND EQUILIBRIUM EUROPEAN VARIABLES

I shall start with a brief investigation of inflation in the core group (π^{eur}). First, it must be noted that the development of π^{eur} depends on the aggregation method used (see Figure 4.2). Due to the large depreciations vis-à-vis the German mark, conversion with current exchange rates places a greater weight on price developments in the traditionally high-inflation countries. This explains why π^{eur}_{cur} surpasses π^{eur}_{bp} up to the mid-1980s. From 1985 onwards, the two measures of European inflation exhibit exactly the same pattern as the size of exchange rate changes decreased to a considerable extent.

Some basic statistics of the depicted inflation data are provided in Table 4.1. Depending on the aggregation method, European inflation amounted to 1.2 and 1.3 percentage points per quarter in the entire time span. The first five years of the EMS were, however, a period of quite rapidly rising prices. As Table 4.1 shows, European prices were increasing by 1.4 and 1.5 percentage points. Thereafter, the average inflation rate in the core group came down considerably to about 0.7 percentage point. The variability of inflation also reached its lowest value in the last subperiod.

The growth rates of real output in the core group together with those in France and Germany are recorded in the second panel of Table 4.1. Here, I have also broken down the whole sample into three subperiods. The substantial nominal exchange rate depreciations against the German mark since the early 1960s are clearly discernible in the European data. In every subperiod considered, the expansion of European real output computed with

Figure 4.2 Annual inflation rates

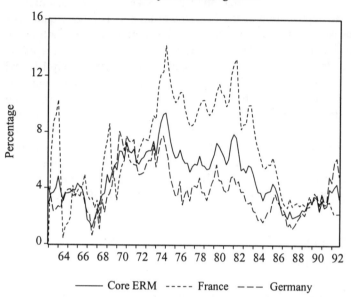

Base period exchange rates

——— Core ERM   - - - - - France   – – – Germany

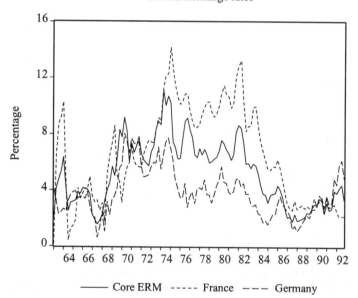

Current exchange rates

——— Core ERM   - - - - - France   – – – Germany

Table 4.1 Inflation and economic growth[a]

Sample	Inflation (in percentages)							
	1961.1–92.4		1961.1–78.4		1979.1–84.4		1985.1–92.4	
	M	SD	M	SD	M	SD	M	SD
Core ERM BP	1.2	0.6	1.3	0.7	1.4	0.5	0.7	0.4
Core ERM Cur	1.3	0.7	1.5	0.8	1.5	0.5	0.7	0.4
France	1.6	1.1	1.7	1.3	2.3	0.8	0.8	0.4
Germany[b]	1.0	0.8	1.1	0.2	0.9	0.4	0.8	0.5
Sample	Growth rates of real GDP (in percentage points)							
	1961.1–92.4		1961.1–78.4		1979.1–84.4		1985.1–92.4	
	M	SD	M	SD	M	SD	M	SD
Core ERM BP	0.8	1.1	1.0	1.2	0.3	0.8	0.6	0.7
Core ERM Cur	0.4	1.6	0.5	1.9	−0.2	1.1	0.5	0.8
France	0.9	1.3	1.1	1.6	0.4	0.7	0.7	0.5
Germany[b]	0.7	1.5	0.9	1.8	0.3	1.1	0.8	0.9

Notes:
a. M denotes the mean and SD stands for the standard deviation of the series multiplied by 100. BP stands for 1985 exchange rates. Cur represents current exchange rates. All national data are quarterly and seasonally adjusted.
b. The German figures are multiplicatively corrected for the breaks in the time series due to German unification in 1990.3.

1985 exchange rates exceeds the growth of European real output based on current exchange rates. Apart from this, the figures display the familiar pattern. After the pre-EMS period of high growth rates, economic activity markedly slowed down. Since the mid-1980s, economic growth accelerated again, but remained well below the average expansion rates realized in the pre-EMS period.

The path of velocity of *M1* and *M3* in the core ERM group is depicted in Figure 4.3. A noteworthy feature of this graph is the different pattern of velocity of narrow and broad money. On the one hand, European *M1*-velocity (V^1_{eur}) has on balance (slightly) risen. This was mainly due divergent developments in the largest core countries; in Germany *M1*-velocity declined, while V^1 increased in France. Owing to these movements, the differential between V^1 in individual countries has almost completely disappeared. On the other hand, European *M3*-velocity (V^3_{eur}) has exhibited a downward tendency throughout the entire sample; it dropped from about 0.5 to approximately 0.4. Individual countries faced the same behaviour in *M3*-velocity, implying that the level of *M3*-velocity has hardly shown any convergence within the core group.[24]

Figure 4.3 Velocity of M1 and M3

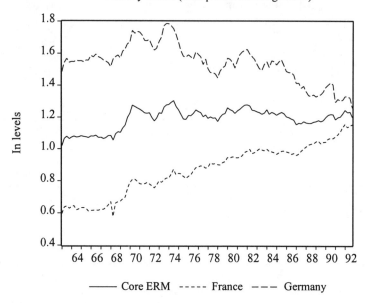

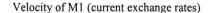

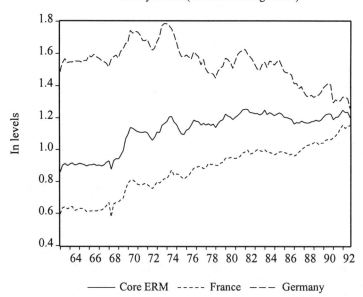

Figure 4.3 Velocity of M1 and M3

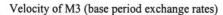

Velocity of M3 (base period exchange rates)

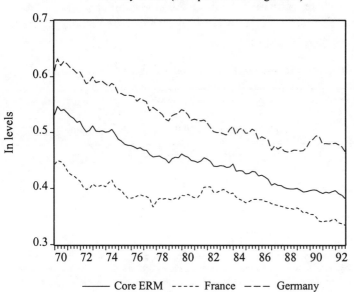

Velocity of M3 (current exchange rates)

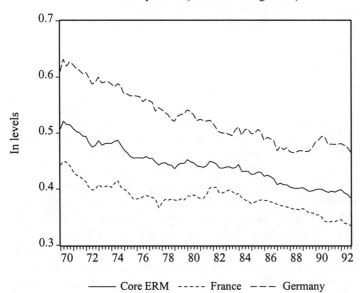

For the calculation of the equilibrium levels of real output and velocity on a European scale, I have followed the same approach as in Chapter 3. Therefore, I do not pay much attention to the methodological and technical issues involved here, but mainly focus on the empirical outcomes and their interpretation. The summary statistics of this exercise are reported in Table 4.2.

Table 4.2 Summary statistics of the forecast errors in Q_{eur}^*, V_{eur}^{1*} *and* V_{eur}^{3*}

	Q_{eur}^*		V_{eur}^{1*}		V_{eur}^{3*}	
	BP	*CUR*	*BP*	*CUR*	*BP*	*CUR*
MAE	0.008	0.013	0.013	0.015	0.008	0.009
RMSE	0.011	0.018	0.017	0.020	0.010	0.010
FOC	0.086	0.184	0.238	0.306	0.112	0.194
DW	1.83	1.63	1.52	1.40	1.78	1.61

Notes: *BP* is the base period exchange rate (base year is 1985). *CUR* denotes the current exchange rate vis-à-vis the German mark. *MAE* denotes the mean absolute error, *RMSE* is the root mean squared error, *FOC* is the first order autocorrelation and *DW* is the Durbin Watson statistic.

Several interesting things emerge from this table. First, the European variables computed with 1985 exchange rates are apparently easier to predict than those calculated with actual exchange rates: the error statistics of the former are substantially lower than those of the latter. Second, the statistics suggest greater variability of V_{eur}^{1*} compared to V_{eur}^{3*}. This observation agrees with the results for the individual countries. However, remarkable differences with the outcomes documented in Table 3.3 are the significant lower values of the mean absolute error and root mean square error for the European trend velocity, regardless of the definition of the money stock. In fact, these values are halved. Summing monetary aggregates across countries seemingly eliminates some of the noise present in national money supplies. More formally, disturbances in any one country's money are probably negatively correlated, so that the variance of the forecast error in the aggregate relationship is less than the corresponding variance in single-country relationships. This result indicates that aggregated money variables can be forecasted with more precision than national monetary aggregates, and in a sense corroborates other empirical work, generally finding an ERM-wide money demand to be more stable than national money demand functions (for example, Cassard et al., 1994; Bayoumi and Kenen, 1993; Fase, 1994; Monticelli and Strauss-Kahn, 1991; Kremers and Lane, 1990).

This feature probably refects the existence of currency substitution between the core ERM countries, which could expand more in the future as deregulation and liberalization of capital flows will progress. Thus, the crucial point is that if economic agents decide to frequently change their portfolio composition causing large outflows or inflows of liquidity in a country, this would tend to make national money demands unstable (with possible attendant difficulties in monetary targeting).[25] Notice that such an interpretation of the outcomes would suggest that the establisment of full monetary union would — further — enhance the stability of the demand for money in the EMU area as a whole (Lane and Poloz, 1992).[26] In this case, exchange rates are permanently fixed making all currencies within the union perfect substitutes in investors' portfolios.

The next stage in the investigation is to figure out what the order of integration of the European variables is.[27] Subsequently, the critical assumption of the P^*-framework that the actual and trend European variables

Table 4.3   ADF unit root tests for the European variables[a,b]

Variable	Log levels ($m = 1$)		Growth rates ($m = 2$)	
	BP	CUR	BP	CUR
p_{eur}	-2.2 $(t, 8)$	-1.6 $(c, 3)$	-0.7 $(n, 3)$	-0.7 $(n, 5)$
q_{eur}	-2.0 $(c, 4)$	-2.4 $(c, 3)$	$-3.7"$ $(c, 3)$	$-4.7"$ $(n, 2)$
V^1_{eur}	-2.1 $(c, 0)$	-1.8 $(c, 0)$	$-4.9"$ $(n, 7)$	$-10.0"$ $(n, 0)$
V^3_{eur}	-3.1 $(t, 0)$	-2.8 $(t, 0)$	$-8.0"$ $(n, 0)$	$-9.0"$ $(c, 0)$

Notes:

a.   The testing equation looks like: $\Delta^m x_t = \tau\, TD + \rho\, \Delta^{m-1} x_{t-1} + \Sigma^s_{j=1} \gamma_j \Delta^m x_{t-j}$. Here, x is the dependent variable, m denotes the order of integration ($m = 1$ or 2) and TD stands for the deterministic variables (intercept and/or time trend). The t-statistic of ρ on the lagged level of the dependent variable is used to determine whether the endogenous variable is stationary or not.

b.   BP stands for base period exchange rates (base year is 1985) and CUR represents current exchange rates vis-à-vis the German mark. The entries show the relevant ADF test statistic. The information in parentheses indicates the use of a constant only, c, or a constant and a trend, t. A specification without an intercept and time trend is indicated as $(n, ...)$. The figure in parentheses shows the number of lagged dependent variables included (j). The symbol " means that the statistic differs significantly from zero at the one percent level.

are cointegrated (meaning that the European gaps are stationary) must be verified. The results of unit root tests are reported in Table 4.3. From this table, it is apparent that only the European price level is I(2), implying that the change in the rate of inflation ($\Delta \pi^{eur}$) is stationary. The other variables are

Figure 4.4 European gaps

European price gap based on M1

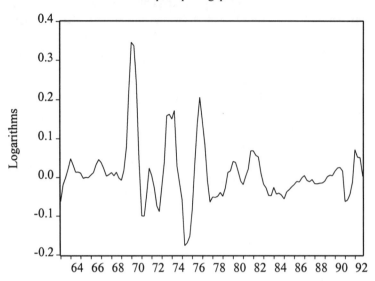

European velocity gap based on M1

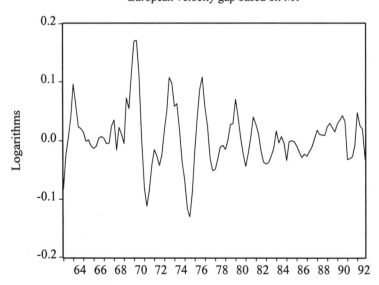

Figure 4.4 European gaps (continued)

European output gap

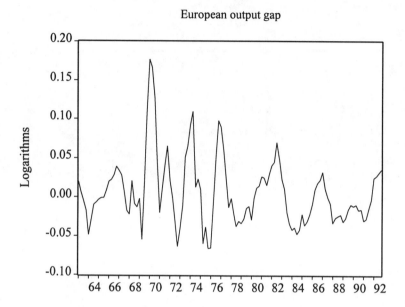

I(1), regardless of the conversion method. Thus, the first difference of the latter time series (in logarithms) is stationary.

Before the European price gaps (GAP_{eur}, GAP_i^{f1} and GAP_i^{f2}) can be inserted in the inflation equations, it must be checked whether these variables also satisfy the stationarity condition. In Table 4.4, ADF cointegration tests are

Table 4.4 Cointegration tests for the European price gaps (GAP$_{eur}$ and GAP$_i^{f1}$)

	Price gap based on *M1*		Price gap based on *M3*	
	BP	CUR	BP	CUR
Belgium	−8.4" (*n*, 0)	−7.0" (*n*, 4)	−6.5" (*n*, 0)	−6.2" (*n*, 5)
France	−9.5" (*n*, 0)	−10.2" (*n*, 0)	−5.1" (*n*, 3)	−5.1" (*n*, 3)
Germany	−7.1" (*n*, 2)	−6.4" (*n*, 0)	−7.1" (*n*, 0)	−5.9" (*n*, 3)
Netherlands	−8.6" (*c*, 0)	−8.1" (*n*, 0)	−7.5" (*n*, 1)	−6.6" (*n*, 1)
Core ERM	-6.9" (*n*, 2)	-6.9" (*n*, 3)	-6.4" (*n*, 0)	-6.3" (*n*, 3)

Notes: *BP* stands for base period exchange rates (base year is 1985) and *CUR* represents current exchange rates vis-à-vis the German mark. For an explanation of the testing equation and other figures and symbols see Table 4.3.

Figure 4.5 Domestic and European price gaps

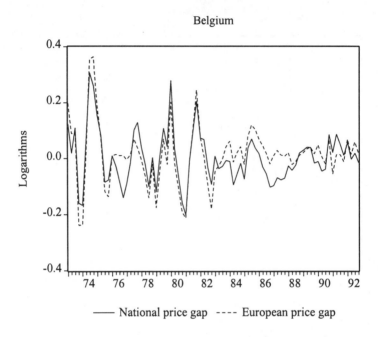

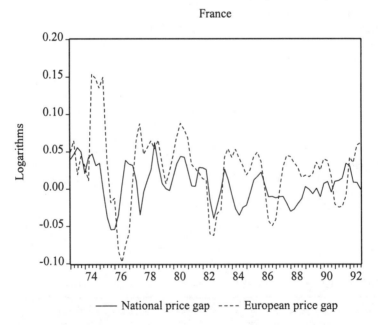

Figure 4.5 Domestic and European price gaps (continued)

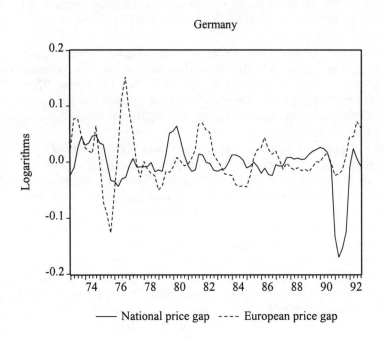

Germany

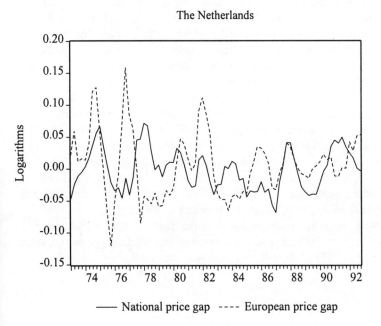

The Netherlands

applied to these price gaps. This table shows these gaps to be stationary at the one percent level in all instances, regardless of the aggregation method and definition of the money stock.[28] Thus, the fundamental P^*-assumption can be accepted.

This stationarity is also clearly visible when plotting the European price gaps (GAP_{eur}; see Figure 4.4): the gaps fluctuate around a zero mean. Relatively large peaks occur in the late 1960s and the first half of the 1970s. These distortions possibly reflect the breakdown of the Bretton Woods System in the early 1970s and perturbations ensuing from supply side shocks (notably the first oil crisis).

Figure 4.5 gives an impression of the size and sign of national and European price gaps over time (GAP_i^d and GAP_i^{fj}, respectively). On the whole, the two gaps do not always move closely together. Moreover, differences in the magnitude of local and European disturbances at a particular date are more a rule than an exception. This observation hints at the existence of country-specific monetary and real shocks or at least a different timing of common shocks across countries. In this respect, the effects of German unification for domestic and European price gaps are illustrative. This event led to a large negative domestic price gap for Germany around 1991. On the other hand, in the European data and in the foreign price gaps, the impact of German unification is less noticeable: the European price gaps are not extremely negative. According to the P^*-model, the negative German price gap around 1991 pointed to inflationary pressures. In retrospect, German inflation did rise shortly after unification, which prompted the Bundesbank to tighten its monetary policy. When looking at the domestic price gaps for the other countries, no direct signs of inflationary tendencies coming from domestic factors were present at this date. On the contrary, the domestic gaps were positive and pointed to a deflationary bias, mirroring the fact that the non-anchor countries had already turned into a recession in 1990. De Grauwe (1994a) argues that the provisions of the EMS had the effect of forcing those countries who stayed within the system to follow an unwelcome restrictive monetary policy (that is, to increase their interest rates) so as to help Germany in its objective of reducing its domestic inflation rate after unification. It is precisely this asymmetric feature of the EMS that is sometimes believed to have been the main factor underlying the loss of credibility of the system and the emergence of large exchange rate tensions in 1992.

The latter observations obviously raise the question whether domestic or foreign price gaps provide a more accurate signal of changes in domestic prices to come. This issue will be addressed empirically in Section 7.

5 TECHNICAL ASPECTS OF THE CONSTRUCTION OF EUROPEAN EQUILIBRIUM VARIABLES

In the following, the emphasis will be on the more technical features of the construction of V^*_{eur} and Q^*_{eur} (both computed with current exchange rates), respectively. First, I pay attention to the models that the MSKF technique has selected in creating these variables over time. Subsequently, I discuss some other noteworthy outcomes of these computations. Here, a comparison with the determination of the equilibrium variables in individual countries evidently comes to mind.

5.1 Trend Velocity in Europe

Figure 4.6 displays the appropriateness of the six implemented models in predicting the velocity of a narrow and broad monetary aggregate over time. In the first two decades of the sample, the relative attractiveness of the models for forecasting V^1_{eur} is prone to large variations as the upper panel of this figure demonstrates. The picture changes in the late 1970s. Since then, model 2 definitely generates the best predictions for V^1_{eur}. The outlier models are activated four times. All large breaks take place in the late 1960s and early 1970s. The well-documented problems in the Bretton Woods System around 1970 are probably largely responsible for the emergence of these outliers.

As pointed out in Section 4, the statistical properties of V^3_{eur} differ from those of V^1_{eur}. This is also evident in the pattern of prior probabilities on the various models, which cannot be attributed to differences in the input parameters chosen for the construction of both equilibrium variables, anyway. Whereas the MSKF method frequently switches between model 2 and 3 in forecasting V^1_{eur} up to the late 1970s, a distinct preference for model 2 in predicting V^3_{eur} exists from the very beginning of the 1970s. In the latter case, the prior probabilities on model 1 and 3 are practically nil throughout the entire sample. This means that forecast errors are predominantly viewed as permanent changes in the level of V^3. The right-hand panels of Figure 4.6 tell us that the outlier models are employed three times in the case of V^1_{eur}, but have no part in the prediction of V^{3*}_{eur}.

With respect to the course of the prior probabilities on the models applied for the calculation of V^{3*} in Germany we have arrived at quite similar conclusions (see Figure 3.6). However, for the Netherlands the prior probabilities on the models exhibit an erratic pattern throughout the sample. The MSKF method regularly switches from one model to another in predicting V^3 in the Netherlands. This could be viewed as a sign of a somewhat less stable Dutch money demand. Moreover, it should not come as a surprise that velocity of *M3* on a European scale in particular 'inherits' the characteristics of the comparable variable in a country whose relative weight

Figure 4.6 Prior probabilities on models for European M1 and M3 velocity

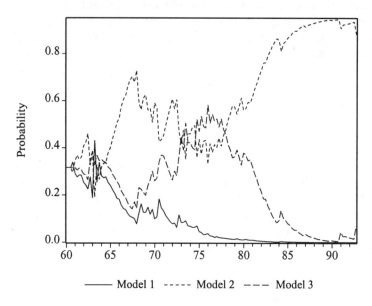

Normal-sized forecast error models for M1 velocity

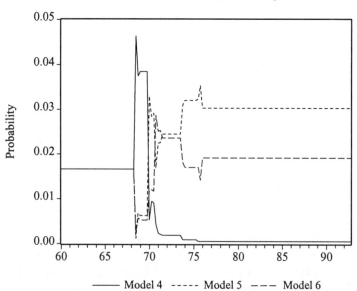

Outlier models for M1 velocity

Figure 4.6 Prior probabilities on models for European M1 and M3 velocity (continued)

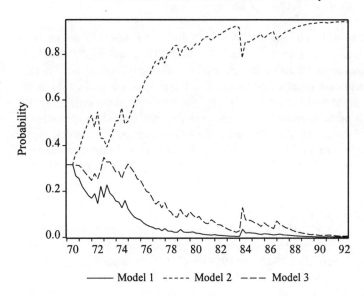

Normal-sized forecast error models for M3 velocity

——— Model 1   ----- Model 2   — — Model 3

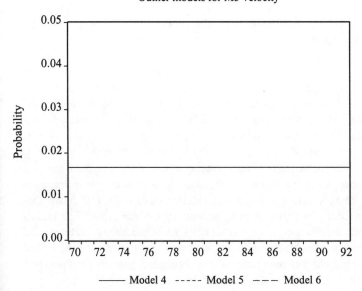

Outlier models for M3 velocity

——— Model 4   ----- Model 5   — — Model 6

in the EU-wide money stock is fairly high. Finally, the shock to German velocity (of *M1* and *M3*) caused by the German unification peter out in the group's monetary aggregate.[29]

5.2   Potential Real Output in Europe

The prior probabilities on the models which the MSKF has used to generate Q^*_{eur} are plotted in Figure 4.7. Until the mid-1970s, the MSKF method alternately uses model 1 and 3 in forecasting real output. In this period, the prediction errors are in turn interpreted as temporary or permanent shifts in both the constant and time trend. Hence, the method cannot convincingly decide which of both models best describes the data generating process of European real output. On the other hand, the MSKF method quickly discovers that model 2, where only the level of real output is hypothesized to change, fails to trace the path of real output adequately. Its prior probability almost immediately falls from the initially assumed 31.3 percent to approximately 10 percent. In 1976, the prior probability of model 3 suddenly jumps to more than 85 percent and then stabilizes around this level.

The outlier models (that is, specification 4, 5 and 6) participated three times in the estimation procedure. The corresponding dates are 1961.1—1962.1, 1963.1—1964.1 and 1968.4—1970.4.[30] Not surprisingly, these dates more or less concur with those that the tracking signal detects in the time series of real output in individual countries (see Table 3.4), except for the break in real output around 1975 associated with the first oil crisis (see footnote 29).

In contrast to the specification of the models for Germany and the Netherlands discussed in Section 3.1 of Chapter 3, experiments with different input parameters to compute Q^*_{eur} illustrate that the results improve to some extent — on the basis of the error statistics (and first order autocorrelation in particular) — if the speed of adjustment of the parameters is set at a slightly higher level. Technically speaking, somewhat better forecasts of European real output are obtained if old observations are relatively quickly disregarded. This finding could mirror the existence of country-specific shocks. Local disequilibria presumably make themselves felt for a relatively long period, because the economic structure of individual countries cannot respond quickly to new situations. Conversely, on a higher aggregation level purely domestic pertubations have, almost by definition, smaller and mostly less prolonged repercussions for the overall economic performance of the group. The reason is that domestic imbalances may be mitigated by adverse idiosyncratic shocks in other countries. This brings us to a related question concerning the nature of the statistical links between national and European gaps in the course of time. In the next section, I shall elaborate on this subject.

Figure 4.7 *Prior probabilities on models for European real output*

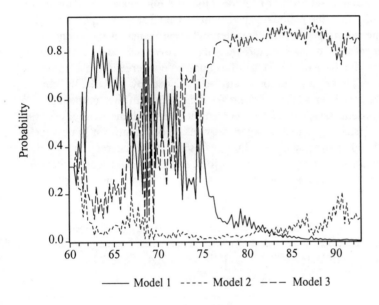

Normal-sized forecast error models

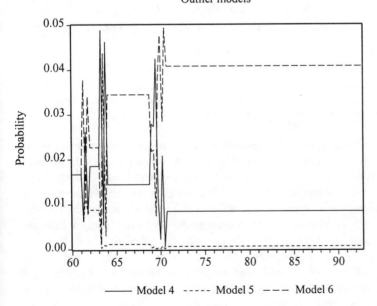

Outlier models

6 ECONOMIC DISTORTIONS IN EUROPE: THEORETICAL AND POLICY CONSIDERATIONS

From the previous sections, it is evident that the European gaps show much less volatility than the national gaps calculated in Chapter 3. Apart from this feature, the question how the character and significance of the connections between local and European disturbances have evolved over time is also rather relevant in the face of the state of economic convergence in Europe. A summary of these associations can be provided by calculating simple correlation coefficients. Table 4.5 presents the results of the computations.[31] The figures demonstrate that in the whole time interval domestic shocks in the real and monetary sphere are in general weakly, but significantly positively correlated with disturbances on a European scale in most cases. This finding is in accordance with my prior expectations, since national economies are on average, but not necessarily to the same extent, hit by common international shocks.

Table 4.5 Correlation between European and national gaps based on M3

	1973.1–1992.4			1973.1–1978.4			1979.1–1992.4		
	PG	*VG*	*OG*	*PG*	*VG*	*OG*	*PG*	*VG*	*OG*
Belgium	0.17	0.65	0.25	0.10	0.49	0.15	0.26	0.73	0.37
France	0.42	0.71	0.27	0.46	0.77	0.27	0.33	0.68	0.29
Germany	0.32	0.70	0.43	0.11	0.52	0.13	0.58	0.79	0.73
Netherlands	−0.05	0.29	0.19	−0.14	0.17	0.01	0.11	0.37	0.39
Average	0.22	0.59	0.29	0.13	0.49	0.19	0.32	0.64	0.45

Notes: *PG*, *VG* and *OG* denote the price, velocity and output gap, respectively. The European variables are calculated with current exchange rates.

When examining the relationship between local and European shocks in different subsamples, several interesting aspects come to the fore. In the first place, individual countries are apparently more economically isolated from other European countries during the 1970s compared to the 1980s since the correlation coefficients are — with a few exceptions — smaller than in the complete sample. Second, for some reasons the economic linkages between European countries have become tighter in the last subperiod, as reflected in higher correlation coefficients. The (unweighted average) correlation coefficient of the output gaps has increased from about 0.3 in the pre-EMS era to approximately 0.45 in the last time interval. Whereas the same statistic for the velocity gaps was already fairly high in the 1970s (0.6), it has risen somewhat further to about 0.65 in the last period. The correlation between both price gaps has moved in the same direction, but remains weaker than the correlations between their constituent parts.

These calculations could mirror an increased symmetry in shocks, which would accord with other scarce empirical evidence suggesting that, in line with the modern international trade theory, the importance of nationally differentiated shocks has diminished over the past decade (Stockman, 1988; Baxter and Stockman, 1989).[32] Moreover, the results can also be connected with an issue being at the forefront of recent theoretical and empirical work on monetary integration which is related to the optimum currency area literature.[33] In this theory, the presence of many country-specific shocks is viewed as a major obstacle for individual countries to fix irrevocably their exchange rates (or to join a monetary union with a common currency).[34] More specifically, this strand of theory emphasizes the point that a common currency area is more efficient the more correlated the underlying shocks, since the more correlated the disturbances the smaller the need for independent macroeconomic policies. These tentative results suggest that the 'macroeconomic cost' of giving up the possibility of accommodating country-specific disequilibria through exchange rate adjustments has decreased for the core group since the formation of the ERM in 1979, because individual countries are to a greater extent exposed to common shocks.[35] In a similar vein, Bayoumi and Eichengreen (1993) find that aggregate (supply) disturbances are more highly correlated for the original European Union members than for the later EU entrants. As a consequence, the relative size of these distortions will be smaller for the core members — Germany and her immediate neighbours — than for the rest of the EU. This may also just reflect the greater homogeneity in technology and industrial structure within the original EU group.

Bayoumi (1992) comes up with an alternative explanation for the greater symmetry in economic distortions in the core countries in the EMS period. He stresses that the fixed exchange rate regime itself may actually have caused idiosyncratic country shocks to become more contemporaneously correlated, since the exchange rate 'buffer' is no longer available.[36] In fact, one of the main arguments in favour of the ERM is that, by reducing monetary independence, it enforces a more coordinated policy response across members which might otherwise be difficult to achieve (see Fratianni and von Hagen, 1992). Bayoumi's study indicates that while the ERM has not affected the nature of the underlying shocks hitting the economies, it has had a significant effect on the response of member countries to these imbalances, making them both more elongated and more similar.

The final remark on Table 4.5 concerns the possibility that the present symmetry of national and European shocks is underestimated to some extent. Actually, I have only calculated the correlation between contemporaneous disturbances. I have not tried to identify the lead and lag structure that generates the highest correlation coefficients. Such a procedure can of course be justified on the ground that some countries (i.c. Germany) are considered to be 'locomotives' whereas other countries — and especially the smaller ones — can be qualified in the same typology as 'wagons'.[37]

Bayoumi and Eichengreen (1994b) argue that it is also of interest to look at the size of the disturbances over time.[38] If distortions are of negligible magnitude, countries may incur only minor costs from forsaking policy autonomy, because real and monetary variables will barely diverge from their equilibrium values. This would imply that the need for the nominal exchange rate to act as a cushion is rather small. To investigate this aspect, I compute the average size of the disturbances for each country and for the core group as a whole in four subperiods (with a more or less equal length). As a proxy for these imbalances, I take the gaps generated by the MSKF method. This enables me to distinguish between disruptions on the real and monetary side of the economy. The average size of the disturbances is measured by calculating the standard deviation of the gaps in the four subperiods and averaging them. Since each shock is normalized to have a standard deviation of one over the entire sample, any dispersion from unity indicates whether the magnitude of the disturbances in the respective subsamples is larger or smaller compared to that in the whole sample. Table 4.6 reports the outcomes of this exercise.

Table 4.6 Magnitude of monetary and real shocks over time

	1963.1—1970.4		1971.1—1978.4		1979.1—1984.4		1985.1—1992.4	
	MS	RS	MS	RS	MS	RS	MS	RS
Belgium	0.7	0.9	1.1	1.0	1.2	1.4	1.0	0.7
France	1.4	1.9	1.5	0.9	0.6	0.6	0.6	0.6
Germany	0.8	1.5	1.2	1.0	1.2	0.9	0.9	0.7
Netherlands	0.7	1.3	1.6	1.0	1.0	1.1	0.7	0.7
Core ERM	1.4	1.6	1.2	1.1	0.7	0.7	0.7	0.7

Notes: MS and RS stand for monetary and real shocks, respectively. The table shows the standard deviation of the disturbances over the relevant period divided by the average standard deviation over the four subperiods. In contrast to Table 4.5, the computations are based on *M1*, since this time series is available for a longer time span than that of *M3*. The figures for Germany have been multiplicatively adjusted for breaks in the data associated with German unification in 1990.3.

The calculations indicate an increase in the size of monetary shocks after the first subperiod, that is, after the Bretton Woods regime broke down. Conversely, the magnitude of the output gaps diminished in the second period compared with the 1960s, despite the economic turbulence caused by the two oil crises. This probably reflects to a certain degree the constraints imposed by a fixed exchange-rate regime to pursue domestic output stabilization policies. Since the creation of the EMS in 1979, a remarkable reduction in the size of monetary and real shocks in almost every country has taken place compared with the 1972–78 period. Belgium is an exception to this rule with a slight rise in the size of real and monetary imbalances in the first years of the EMS (1979-84). In the last subperiod, the countries are generally faced with the smallest disruptions in both the real and monetary side of the economy. All in all, there has been an obvious downward trend in the magnitude of monetary and real shocks within the core group over time. The policy conclusion is that these countries of course limit the short-run flexibility of relative prices by fixing the exchange rate or adopting a common currency, but the decreased size of the shocks has made the occurrence of future policy conflicts among these countries less likely (provided that major, unprecedented shocks will not or just occasionally happen[39]).

So far, I have exclusively focused on the association between, and the size of, national and European gaps in the course of time. In the next section, I shall test whether European gaps exert any influence whatsoever on inflation in individual countries.

7 REGRESSION RESULTS

Analogous to the empirical research in Chapter 3, I shall test the validity of the P^*-framework with European gaps in two constellations. In the first model, I define inflation as the quarterly change in the GDP price deflator ($\pi = p_t - p_{t-1}$). In the second specification, inflation is measured as the annual change in p ($\Delta_4 p = p_t - p_{t-1}$). As a starting point, I have chosen the following equations:

$$\Delta \pi_t^i = \alpha_0 + \alpha_1 GAP_{i,t-n}^{f1} + \sum_{j=1}^{4} \beta_j \Delta \pi_{t-j}^i + \tau \Delta \, p_{i,t-m}^{en} \tag{4.13}$$

$$\alpha_1 < 0$$

$$\Delta \Delta_4 \, p_t^i = \alpha_0 + \alpha_1 \sum_{j=1}^{4} GAP_{i,t-j}^{f1} + \sum_{j=1}^{4} \beta_j \Delta \Delta_4 \, p_{t-j}^i + \tau \Delta_4 \, p_{i,t-m}^{en} \tag{4.14}$$

$$\alpha_1 < 0$$

In these expressions, the endogenous variable depends on its own lagged values, representing the inherent dynamics of the inflation process, and growth rates of energy prices. In order to save degrees of freedom, I have pursued a 'general-to-specific' estimation approach, commencing with the equations above and then sequentially removing insignificant lagged dependent variables, taking care at each step to test for any misspecification. Further, the benchmark equations for individual countries are allowed to differ with respect to the lags with which the gaps influence domestic inflation. In this way, I implicitly account for possible varying speeds of adjustment in response to shocks across countries. In the upper half of the tables the outcomes for *M1* are shown, whereas the lower part of each table documents the results for *M3*. As is apparent from Section 6, the correlation between national and EU-wide shocks has increased in the course of time. For this reason, I perform estimations over different subperiods.[40]

In the second part of each subsection, I ask myself whether European gaps possess more information value for future price developments than national gaps. This aspect is extremely relevant for monetary policy makers in Europe. Indeed, if domestic inflation is more strongly correlated with European shocks, monetary spillover effects exist and a European monetary aggregate will ultimately determine the country's long-run price level. In fact, there are two ways to cope with this issue. The first alternative is to test whether a specification with just the domestic or European gap (as defined in equation (2.3) or (4.7), respectively) is more capable in explaining domestic inflation. The second option is to include both gaps simultaneously in the estimation equation (in conformity with equation (4.8)). For the sake of completeness, I record the outcomes of both approaches. Since the application of this procedure for every model mentioned above would generate an enormous quantity of statistical output, only the specification where inflation is defined as $\Delta\pi$ and the price gap is calculated with *M3* will be re-estimated. Reassuringly, the overall conclusions do not really change if another model had been selected.

In Section 7.5, I report the empirical results for the core ERM group as a whole. Here, the aggregate European inflation derived from equation (4.12) acts as the dependent variable, while the price gap is calculated according to equation (4.3).

7.1   Empirical Outcomes for Belgium

The estimations for Belgium are presented in Table 4.7. In the whole sample, the results are somewhat ambiguous. The gaps calculated with base year exchange rates (GAP_{bp}^{fl}) are in three cases (weakly) significant, whereas no causal relation between European gaps based on current exchange rates (GAP_{cur}^{fl}) and domestic price developments exists. On the other hand, the coefficients on the gaps do carry the theoretically expected negative signs in all instances.

In the entire EMS period, the information value of the gaps is very low and only one coefficient is significantly different from zero (that is, GAP_{cur}^{fl} in model I_{m3}). By iteratively moving the beginning of the estimation period closer toward the end of the sample, that is, 1992.4, the European gaps

Table 4.7 *Regression results for Belgium*

| Model | DV | Sample | Price gap (GAP^{fl}) | | Energy prices | LDV | R^2 | SE | Q(8) | HET | Chow$_{79}$ | Chow$_{82}$ |
			BP	CUR								
I$_{m1}$	$\Delta\pi$	63.1–92.4	−0.045 (1.4)	−0.023 (1.1)	0.013 (2.3')	12 4	0.31	0.59	7.5	8.0	11.9°	8.1
I$_{m1}$	$\Delta\pi$	79.1–92.4	−0.029 (1.0)	−0.074 (2.1')		1234	0.48	0.48	3.9	5.3		
I$_{m1}$	$\Delta\pi$	85.1–92.4	−0.087 (3.0")	−0.097 (3.2")		4	0.19	0.40	10.3	2.1		
II$_{m1}$	$\Delta\Delta_4 p$	63.1–92.4	−0.079 (2.5')	−0.023 (1.1)	0.007 (2.1')	1 34	0.36	0.68	23.4"	16.4"	7.9	5.3
II$_{m1}$	$\Delta\Delta_4 p$	79.1–92.4	−0.031 (1.0)	−0.017 (0.5)		1 4	0.20	0.54	7.0	5.7		
II$_{m1}$	$\Delta\Delta_4 p$	85.1–92.4	−0.052 (1.8°)	−0.069 (2.0')		12	0.39	0.44	8.0	3.2		
I$_{m3}$	$\Delta\pi$	73.1–92.4	−0.073 (1.9°)	−0.046 (1.3)	0.011 (2.0')	1 34	0.30	0.55	5.1	5.9	18.7"	10.8"
I$_{m3}$	$\Delta\pi$	79.1–92.4	−0.045 (0.8)	−0.107 (2.1')		1234	0.48	0.48	3.5	7.0		
I$_{m3}$	$\Delta\pi$	85.1–92.4	−0.153 (3.4")	−0.141 (3.6")		4	0.22	0.39	6.0	3.9		
II$_{m3}$	$\Delta\Delta_4 p$	73.1–92.4	−0.094 (2.4')	−0.054 (1.4)	0.006 (2.1')	1 4	0.49	0.62	9.9	11.4	16.0"	11.1'
II$_{m3}$	$\Delta\Delta_4 p$	79.1–92.4	−0.038 (0.8)	−0.017 (0.4)		1 4	0.20	0.54	7.2	4.9		
II$_{m3}$	$\Delta\Delta_4 p$	85.1–92.4	−0.109 (2.0')	−0.136 (2.3')		12	0.44	0.43	9.7	2.8		

Notes: The price gaps enter model 1 with a three quarter lag. *DV* denotes the dependent variable. *BP* and *CUR* indicate whether the European variables are computed with base period or current exchange rates. Heteroskedasticity-consistent t-values are shown behind the coefficients. *LDV* represent the significant lags of the dependent variable. For instance, 1 34 means that the first, third and fourth lags of the endogenous variable are significant and included. The diagnostic test statistics refer to the equations where the national variables are added with current exchange rates. SE is the standard error of the regression. Q(8) is the Box-Pierce statistic for serial correlation in the residuals. HET is White's statistic for heteroskedasticity and is distributed as χ^2. Chow$_{79}$ and Chow$_{82}$ are Chow tests for breaks in 1979 and 1982, respectively. The reported statistic is the likelihood ratio. The symbols °, ' and " denote that the statistic is significantly different from zero at the ten, five and one percent level, respectively.

gradually start exerting a significant influence on the dependent variable. From 1985 onwards, every gap has predictive value in explaining price movements.[41]

Although the above findings lend support for the view that the inflationary process in Belgium nowadays more heavily depends on European distortions, domestic gaps could in principle still be a more appropriate indicator for future price movements. In order to investigate the relative importance of both gaps over time, I have re-estimated model I_{m3} for the same subperiods as in Table 4.7. For the sake of clarity, only the parameters of the gaps and two descriptive statistics are presented. Several conclusions can be inferred from Table 4.8. In the first place, the usefulness of the domestic price gap as an indicator for inflationary threats is beyond question in the entire time span. Conversely, inflation is unrelated to distortions on a European level in the full sample. These conclusions do not hold for the second and third time interval. Since the inception of the EMS, the significant causal relationship between ERM-wide distortions and the rate of inflation catches the eye, while the national price gap has no predictive power for domestic inflation anymore. Institutional and macroeconomic policy changes (perhaps to some extent motivated by the provisions and characteristics of the EMS) are possibly partly responsible for this. In other words, the regression results imply that from 1979 onwards the growth of the European money stock ($M3$) affects inflation in Belgium.

Table 4.8 Regression results with domestic and/or European price gaps for Belgium

Model	1973.1–1992.4			1979.1–1992.4			1985.1–1992.4		
	GAP^d	$GAP^{f1/f2}$	R^2 (SE)	GAP^d	$GAP^{f1/f2}$	R^2 (SE)	GAP^d	$GAP^{f1/f2}$	R^2 (SE)
A	−0.129		0.53	−0.061		0.44	−0.057		0.15
	(2.4′)		(0.59)	(1.3)		(0.54)	(0.8)		(0.42)
B		−0.046	0.30		−0.107	0.48		−0.141	0.22
		(1.3)	(0.55)		(2.1′)	(0.48)		(3.6″)	(0.39)
C	−0.103	−0.032	0.32	−0.058	−0.102	0.48	−.023	−0.162	0.20
	(2.2′)	(1.0)	(0.55)	(1.0)	(2.1′)	(0.47)	(0.2)	(2.9″)	(0.39)

Notes: Model A contains the domestic price gap as defined in equation (2.3). Model B includes GAP^{f1} from expression (4.7) (see Table 4.7). In model C, both gaps are inserted simultaneously where GAP^{f2} does not comprise Belgian data (equation (4.8)). Heteroskedasticity consistent t-values are recorded below the coefficients in parentheses. SE is the standard error of the regression. The gaps are inserted with a lag of three quarters. The symbols °, ′ and ″ denote significance at the ten, five and one percent level, respectively.

Table 4.9 Regression results for France

Model	DV	Sample	Price gap (GAP^{fl}) BP	CUR	Energy prices	LDV	R^2	SE	Q(8)	HET	Chow$_{79}$	Chow$_{82}$
I$_{m1}$	$\Delta\pi$	63.1–92.4	−0.049 (2.3')	−0.042 (1.4)	0.016 (4.5")	123	0.29	0.92	12.4	18.3	2.6	3.8
I$_{m1}$	$\Delta\pi$	79.1–92.4	−0.032 (0.9)	−0.049 (1.4)	0.014 (3.9")	1234	0.34	0.47	4.2	12.2		
I$_{m1}$	$\Delta\pi$	85.1–92.4	−0.025 (2.0')	−0.029 (2.0')	0.011 (4.3")	12	0.60	0.31	2.4	6.7		
II$_{m1}$	$\Delta\Delta_4 p$	63.1–92.4	−0.046 (2.3')	−0.068 (1.9°)	0.012 (5.8")	1 34	0.34	1.02	10.5	5.8	3.3	4.1
II$_{m1}$	$\Delta\Delta_4 p$	79.1–92.4	−0.045 (1.8°)	−0.072 (2.4)	0.012 (5.0")	34	0.43	0.54	8.9	12.9		
II$_{m1}$	$\Delta\Delta_4 p$	85.1–92.4	−0.052 (1.9°)	−0.057 (2.2)	0.008 (2.7")	234	0.41	0.36	3.1	7.4		
I$_{m3}$	$\Delta\pi$	73.1–92.4	−0.031 (1.1)	−0.033 (1.0)	0.016 (3.8")	1234	0.32	0.52	3.4	15.7	8.5	9.2
I$_{m3}$	$\Delta\pi$	79.1–92.4	−0.043 (1.0)	−0.079 (1.7°)	0.014 (4.1")	1234	0.35	0.47	3.8	11.7		
I$_{m3}$	$\Delta\pi$	85.1–92.4	−0.037 (2.1')	−0.052 (2.6)	0.012 (4.6")	12	0.61	0.30	2.0	6.7		
II$_{m3}$	$\Delta\Delta_4 p$	73.1–92.4	−0.031 (1.6)	−0.055 (1.9°)	0.010 (5.9")	4	0.36	0.60	13.5°	3.3	3.6	5.4
II$_{m3}$	$\Delta\Delta_4 p$	79.1–92.4	−0.060 (2.0')	−0.110 (2.7)	0.012 (5.3")	34	0.44	0.53	8.6	12.4		
II$_{m3}$	$\Delta\Delta_4 p$	85.1–92.4	−0.086 (2.3')	−0.109 (2.7)	0.008 (3.1")	234	0.45	0.35	2.6	7.3		

Notes: The price gaps enter model I with a three quarter lag. *DV* denotes the dependent variable. *BP* and *CUR* indicate whether the European variables are computed with base period or current exchange rates. Heteroskedasticity-consistent t-values are shown behind the coefficients. *LDV* represent the significant lags of the dependent variable. For instance, 1 34 means that the first, third and fourth lags of the endogenous variable are significant and included. The diagnostic test statistics refer to the equations where the national variables are added with current exchange rates. SE is the standard error of the regression. Q(8) is the Box-Pierce statistic for serial correlation in the residuals. HET is White's statistic for heteroskedasticity and is distributed as χ^2. Chow$_{79}$ and Chow$_{82}$ are Chow tests for breaks in 1979 and 1982, respectively. The reported statistic is the likelihood ratio. The symbols °, ' and " denote that the statistic is significantly different from zero at the ten, five and one percent level, respectively.

In some respect, these findings buttress the (theoretical) notion that in countries with an exchange rate target money supply becomes fully endogenous under certain conditions.[42] In this circumstance, domestic monetary authorities put their policy actions predominantly at the service of the exchange rate objective and consequently lose control over total domestic monetary expansion. From this perspective, it should not come as a great surprise that a relationship between domestic money measures and domestic price trends does not exist in the EMS period.

7.2   Empirical Outcomes for France

The results for France, which are tabulated in Table 4.9, can be summarized as follows. The models with *M1* indicate that European disturbances have a (weak) significant impact on French inflation over the period 1963.1—1992.4. On the other hand, the regressions with *M3* conducted over the sample 1973.1—1992.4 do not point to any significant influence of European price gaps on domestic price movements.[43] The results for the other subperiods show that the informative value of the gaps has clearly improved over time. In the time span 1985.1—1992.4, the parameters of the European price gaps are generally different from zero at the five percent level in every model. Hence, French inflation has gradually become more sensitive for disturbances on a European scale. Be that as it may, one cannot rule out beforehand the

Table 4.10 Regression results with domestic and/or European price gaps for France

Model	1973.1—1992.4 GAP^d	$GAP^{f1/f2}$	R^2 (SE)	1979.1—1992.4 GAP^d	$GAP^{f1/f2}$	R^2 (SE)	1985.1—1992.4 GAP^d	$GAP^{f1/f2}$	R^2 (SE)
A	−0.089		0.47	−0.102		0.36	−0.065		0.62
	(2.0′)		(0.52)	(1.6)		(0.46)	(1.6)		(0.30)
B		−0.033	0.32		−0.079	0.35		−0.052	0.61
		(1.0)	(0.52)		(1.7°)	(0.47)		(2.6′)	(0.30)
C	−0.113	−0.027	0.35	−0.057	−0.061	0.36	−0.057	−0.045	0.61
	(2.8″)	(1.1)	(0.51)	(1.1)	(1.0)	(0.46)	(1.2)	(2.0′)	(0.30)

Notes: Model A contains the domestic price gap as defined in equation (2.3). Model B includes GAP^{f1} from expression (4.7) (see Table 4.9). In model C, both gaps are inserted simultaneously where GAP^{f2} does not comprise French data (equation (4.8)). Heteroskedasticity consistent t-values are recorded below the coefficients in parentheses. SE is the standard error of the regression. The gaps are inserted with a lag of three quarters. The symbols °, ′ and ″ denote significance at the ten, five and one percent level, respectively.

possibility that these shocks — as yet — contain less relevant information for the future path of inflation than local disturbances. Just like in the previous subsection, I shall address this issue by re-estimating model I_{m3}. The estimation results are reported in Table 4.10.

A number of key points emerges from this table. First, the estimations illustrate that local distortions exercise a significant impact on inflation in the whole time span. A positive price gap of 1 percentage point leads to a fall in inflation of approximately 0.16 percentage point. Disturbances on a European level are apparently not relevant for domestic price movements during this period. This picture is reversed in the entire EMS-period. Now, the explanatory power of local gaps is statistically negligible, while the European gap starts to convey information for future inflation. The estimations pertaining to the third period indicate that the information content of ERM-wide shocks has improved further. A plausible explanation for the observed shift in relative importance of both gaps could be that French macroeconomic policies are nowadays more in line with those in other core ERM countries (see Sachs and Wyplosz, 1986).[44]

The monetary policy aspects ensuing from these results clearly stand out. As elaborated in Section 4.2 of Chapter 3, French monetary authorities have always set both exchange rate and monetary targets since the mid-1980s, although the constraints associated to ERM membership clearly placed the exchange rate at the center of monetary policy (Jozzo, 1993; Quintyn, 1993).[45] The underlying philosophy of publically announcing annual target ranges for the growth of a selected monetary aggregate is to reinforce the credibility of the anti-inflationary commitment and to moderate inflationary expectations (Icard, 1994). However, these results partly take the edge off this view, since they can be interpreted to mean that undershooting or overshooting the internal objective does not seem to have any noticeable direct implications for French inflation in the 1980s. This is in conformity with the notion that the acceptance of the German leadership in the ERM largely limits the scope for monetary authorities in other participating countries to run an independent monetary policy.

7.3 Empirical Outcomes for Germany

For Germany, European gaps do not translate into national price movements in the entire time interval (Table 4.11). Besides, the parameters of the gaps sometimes carry the wrong sign. This situation changes in the entire EMS period where several significant coefficients can be discovered. In the third sample period, there is a significant pass-through from European distortions to domestic prices in every model.

The evolution of the parameters of European gaps nicely comes to the fore if I subsequently drop one year after another from the second subperiod. In Figure 4.8, the estimated gap coefficients in model II are depicted for the time

Table 4.11 Regression results for Germany

Model	DV	Sample	Price gap (GAP^f)		Energy prices	LDV	R^2	SE	Q(8)	HET	Chow$_{79}$	Chow$_{82}$
			BP	CUR								
I_{m1}	$\Delta\pi$	63.1–92.4	−0.013 (0.2)	0.045 (1.4)		123	0.68	0.69	7.6	39.2"	4.9	6.2
I_{m1}	$\Delta\pi$	79.1–92.4	−0.105 (1.3)	−0.093 (1.1)		1234	0.59	0.51	1.6	10.0		
I_{m1}	$\Delta\pi$	85.1–92.4	−0.201 (6.3")	−0.195 (4.8")		1 4	0.44	0.50	4.9	4.3		
II_{m1}	$\Delta\Delta_4 p$	63.1–92.4	0.018 (0.6)	0.016 (1.2)		4	0.12	0.72	9.1	12.6'	3.1	4.5
II_{m1}	$\Delta\Delta_4 p$	79.1–92.4	−0.077 (1.7°)	−0.057 (1.8°)		2 4	0.21	0.54	5.4	12.2		
II_{m1}	$\Delta\Delta_4 p$	85.1–92.4	−0.161 (4.4")	−0.139 (4.3")	0.009 (2.2')	23	0.50	0.46	7.4	14.0°		
I_{m3}	$\Delta\pi$	73.1–92.4	−0.139 (1.4)	−0.007 (0.1)		1234	0.56	0.59	4.0	28.5"	8.5	9.2
I_{m3}	$\Delta\pi$	79.1–92.4	−0.211 (2.2')	−0.139 (1.7°)		1234	0.59	0.51	1.2	9.9		
I_{m3}	$\Delta\pi$	85.1–92.4	−0.306 (4.7")	−0.278 (3.6")		1 4	0.46	0.49	6.6	5.0		
II_{m3}	$\Delta\Delta_4 p$	73.1–92.4	−0.036 (0.7)	0.007 (0.3)		2 4	0.14	0.65	3.9	7.7	8.9°	7.8
II_{m3}	$\Delta\Delta_4 p$	79.1–92.4	−0.104 (1.7°)	−0.070 (2.2')		2 4	0.23	0.54	4.9	1.9		
II_{m3}	$\Delta\Delta_4 p$	85.1–92.4	−0.298 (4.2")	−0.202 (4.1")		23	0.38	0.51	4.0	6.5		

Notes: The price gaps enter model I with a three quarter lag. *DV* denotes the dependent variable. *BP* and *CUR* indicate whether the European variables are computed with base period or current exchange rates. Heteroskedasticity-consistent t-values are shown behind the coefficients. *LDV* represent the significant lags of the dependent variable. For instance, 1 34 means that the first, third and fourth lags of the endogenous variable are significant and included. The diagnostic test statistics refer to the equations where the national variables are added with current exchange rates. SE is the standard error of the regression. Q(8) is the Box-Pierce statistic for serial correlation in the residuals. HET is White's statistic for heteroskedasticity and is distributed as χ^2. Chow$_{79}$ and Chow$_{82}$ are Chow tests for breaks in 1979 and 1982, respectively. The reported statistic is the likelihood ratio. The symbols °, ' and " denote that the statistic is significantly different from zero at the ten, five and one percent level, respectively.

Figure 4.8 Estimated gap coefficients and their significance

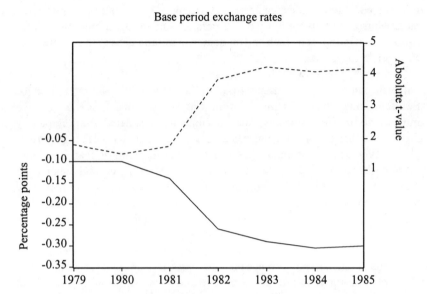

Base period exchange rates

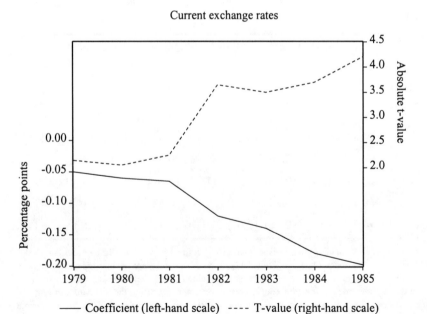

Current exchange rates

span 1979/85—92. The sample period was not shortened further to retain sufficient degrees of freedom. The t-values of the gap coefficients enter the five percent significance area around 1981. Indeed, the significance of most parameters even falls within the one percent domain in shorter subperiods. Moreover, the impact of each gap on domestic inflation has gradually become stronger in the 1980s.

Hence, the results with the European gaps are not only rather satisfactory but also paint a fairly consistent picture compared with the outcomes for Belgium and France. No matter from which angle one looks at it, price movements in Germany have also become less insulated from monetary factors in other European countries than a decade ago. This is an important observation since it implies that inflation in the country that is widely acknowledged as the de facto anchor of the ERM is increasingly subject to monetary spill-over effects from the non-anchor countries. These monetary interdependencies probably originate from the phenomenon of currency substitution together with the convergence of monetary policies and/or inflation preferences in the core group. Whether monetary growth in the core countries could have functioned as an (additional) ingredient in the delineation of German monetary policy since the mid-1980s remains to be seen, though.[46] The relationship between domestic price developments and the current intermediate target of the Bundesbank (Buba) could still be much stronger

Table 4.12 Regression results with domestic and/or European price gaps for Germany

Model	1973.1—1992.4			1979.1—1992.4			1985.1—1992.4		
	GAP^d	$GAP^{f1/f2}$	R^2 (SE)	GAP^d	$GAP^{f1/f2}$	R^2 (SE)	GAP^d	$GAP^{f1/f2}$	R^2 (SE)
A	−0.102		0.64	−0.113		0.64	−0.114		0.47
	(4.8")		(0.52)	(5.6")		(0.48)	(5.9")		(0.49)
B		−0.007	0.56		−0.141	0.59		−0.278	0.46
		(0.1)	(0.59)		(1.7°)	(0.51)		(3.6")	(0.49)
C	−0.113	0.041	0.60	−0.098	−0.042	0.63	−0.072	−0.163	0.47
	(4.2")	(0.7)	(0.56)	(3.5")	(0.6)	(0.48)	(2.1')	(2.0')	(0.49)

Notes: Model A contains the domestic price gap as defined in equation (2.3). Model B includes GAP^{f1} from expression (4.7) (see Table 4.11). In model C, both gaps are inserted simultaneously where GAP^{f2} does not comprise German data (equation (4.8)). Heteroskedasticity consistent t-values are recorded below the coefficients in parentheses. SE is the standard error of the regression. The gaps are inserted with a lag of three quarters. The symbols ·°, ' and " denote significance at the ten, five and one percent level, respectively.

than the connection between domestic inflation and monetary expansion in Europe. Table 4.12 sheds light on this issue.

A glance at this table immediately tells us that the regression results sharply contrast with those for Belgium and France. In the entire time interval, the story is analogous to that for the latter countries; only the national price gap significantly influences the path of inflation. However, in the second time span, this variable still possesses explanatory power in the case of Germany, whereas national disturbances have — almost completely — lost their informative value in the latter countries. Be that as it may, the parameters on the European price gaps and their significance have also clearly risen in absolute terms in the course of time. Nowadays, distortions elsewhere in the core group significantly show up in German inflation rates. Thus, both gaps contain useful information for detecting inflationary trends in Germany.

How can these empirical results be interpreted from a monetary perspective? To begin with, the lasting stable link between domestic price developments and national money growth is a clear sign of asymmetry in the EMS[47] or, equivalently, a confirmation of a weak version of the German-leadership proposition. The latter hypothesis implies that Germany plays a dominant, but not unique, role in coordinating monetary policy in the EMS in the long run (Haldane, 1991).[48] More specifically, the fact that Germany has actually never pegged the German mark to any other currency, thereby preserving the freedom to pursue an independent monetary policy, has presumably largely accounted for the continuing significant negative impact of local gaps on its inflation rate. This also implies that the current intermediate target of the Buba, that is, *M3*, still pins down to a large degree the long-run price level in Germany.

However, this is just a part of the story. The results with the European gaps again illustrate the burgeoning economic integration in the early 1980s, which eventually became firmly-embedded in Europe.[49] Nowadays, monetary conditions in the other core ERM countries also convey information for future price developments in Germany, suggesting that a European money stock can serve as an additional indicator supplementing the existing target for German *M3*. As such, the growth of a European monetary aggregate might at times have put a different complexion on monetary developments in Germany. In concrete, this could imply that when monetary developments in Germany were distorted by identifiable transitory factors, while at the same time the European money supply was growing at an acceptable pace, more weight should have been placed on the latter variable in formulating and implementing monetary policy in Germany. Such an informal adjustment of the Buba's strategy would seem logical, given the convergence reached in policy preferences regarding inflation and the traditionally high degree of openness of the German economy coupled with its integration in international financial markets. It is possible that the Buba has already implicitly taken into account monetary developments in the entire EMS area for a long time,

Table 4.13 Regression results for the Netherlands

Model	DV	Sample	Price gap (GAP^{fi})		Energy prices	LDV	R^2	SE	Q(8)	HET	Chow$_{79}$	Chow$_{82}$
			BP	CUR								
I_{m1}	$\Delta\pi$	63.1—92.4	−0.051 (0.8)	−0.070 (1.2)	0.024 (2.1')	1234	0.52	1.21	6.5	16.6	11.2	10.1
I_{m1}	$\Delta\pi$	79.1—92.4	−0.096 (1.1)	−0.101 (1.2)	0.040 (3.6")	1234	0.48	1.11	2.5	19.1°		
I_{m1}	$\Delta\pi$	85.1—92.4	−0.185 (2.4')	−0.196 (2.3')	0.046 (3.8")	1234	0.50	1.09	5.9	21.2'		
II_{m1}	$\Delta\Delta_4 p$	63.1—92.4	−0.212 (3.1")	−0.147 (2.6")	0.016 (4.3")	1 4	0.32	1.34	15.9°	6.4	3.5	7.8
II_{m1}	$\Delta\Delta_4 p$	79.1—92.4	−0.190 (2.3')	−0.252 (2.4")	0.026 (3.7")	12 4	0.41	1.19	8.1	14.6		
II_{m1}	$\Delta\Delta_4 p$	85.1—92.4	−0.273 (2.1')	−0.250 (2.1')	0.042 (4.6")	12 4	0.60	1.05	8.2	25.7"		
I_{m3}	$\Delta\pi$	73.1—92.4	−0.133 (1.7°)	−0.157 (2.2')	0.024 (3.1")	1234	0.48	1.07	4.0	16.0	12.4°	6.1
I_{m3}	$\Delta\pi$	79.1—92.4	−0.261 (2.3')	−0.279 (3.3")	0.039 (3.9")	1234	0.54	1.05	3.4	20.6°		
I_{m3}	$\Delta\pi$	85.1—92.4	−0.435 (2.2')	−0.484 (2.1')	0.044 (4.1")	1	0.40	1.20	10.9	1.9		
II_{m3}	$\Delta\Delta_4 p$	73.1—92.4	−0.086 (1.5)	−0.166 (2.5')	0.016 (4.2")	12 4	0.36	1.27	6.3	15.2	11.3°	17.4"
II_{m3}	$\Delta\Delta_4 p$	79.1—92.4	−0.233 (1.9°)	−0.278 (2.3')	0.024 (3.7")	12 4	0.41	1.19	8.7	11.0		
II_{m3}	$\Delta\Delta_4 p$	85.1—92.4	−0.478 (2.7')	−0.350 (2.3')	0.039 (4.8")	12 4	0.60	1.03	8.0	22.7'		

Notes: The price gaps enter model I with a three quarter lag. DV denotes the dependent variable. BP and CUR indicate whether the European variables are computed with base period or current exchange rates. Heteroskedasticity-consistent t-values are shown behind the coefficients. LDV represent the significant lags of the dependent variable. For instance, 1 34 means that the first, third and fourth lags of the endogenous variable are significant and included. The diagnostic test statistics refer to the equations where the national variables are added with current exchange rates. SE is the standard error of the regression. Q(8) is the Box-Pierce statistic for serial correlation in the residuals. HET is White's statistic for heteroskedasticity and is distributed as χ^2. Chow$_{79}$ and Chow$_{82}$ are Chow tests for breaks in 1979 and 1982, respectively. The reported statistic is the likelihood ratio. The symbols °, ′, and ″ denote that the statistic is significantly different from zero at the ten, five and one percent level, respectively.

although it has never openly admitted this (presumably fearing to lose some credibility). A Bundesbank official obliquely states that this conjecture indeed makes some sense (Goos, 1994) when he points to the fact that since the adoption of monetary targeting in 1975, the Buba has failed to meet its monetary growth targets almost as often as it has attained them.

7.4   Empirical Outcomes for the Netherlands

The outcomes for the Netherlands are different from those for the other countries (see Table 4.13). With the exception of model I, significant connections between European disturbances and domestic price developments are found in the entire time span. Moreover, since the establishment of the EMS, domestic inflation has become even more sensitive to European shocks. This process is reflected in a continuous rise in the parameters of the gaps and their significance. In the last subperiod, every coefficient is significant at the five percent level.

At this point, the same question arises as in the preceding subsections: do domestic gaps provide more accurate information about the future development of Dutch inflation than European imbalances? Empirical evidence on this issue is presented in Table 4.14.

Table 4.14 Regression results with domestic and/or European price gaps for the Netherlands

Model	\multicolumn{3}{c}{1973.1—1992.4}			\multicolumn{3}{c}{1979.1—1992.4}			\multicolumn{3}{c}{1985.1—1992.4}		
	GAP^d	$GAP^{f1/f2}$	R^2 (SE)	GAP^d	$GAP^{f1/f2}$	R^2 (SE)	GAP^d	$GAP^{f1/f2}$	R^2 (SE)
A	−0.255 (3.2")		0.53	−0.246 (1.05)	(1.8°)	0.51	−0.231 (1.08)	(1.4)	0.50 (1.10)
B		−0.157 (2.2')	0.48 (1.07)		−0.279 (3.3")	0.54 (1.05)		−0.484 (2.1')	0.53 (1.00)
C	−0.214 (2.1')	−0.142 (2.0')	0.50 (1.04)	−0.177 (1.2)	−0.243 (2.7")	0.54 (1.04)	−0.212 (1.6)	−0.372 (2.1')	0.52 (1.02)

Notes: Model A contains the domestic price gap as defined in equation (2.3). Model B includes GAP^{f1} from expression (4.7) (see Table 4.13). In model C, both gaps are inserted simultaneously where GAP^{f2} does not comprise Dutch data (equation (4.8)). Heteroskedasticity consistent t-values are recorded below the coefficients in parentheses. SE is the standard error of the regression. The gaps are inserted with a lag of three quarters. The symbols °, ' and " denote significance at the ten, five and one percent level, respectively.

All things considered, I could, at least partly, simply repeat the analysis of the outcomes for the other countries. In the entire time span, national price gaps appear to matter for domestic inflation. Since the inception of the EMS, the information content of the domestic gap deteriorates gradually and eventually becomes negligible. However, in contrast to the results for the other countries, I find a link between foreign monetary conditions and domestic inflation in the full sample as well. The long-standing monetary strategy of trying to stabilize the exchange rate of the guilder against the German mark, coupled with the small size and the historically high degree of openness of the Dutch economy, has possibly rendered domestic inflation much sooner sensitive to foreign monetary conditions.

Overall, the results with European gaps are supportive of the view that international distortions bring about significant changes in the rate of inflation in those countries where monetary policy is exclusively focused on maintaining a fixed exchange rate. It also offers evidence for the view that monetary authorities in the latter countries are hardly able to determine their own long-run equilibrium price level.[50] Instead, domestic price movements are largely caused by monetary developments abroad.

7.5   Empirical Outcomes for the Core Group as a Whole

The validity of the P^*-framework on a European level is generally accepted by the data, both in the entire period and in the subsamples (Table 4.15). Only in the specifications with M_{eur}^l, the link between European price gaps and European inflation is rejected in the sample 1963.1–1992.4. Hence, the overall results point to a fairly stable long-run relationship between European inflation and the European price gaps (GAP_{eur}). In this respect, it is irrelevant which conversion method is employed.

Economically, the findings suggest that the overall European inflation rate could be influenced by concerted monetary policy actions if national central banks have effective instruments at their disposal.[51] In a sense, the estimation results thus lend support for moving towards policies based on targeting an ERM-wide monetary aggregate. This would require closer coordination of monetary policies throughout the region within an adequately developed institutional framework. Monticelli (1993b, 1995) has formulated theoretical schemes of monetary coordination. Here, it is demonstrated that this coordination can take place in either an asymmetric or symmetric fashion, mainly depending on the (in)stability of national and European money demand functions. In this theoretical setting, the adoption of monetary targeting at the area level would not necessarily entail the decline of the anchor role of Germany in the ERM. Viewed in this light, the finding that the European money supply is a key variable in determining inflation on a European level could to a certain extent hinge on the strong and lasting money—price

Table 4.15 *Regression results with the (weighted) European price level*

Model	DV	Sample	Price gap (GAP^{eur}) BP	CUR	Energy prices	LDV	R^2	SE	Q(8)	HET	Chow$_{79}$	Chow$_{82}$
I_{m1}	$\Delta\pi^{eur}$	63.1–92.4	−0.043 (1.1)	−0.057 (3.3")	0.009 (1.6°)	12	0.34	0.61	6.7	9.1	4.3	6.0
I_{m1}	$\Delta\pi^{eur}$	79.1–92.4	−0.107 (3.3")	−0.070 (2.0)	0.009 (2.9")	12	0.36	0.42	8.2	6.5		
I_{m1}	$\Delta\pi^{eur}$	85.1–92.4	−0.092 (3.1")	−0.095 (3.2")	0.085 (1.9°)	12	0.49	0.37	6.7	1.0		
II_{m1}	$\Delta\Delta_4 p^{eur}$	63.1–92.4	−0.034 (1.0)	−0.042 (1.2)	0.008 (3.3")	4	0.27	0.70	13.4	12.2	6.0	7.0
II_{m1}	$\Delta\Delta_4 p^{eur}$	79.1–92.4	−0.084 (2.3)	−0.095 (2.8")	0.008 (2.9")	4	0.40	0.44	6.2	9.8		
II_{m1}	$\Delta\Delta_4 p^{eur}$	85.1–92.4	−0.065 (2.1)	−0.055 (1.6)	0.008 (2.9")	4	0.41	0.43	6.7	11.3		
I_{m3}	$\Delta\pi^{eur}$	73.1–92.4	−0.175 (4.2")	−0.124 (3.8")	0.008 (2.1)	2 4	0.47	0.47	3.3	32.5"	2.3	3.1
I_{m3}	$\Delta\pi^{eur}$	79.1–92.4	−0.182 (4.0")	−0.149 (3.1")	0.009 (2.0)	4	0.45	0.39	3.7	8.9		
I_{m3}	$\Delta\pi^{eur}$	85.1–92.4	−0.131 (3.3")	−0.126 (2.4)	0.008 (1.8°)	4	0.47	0.38	3.0	12.0		
II_{m3}	$\Delta\Delta_4 p^{eur}$	73.1–92.4	−0.128 (2.3)	−0.113 (2.7")	0.004 (2.1)	2 4	0.42	0.55	13.8	6.2	4.1	3.6
II_{m3}	$\Delta\Delta_4 p^{eur}$	79.1–92.4	−0.156 (2.5")	−0.143 (3.6")	0.007 (3.1")	4	0.43	0.43	7.4	9.8		
II_{m3}	$\Delta\Delta_4 p^{eur}$	85.1–92.4	−0.116 (1.9°)	−0.087 (1.3)	0.007 (2.5")	4	0.41	0.43	6.9	15.0		

Notes: The European price gaps enter model I with a three quarter lag. *DV* denotes the dependent variable. *BP* and *CUR* indicate whether the European variables are computed with base period or current exchange rates. Heteroskedasticity-consistent t-values are shown behind the coefficients. *LDV* represent the significant lags of the dependent variable. For instance, 1 34 means that the first, third and fourth lags of the endogenous variable are significant and included. The diagnostic test statistics refer to the equations where the national variables are added with current exchange rates. SE is the standard error of the regression. Q(8) is the Box-Pierce statistic for serial correlation in the residuals. HET is White's statistic for heteroskedasticity and is distributed as χ^2. Chow$_{79}$ and Chow$_{82}$ are Chow tests for breaks in 1979 and 1982, respectively. The reported statistic is the likelihood ratio. The symbols °, ' and " denote that the statistic is significantly different from zero at the ten, five and one percent level, respectively.

relationship in Germany, given the weight of Germany in European aggregates (Mayer and Fels, 1995).

De Grauwe (1994a) favours monetary targeting on a European level on recent EMS experiences. He states that the EMS served the interests of all participating members during the greater part of the 1980s, because most of the non-anchor countries pursued anti-inflationary strategies and saw the EMS as a device making this disinflation easier to achieve. Things changed dramatically in the early 1990s when inflation dropped to historically low levels (except for Germany) and the recession became the major problem. It then appeared that the asymmetric monetary arrangement inherent in the EMS intensified the deflationary forces of the recession. A symmetrical monetary arrangement, that is, targeting the sum of the money stocks in the EMS countries, would therefore have reduced the need to follow tight, or even deflationary, monetary policies in the non-anchor countries after the occurrence of asymmetric shocks in Germany resulting from monetary unification. In this way, much of the turmoil in 1992—93 could have been avoided.

These encouraging outcomes should not, however, divert attention away from the fact that our European monetary aggregate is just an estimate, never used for any purpose in monetary policies. A widespread and theoretically well-founded opinion among monetary theorists is that the major threat of instability and breakdown of an otherwise good relationship between European money and prices comes from the very fact that this European money supply is actually used as a target (Sardelis, 1993).

8 CONCLUDING REMARKS

In this chapter, I have focused on some aspects that play a prominent role in the current debate on the move towards EMU. One of the issues concerns the selection of an effective strategy for monetary policy in Stage Three. This topic has motivated a large and growing literature on the stability and predictability European money demand functions (see Bayoumi and Kenen, 1993; Fase, 1994; Kremers and Lane, 1990; and Monticelli and Strauss-Kahn, 1991, among others).[52] In general, these studies pay hardly any attention to the relationship between European monetary aggregates and the final objective of monetary policy, that is, price stability. I have therefore followed a different approach in the sense that I have explored this link explicitly and in a one-step procedure by using a modified version of the original P^*-concept.

The results of my empirical research can be summarized as follows. First, it turns out that local real and monetary shocks have become more symmetric over time since their correlation with European-wide disturbances has risen in recent years. This is good news for the proponents of EMU, because it suggests that the major potential cost involved in forming a monetary union, namely foregoing the use of the nominal exchange rate as a tool for macroeconomic adjustment, has decreased for the countries in question.[53] One of the explanations could be that national policies are nowadays closer coordinated.[54] On the other hand, the findings could also just reflect the worldwide observed tendency of increasing economic interdependencies between industrialized countries.

Testing the validity of the P^*-model with European price gaps also points to increasing monetary interdependencies in the core countries. In the longest possible estimation period, European imbalances are generally no sign of movements in domestic prices to come in individual countries. Hence, the estimations give no reason to expect that a surge or shortfall of money growth in the core group carries over in domestic price developments. For most of the countries, the information content of European distortions for future movements in inflation gradually improves since the inception of the EMS. In the period 1985—92, lagged European price gaps exert a significant influence on domestic inflation rates in most instances. Since a variety of specifications points in the same direction, some confidence can be placed in these results.[55]

Although these estimations provide important insights, the key question is of course whether the appropriateness of European price gaps for predicting inflationary threats differs from that of national gaps. My findings indicate that the explanatory power of purely national gaps has eroded considerably from the beginning of the EMS in 1979 for the non-anchor countries. Since the early 1980s, local disturbances do not translate into price movements at all. Thus, the evidence suggests that the long-run price level toward which domestic prices adjust is nowadays predominantly determined by the European money stock instead of national monetary aggregates.

For Germany, the anchor country in the EMS, I obtain somewhat different results. I find that the domestic price gaps still exercise a significant effect on German inflation in the 1980s. This outcome underlines the special position of Germany in the ERM. Although Germany still has a certain degree of monetary independence, the estimations show that monetary conditions in Germany's immediate neighbours increasingly matter for inflation in Germany; European price gaps also impact on price movements since the start of the EMS, as is the case in the non-anchor countries. The implication is that the long-run equilibrium price level in Germany is increasingly determined by monetary conditions in Europe.

The factors underlying the increased usefulness of foreign price gaps for discovering inflationary pressures are presumably the lifting of capital controls and the closer policy coordination in response to economic shocks originating outside the core countries. Another explanation could be the drastic changes in fiscal and monetary policy in some non-anchor countries in the course of the 1980s in order to ensure a smooth operation of the EMS, which in turn has contributed to the monetary convergence in the core group.

Thus, the countries' estimations suggest that a European money stock can function as a reliable, additional indicator in the formulation and execution of monetary policy in the core group. It surely points to the need for greater attention for the development of aggregate European monetary conditions by all countries, including Germany, and closer coordination of monetary policy. The estimation of the P^*-model at the European level yields significant and stable relationships between European inflation and the European price gaps in the entire period and in the subsamples. Combining all empirical evidence, thus, provides preliminary support for monetary targeting by the ESCB.

Here, I have to spell out that the usual problems relating to the Lucas–Goodhart critique apply, of course, to our results as well. After all, the regime shift ensuing from irrevocably fixing the exchange rates (or the introduction of a single currency) may lead to significant changes in liquidity preferences for the area as a whole, complicating the management of monetary policy from the very start of Stage Three.[56] What is more, the use of a European money supply as an additional indicator or the possible transition to controlling the European money supply can destabilize a previously stable relationship between prices and European monetary aggregates. In this connection, it is important to recognize that at present in many European countries no monetary target is pursued but rather an exchange rate target.

If these potential problems with monetary targeting at a European level or in EMU actually emerge, a different monetary strategy is perhaps warranted. A monetary philosophy that obviously comes to mind as an alternative for monetary targeting is direct inflation targeting. The latter approach has recently gained much popularity throughout the Western world. Chapter 6 details the exact modalities of such a direct inflation targeting framework and compares empirically the inflation performance of countries with different monetary approaches.

NOTES

1. However, it is undeniable that the system's successful performance in the 'phase of consolidation', a term invented by Padoa-Schioppa (1988) to characterize the period 1979–87, owed something to the help of special factors and circumstances. For example, the strong dollar attenuated intra-EMS pressures by diverting financial flows away from DM-denominated assets. Further, capital controls reduced the exchange-rate pressures associated with the higher inflation rates in France and Italy.
2. Viñals (1994) discusses some issues which are of importance during the transition period.
3. In principle, there is a wide range of potential candidates that can serve as intermediate targets, for example, real or nominal interest rate objectives (Barro, 1989), nominal income targets (Garganas, 1993), exchange rate targets, money and/or other indicators as information variables (Friedman, 1994). Conversely, since the ultimate objective of monetary policy is to control inflation, some countries attempt to achieve their actual target, that is, price stability, directly (see Chapter 6). However, theoretical and empirical studies in this field

clearly demonstrate that both indirect and direct procedures are fraught with conceptual and/or operational difficulties, for instance regarding the controllability, transparency and simplicity of direct and indirect targets.

4. This issue is closely associated with the controversy among economists about policy rules or discretionary policies. In fact, the Statute of the ESCB does not provide guidance as to whether policy rules are to be preferred to discretion and, in the former case, what sort of rules (that is, feedback vs. non-feedback; variables determining the nature of the feedback) have to be adhered to. Furthermore, which type of policy gives the 'best' results remains an open question. In this connection, Bernanke and Mishkin (1992) conclude that the use of a 'hybrid' strategy, containing both elements of rules and discretion, seems to generate more favourable outcomes in terms of inflation. Generally speaking, studies on this subject are in a way variations on the path-breaking articles of Kydland and Prescott (1977) and Barro and Gordon (1983). For more recent studies on this subject see Bertocchi and Spagat (1994), Dwyer (1993), Giovannini (1993) and McCallum (1994) to name but a few.

5. According to the game theoretic literature, a credible commitment to combat inflation firmly reduces the inflationary bias resulting from the time-consistency problem (Kydland and Prescott, 1977; Barro and Gordon, 1983) and the short-term output costs of converging towards price stability.

6. In the past, the German monetary authorities were probably not so reluctant to target only the European money supply. The reason is that it could have harmed the Buba's outstanding anti-inflation reputation (Weber, 1992) because it was, in fact, unable to control the overall monetary conditions in other countries directly.

7. Giovannini and Turtelboom (1992) review the extensive theoretical and empirical literature on currency substitution.

8. The Deutsche Bundesbank (1995) opposes this view. By examining the effect of currency substitution on domestic monetary aggregates, the Bundesbank reaches the conclusion that this phenomenon has virtually no impact on the stability of German *M3*.

9. The construction of the European variables is explained in Section 3.

10. This hypothesis is generally accepted by recent empirical studies indicating that a European demand for money function is on the whole more stable than money demand in individual countries (Bekx and Tullio, 1989; Kremers and Lane, 1990; Artis et al., 1993; Monticelli and Strauss-Kahn, 1991; Fase and Winder, 1993). On the other hand, Arnold (1994) asserts that the existence of a stable European demand for money is a mere statistical artifact. For earlier work on the demand for money in European countries, see den Butter and Fase (1981).

11. $GAP_i^{p'}$ can, however, only be given empirical content if a measure for the equilibrium value of the real exchange rate is available. Since er_i^* is an unobservable variable, I have also used the Multi State Kalman Filter method to obtain an estimate of the equilibrium component of the real exchange rate. To this end, one can write the actual real exchange rate (er_i) as:

$$er_i = e_i + p_{eur} - p_i = er_i^* + u \qquad \text{(i)}$$

where u is a stationary, unobservable error term. The calculated equilibrium component of the real exchange rate is included in equation (4.7).

12. In 1991, the Economic Unit made an inventory of the differences and similarities of broad monetary aggregates in all EU countries as part of a harmonization project. An interesting conclusion was that these aggregates were at that time already quite similar in terms of the types of assets they comprised.

13. The most salient features of recent developments in CBHs are discussed by the Economic Unit of the Committee of Governors of the Central Banks of the Member States of the European Economic Community (1993). The effect of cross-border deposits on the stability of the relation between monetary aggregates and nominal GDP at the national level is examined in Angeloni et al. (1991). One of the findings of this paper (p. 23) is that the 'best' definition of money (including or excluding CBHs) in the five largest EU countries is not

empirically identifiable in the period 1982.1–1990.4.

14. Other empirical studies also come across statistical limitations (for example, Angeloni et al., 1991). In fact, the quality of data on CBHs appears to be fairly poor before 1982.

15. These methods are each other's equivalent under certain conditions. If the nominal exchange rates are stable over time, the first technique is identical to the second. In cases where the core ERM countries have (had) the same rate of inflation, the second and third methods yield similar results, while in cases where PPP holds permanently, the first and third alternatives give the same outcomes.

16. However, existing studies on money demand on a European scale sometimes conclude that the estimation results are fairly robust to different methods of adding up national variables (Monticelli and Strauss-Kahn, 1991; Cassard et al., 1994).

17. From a methodological perspective, it seems more sensible to aggregate national nominal variables (money supply and nominal income) with current exchange rates and to use base-period exchange rates for adding national real output. The reason is that exchange rate movements will eventually largely show up in nominal variables through changes in the price component. On the other hand, real output in individual countries is valued at constant (base-year) prices and measures the quantity of output. Hence, aggregation of national real income variables should — intuitively — take place with exchange rates in the same base year. Indeed, national real variables are — implicitly — adjusted for exchange rate developments. However, like other studies of money demand on a European scale (for example, Kremers and Lane; 1990; Fase and Winder, 1993), I employ the same method for adding both nominal and real variables for individual countries, because the use of different conversion factors would seriously hamper the interpretation of the 'European' price level (see equation (4.12)).

18. The Bayoumi and Kenen approach was not employed because the use of levels in aggregation is required within the context of the P^*-model. Nevertheless, the European inflation rates resulting from the Bayoumi and Kenen aggregation method are almost identical to my inflation rates.

19. Gros and Thygesen (1992) present an overview of the events on the exchange front under the Bretton Woods regime in the 1960s.

20. Berk and Winder (1994) provide some proof for the success of Dutch monetary policy in maintaining a stable exchange rate of the guilder vis-à-vis the Deutsche mark in the period 1961.1–1991.12. Using cointegration techniques, they find a stable long-run relationship between Dutch and German prices.

21. Sachs and Wyplosz (1986) claim that this was prompted by the disciplinary working of the exchange rate commitment within the European Monetary System. However, this 'classical' example of the discipline theory of the EMS is contested by other economists (for example, Fratianni and von Hagen, 1992).

22. See Artis and Taylor (1994), Edison and Kole (1994), Giavazzi and Giovannini (1989, Ch. 3) and Ungerer et al. (1986) for empirical analyses of the effect of the ERM on the behaviour of exchange rates.

23. Although a broad theoretical and empirical literature on the EMS has developed over the years, its inconclusiveness with regard to the role played by the ERM on inflation convergence in the European Union stands out (Artis and Nachane, 1990; Bini Smaghi, 1994; Collins and Giavazzi, 1993; Ungerer et al., 1986).

24. There is a huge body of literature on the factors influencing the velocity of money (see for instance Bordo and Jonung, 1987; Boughton, 1992; Goodhart, 1989; Judd and Scadding, 1982).

25. Kremers and Lane (1992) analytically explore the bias that currency substitution and international portfolio diversification may introduce into single-country money demand estimates.

26. Garganas (1993) opposes to this inference. He believes that this stability is unlikely to persist, as the benefits of aggregation in respect to currency substitution effects may be insufficient to compensate for other destabilizing aspects of the ongoing changes in the financial structure

of these countries associated with the process of financial integration and innovation. Moreover, Arnold (1994) argues that the greater stability of aggregated money demand functions compared to national money-demand relations found in recent empirical studies is just a statistical artifact.

27. For a description of unit root tests, I refer to Appendix 2A.

28. In Section 7.5, I investigate whether these European price gaps are accurate indicators for future movements in the European price level.

29. At first sight, this outcome may look a little bit strange. However, only when the nature of large local distortions and the date at which they occur are more or less identical across countries, national disturbances are generally also discovered in the aggregated figures (other things being equal). In this connection, it is also important to realize that the share of German *M3* in the total European money supply at the time of the German unification was approximately 50 percent.

30. The break signal has the same value as in Chapter 3 (0.5). Moreover, the same breakpoints are also found in other sets of models used to calculate Q_{eur}^*.

31. For the sake of surveyability, the table only contains the results for the gaps based on *M3*. In fact, the overall picture remains virtually the same if the gaps with *M1* had been displayed.

32. According to this trade theory, trade develops even between countries with identical capital/labour ratios. However, this trade consists of the two-way exchange of slightly differentiated goods produced under economies of scale so that each country simultaneously exports and imports very similar products.

33. Tavlas (1994) presents a brief overview of the recent theoretical and empirical literature focusing on the identification of the incidence of shocks and the isolation of their underlying determinants in the light of the suitability of countries for currency union participation.

34. The theoretical explanation is that the possible modification of the real exchange rate (as part of a current-account adjustment) might be easier to achieve through a change in the nominal exchange rate than through a change in domestic wages and/or prices. The reason is that the exchange rate can be moved instantaneously at the discretion of the authorities, whereas the second adjustment channel only works slowly and could be accompanied by undesirable labour market effects.

35. This argument builds on Kenen's paper (1969) on optimum currency areas. His article suggested that countries with similar production structures are better candidates for currency area participation than countries whose production structures are different, since the former group of countries is more likely to experience symmetric shocks. Indeed, if countries are confronted with common disturbances, a common policy response will suffice, and no threat will be posed to a fixed-rate system or currency area. For a detailed evaluation of the — potential — economic costs and benefits of a European Monetary Union, see Emerson et al. (1992).

36. Sapir and Sekkat (1995) also provide indirect empirical support for this hypothesis. They find that, by reducing misalignments, the EMS has enhanced the process of trade adjustment during the 1980s through affecting the pricing behaviour of producers. Moreover, Sapir et al. (1994) find clear evidence in favour of the trade promotion aspects of systems of limited exchange rate flexibility, such as the EMS. Hence, these findings suggest less divergent economic disturbances between ERM countries compared to non-ERM countries.

37. The latter phenomenon can perhaps partly explain the unexpected negative correlation between the Dutch and European price gaps in the entire sample period.

38. Another criterion that is useful in gauging the suitability of countries for joining in monetary unions is the speed of domestic adjustment to macroeconomic disturbances (van Bergeijk et al., 1993; Bayoumi and Eichengreen, 1994b).

39. Indeed, the exchange rate turmoil in 1992 and 1993 can be seen as an example of this, with the ERM structure making it difficult for relative prices in the EU to respond sufficiently quickly to the rise in demand for West German products caused by German unification (Bayoumi and Thomas, 1994).

40. I am well aware of the potential drawbacks of this 'approach'. One of them has recently been put forward by Bullard (1994), though in a completely different context. The entire data set includes, broadly speaking, a period of increasing inflation up to about 1980 and a period of disinflation thereafter. By shortening the sample period, one runs the risk of examining a period in which insufficient variation in inflation is present. In this case, an investigation of the data could be uninformative, because it is difficult to discern the effects of European gaps on inflation if there have been negligible changes in the latter variable. A closely related potential problem is that the order of integration of the price level is not identical in different subsamples. This could necessitate the use of different dependent variables, which in turn hampers a straightforward interpretation of the regression results and the test statistics. To circumvent the latter problem, I report estimations over different subperiods without changing the dependent variable. Fortunately, the parameters of primary interest, that is, those on the price gaps, do not appear to be very sensitive to the selection of the endogenous variable.

41. Another feature is that the parameters on the price gaps based on *M1* are much smaller, due to the relatively greater fluctuations of narrowly defined monetary aggregates. Notice that this is consistent with my findings in Chapter 3.

42. There is no monetary autonomy left to non-anchor countries in the ERM when the following conditions are simultaneously satisfied: the country does not exert a significant influence on the level of international interest rates; there is perfect international capital mobility; and there is perfect substitutability between domestic and foreign assets (Goodhart and Viñals, 1994).

43. These opposite findings may be due to the fact that the former full sample covers more years in which a fixed exchange rate regime prevails.

44. These findings support the observations in Section 4.2 of Chapter 3. Here, it was concluded that the closed-economy version of the P^*-model is more applicable for France in periods when the French franc was allowed to float.

45. In 1979, France started to pursue both an exchange rate and monetary target. During the first EMS years, the French commitment to a stable exchange rate was not very firm. However, in 1983 the French economic policy stance changed dramatically in favour of establishing a strong anti-inflation reputation.

46. The theoretical and empirical foundations of German monetary policy are briefly discussed in Issing (1992) (see also Section 4.3 of Chapter 3).

47. Many studies are devoted to this subject (see for example, de Grauwe, 1989; Artus et al., 1991; Henry and Weidmann, 1994; Herz and Röger, 1992; Gardner and Perraudin, 1993; Giavazzi and Giovannini, 1989).

48. Fratianni and von Hagen (1992) present evidence which suggests that the EMS is a largely interactive arrangement. This means that the Bundesbank has not completely constrained the actions of the other central banks in the system and it does not act altogether independently of other EMS countries. In this respect, Goos (1994) and Schlesinger (1994) maintain that, like any other central bank, the Buba does not neglect the external implications and repercussions of its own policies for other countries, considering in particular the Deutsche mark's role as the anchor currency in the ERM and its role as a widely-held international investment and reserve currency.

49. This increased interdependence is partly brought about by lifting capital controls and by closer policy coordination in response to economic shocks originating outside the region. In addition, rather drastic changes in fiscal and monetary policy have been implemented in some countries in order to ensure a smooth operation of the EMS and thereby contributing to economic integration (see, for example, the French experience in the early 1980s; Trichet, 1992; Blanchard and Muet, 1993).

50. By deliberately choosing to anchor their currencies to the Deutsche mark, other ERM members theoretically not only import Germany's low inflation but also accept the monetary policy course of the Bundesbank making their long-run rate of inflation predominantly determined by the long-run growth rate of the German money supply. This hypothesis can be tested by replacing the national gaps for German gaps in the inflation equations for the

non-anchor countries (see Kool and Tatom, 1994).

51. A nice preliminary overview of practical and technical difficulties attached to area-wide monetary control is provided in Monticelli and Viñals (1993) and Sardelis (1993).

52. The results of these studies give reasons for optimism, because they generally conclude that the European demand for money function is more stable than money-demand in individual countries.

53. This is of course just one of the economic costs of a common currency. A brief overview of other costs (and benefits) of a monetary union is recorded in Thygesen (1994) and Viñals (1994) among others.

54. Indeed, the EMS was intended initially as an instrument to strengthen the coordination of monetary policies among the European economies to overcome the unsatisfactory performance of the uncoordinated regime of flexible exchange rates (Fratianni and von Hagen, 1992). In practice, the ERM quickly evolved in an asymmetric system with Germany playing the role of the anchor. The origin of this asymmetric functioning is generally considered to be due to both inherent and intentional factors (Haldane, 1991).

55. In Groeneveld et al. (1997) the same exercise is carried out over the period 1973.1—1994.4, including Italy. Here, the same general tendencies are observed.

56. However, the controllability of the money supply at the area level could be higher than it is at present at the national level for some countries, where monetary growth is to various extents endogenous as a consequence of the constraints imposed by the ERM (Monticelli and Viñals, 1993).

5. Monetary Spillover Effects from the ERM to Austria

*For a rule based policy, the advocates of the hard currency
policy had a well-founded theoretical line of argumentation:
The economy of a small open country has to adjust to the
exchange rate rather than vice versa.*

Hochreiter and Winckler (1995), p. 92

1 INTRODUCTION

In January 1995, Austria, Finland and Sweden joined the European Union. Unlike the other new entrants, Austria also decided to join the Exchange Rate Mechanism (ERM) of the European Monetary System (EMS) as from 9 January 1995.[1] This means that Austrian monetary policy will be predominantly aimed at keeping the schilling within the current fluctuation bands of this arrangement until the establishment of EMU. The participation of Austria in the ERM did not necessitate fundamental changes in the preparation and implementation of monetary policy, because the main policy objective of the Austrian monetary authorities since the late 1970s has been to keep the value of the schilling within very narrow margins against the German mark (see Hochreiter and Winckler, 1995).[2] Hence, the (intermediate) goal of Austrian monetary policy has actually been identical to that of monetary policy in other relatively small countries which joined the ERM at the start in 1979, for example, Belgium and the Netherlands.

Although Austria has only recently become an 'active' member of the ERM, it is conceivable that its monetary tradition has rendered domestic price developments more sensitive to 'ERM-wide' rather than purely domestic monetary developments in the course of time. In a sense, this would be consistent with the theoretical notion that in countries with an exchange rate target, domestic money supply becomes fully endogenous under certain conditions. Moreover, Austria has also committed itself to the achievement of the convergence criteria laid down in the Maastricht Treaty. When Austria succeeds in meeting these conditions, it qualifies for participation in the third and final stage of Economic and Monetary Union (EMU) when the currencies of the participating countries will be irrevocably fixed. In this respect, the optimum currency area literature distinguishes several criteria for gauging the suitability of countries for joining in monetary unions. This strand of theory emphasizes the point that a common currency area is more efficient the more correlated the underlying shocks hitting the national economies, since the more correlated the disturbances the smaller the need for independent macroeconomic policies. In fact, this comes down to examining the relative importance of country-specific and ERM-wide economic disturbances for national economic variables (Bayoumi and Eichengreen, 1994b; Kenen, 1969; Tavlas, 1994).

Against these backgrounds, Austria's recent entry into the EMS and the ERM gives reason for exploring empirically to what extent Austria is integrated in Europe from a monetary perspective.[3] As in Chapter 4, I address this question within an extended version of the original P^*-framework.[4] More specifically, I repeat exactly the same exercise as in Chapter 4 to test whether inflation behaviour in Austria is dominated by domestic or ERM-wide monetary factors. This analysis provides insights into possible monetary spillover effects from original ERM members. Moreover, if a link between Austrian prices and European monetary developments is absent, the situation in which a European monetary supply is used in the monetary policy making process in Stage Two or Three of EMU may be less desirable from Austria's point of view.

Since this chapter uses the same theoretical and methodological setup as Chapter 4, I only focus on the empirical outcomes. This chapter proceeds as follows. In Section 2, I take a look at the key variables in the P^*-model for Austria. Here, I also succinctly pay attention to comparable variables in Belgium and the Netherlands. Section 3 contains the empirical results. The final section concludes.

2   A PRELIMINARY LOOK AT THE DATA AND THE PRICE GAPS FOR AUSTRIA

In this section, the relevant variables within the P^*-framework for Austria are compared with those for two other relatively small European countries, namely Belgium and the Netherlands. Monetary policies in the latter countries have also been primarily focused on trying to stabilize the national currency against the German mark in the past decades.[5] The decision to peg their currencies to the mark is predominantly motivated by Germany's outstanding inflation record coupled with the fact that it is their largest trading partner. By locking their currencies to the D-mark, these countries in fact import Germany's low inflation.

Figure 5.1 provides an indication of the degree of success of each country in stabilizing its nominal exchange rate vis-à-vis the D-mark, with the 1970 exchange rate indexed to 100. As is apparent from this figure, the schilling

Figure 5.1 Nominal and real exchange rate against the German mark

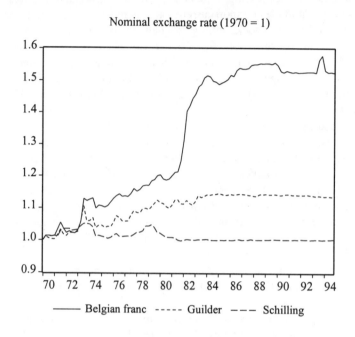

Nominal exchange rate (1970 = 1)

——— Belgian franc - - - - - Guilder – – – Schilling

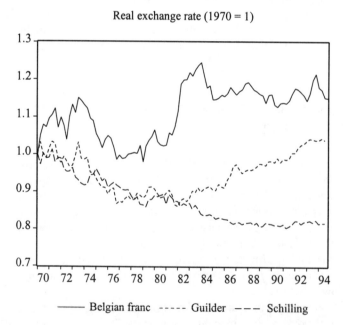

Real exchange rate (1970 = 1)

——— Belgian franc - - - - - Guilder – – – Schilling

depreciated slightly in the 1970s, but returned to its 1970 level in the early 1980s. The strengthening of the schilling towards the end of the 1970s was set in motion by the adoption and subsequent public acceptance of the so-called hard currency strategy of the Austrian monetary authorities (Hochreiter and Winckler, 1995). This policy concept was put into practice by revaluing the schilling against the German mark by 1.5 percent in September 1979. The rationale for this policy step was to dampen wage increases which could ensue from the second oil price hike in 1979. Since then, credibility has risen considerably and helped to maintain a very close link between the schilling and the German mark. Up to the beginning of the 1980s, the guilder gradually lost some ground vis-à-vis the German mark, whereas the Belgian franc experienced a considerable depreciation until the mid-1980s. All in all, the guilder and Belgian franc have depreciated by about 14 and 53 percent respectively since 1970. As Figure 5.1 illustrates, the depreciation of the latter nominal exchange rates largely took place before 1985.[6] The temporary fall and subsequent recovery of the Belgian franc in the 1990s obviously reflect the turbulence in the ERM around 1992. These movements also suggest that the Belgian monetary authorities took appropriate steps to restore confidence.

Figure 5.1 also shows that real exchange rate movements have on balance been much smaller. The virtually constant value of the schilling combined with the fact that Austrian inflation has exceeded German inflation to some extent has led to a real appreciation of the Austrian currency of nearly 20 percent since 1970. On the other hand, the guilder and the Belgian franc have undergone a real depreciation of approximately 4 and 15 percent, respectively.

Table 5.1 presents the average real growth, inflation and monetary expansion in several subperiods. Here, as in the remainder of this chapter, inflation is measured as the quarterly change in the GDP deflator, while money growth represents the quarterly change in broad money *M3*. All the data are seasonally adjusted.

In the full sample, inflation was highest in Belgium, followed by Austria and the Netherlands. Interestingly, this picture remains almost the same in different subperiods. Moreover, inflation reached its highest level in the 1970s and its lowest value in the period 1986.1—1994.4 in every country. Concerning real economic growth, Austria and the Netherlands experienced a quarterly growth rate of about 0.6 percent in the entire time span. On the other hand, economic growth in Belgium was somewhat lower. However, this is not the case in different subsamples. In the first subperiod, the Austrian and Belgian economies expanded by 0.6 percent, whereas economic growth in the Netherlands amounted to 0.8 percent. Since 1979 this situation has been reversed. In this subperiod, the Austrian economy exhibited the largest growth, due to its relatively favourable performance in the early 1980s. Taken together, the real appreciation of the schilling does not seem to have influenced the overall economic performance in Austria in a negative way.

Finally, in every period considered, the average increase of the money stock lies in the same order of magnitude. The strongest monetary expansion took place in the 1970s, when prices were rising quite rapidly, too. Thereafter, the growth of the money supply gradually slowed down. In the last subsample, monetary expansion in the three countries varied between 1.5 and 2.1 percent.

Table 5.1 Average inflation, economic growth and monetary expansion

Sample	Inflation			Economic growth			Growth of *M3*		
	AUS	BEL	NET	AUS	BEL	NET	AUS	BEL	NET
73.1—94.4	1.1	1.3	1.0	0.6	0.5	0.6	2.1	2.1	2.0
73.1—78.4	1.6	2.1	1.9	0.6	0.6	0.8	3.0	2.9	2.8
79.1—94.4	1.0	1.0	0.6	0.6	0.4	0.5	1.8	1.8	1.6
79.1—85.4	1.2	1.3	0.9	0.5	0.2	0.3	2.1	1.5	1.6
86.1—94.4	0.8	0.8	0.3	0.6	0.6	0.6	1.5	2.1	1.7

Notes: AUS, BEL and NET stand for Austria, Belgium and the Netherlands, respectively.

The next step in the empirical research is the examination of the time series properties of the key variables in the conventional and extended P^*-framework. To this end, I have performed standard augmented Dickey-Fuller (ADF) tests to determine the order of integration by following the procedure proposed by Dickey and Pantula (1987).[7] The ADF results suggest that the price level (p) generally contains two unit roots, indicating that equation (2.5) is the most appropriate specification. Conversely, real output and the velocity of money appear to have just one unit root. This implies that their equilibrium counterparts cannot simply be proxied by means of a regression with a deterministic time trend. Indeed, measures of Q^* and V^* constructed in this way are not useful because the resulting p^* measure is likely to yield a nonstationary price gap which would violate the main assumption of the P^*-model that deviations between p and $p*$ are only transitory.[8] In this chapter, the long-term variables are again constructed with the so-called multi-state Kalman filter technique (see Section 3.2 of Chapter 2).

Figure 5.2 gives an impression of the development of the domestic and European price gap for Austria over time. It should be noted that the European price gap is calculated according to equation (4.7). The national variables are converted into German marks by using current exchange rates against the German mark. Subsequently, they are summed, yielding the European variables (see Section 3 of Chapter 4) which are employed to proxy the European price gap. Apart from the Austrian data, the European variables used to compute this gap comprise data for four initial ERM countries, that is, Belgium, France, Germany and the Netherlands. To start with, Figure 5.2

Figure 5.2 Domestic and European price gap

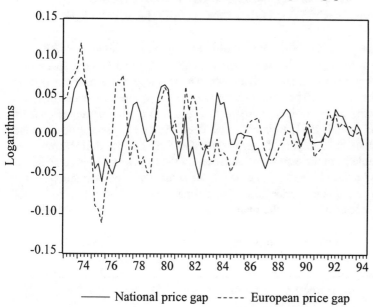

National price gap   ----- European price gap

illustrates that both gaps tend to move around zero, suggesting that both variables are stationary. Formal econometric tests indeed confirm this visual conclusion. Second, the graph reveals that the pattern of purely national distortions generally differs from that of economic imbalances on a European scale.[9] The largest economic distortions are concentrated in the first part of the sample. This may stem predominantly from shocks originating from the supply side of the economy, notably the first oil crisis. During this period, however, the swings in the European price gap are even more pronounced. This is to some extent caused by fairly strong fluctuations in nominal exchange rates at that time. Thereafter, the magnitude of both domestic and European price gaps decline in absolute terms.

The mostly divergent development of domestic and European price gaps logically raises the question which variable is the most appropriate indicator for potential inflationary threats in Austria. In Section 3, I address this issue by investigating the information content of purely domestic and European monetary conditions on the dynamics of inflation in Austria. Here, I also take into account — by considering different estimation periods — the possibility that the relative importance of both gaps may have altered over time due to the ongoing process of monetary integration witnessed in the past decades.

3 THE IMPACT OF NATIONAL AND EUROPEAN MONETARY FACTORS ON AUSTRIAN PRICES

To assess the empirical applicability of the conventional and extended P^*-concept for Austria, I use equations (3.1), (4.13) and (4.8), respectively, to model short-run inflation dynamics. Then, I drop those terms that were insignificant at the 10 percent level. Initially, energy prices were also included in the statistical analysis because their influence is often a matter of concern (Kole and Leahy, 1991; Reimers and Tödter, 1994). However, I never found a significant direct impact of energy prices on Austrian inflation so I removed this variable from the estimation equation. In the following, I first discuss the results with the domestic price gaps. Subsequently, I pay attention to the results with European price gaps. The estimations are subject to a battery of diagnostic tests of which the main results are also recorded in Table 5.2.

Table 5.2 Regression results with domestic and/or European price gaps (based on M3 *and calculated with current nominal exchange rates)*

Sample	Domestic price gap		European price gap		LDV	R^2	SE	Q(8)	HET
73.1—94.4	−0.160	(2.4")			12	0.59	0.89	8.1	12.8'
79.1—94.4	−0.124	(1.6°)			12	0.64	0.79	4.6	9.1
86.1—94.4	−0.047	(0.5)			12	0.44	0.65	4.4	13.7'
73.1—94.4			−0.109	(1.4)	12	0.58	0.89	9.3	12.8'
79.1—94.4			−0.149	(2.0')	12	0.65	0.79	6.4	12.7'
86.1—94.4			−0.219	(2.0')	12	0.50	0.62	11.0	10.7°
73.1—94.4	−0.128	(1.9°)	−0.063	(0.8)	12	0.59	0.89	7.5	13.4°
79.1—94.4	−0.086	(1.0)	−0.104	(1.3)	12	0.65	0.79	5.0	12.7°
86.1—94.4	0.017	(0.2)	−0.219	(1.9°)	12	0.48	.63	12.0	14.7'

Notes: The price gaps are included with a lag of three quarters in all instances. Heteroskedasticity-consistent t-values are recorded behind the estimated coefficients. LDV denotes the significant lags of the dependent variable ($\Delta\pi$). 12 means that the first and second lags of the change in the inflation rate are significant and included. SE is the standard error of the regression multiplied by 100. Q(8) is the Box-Pierce statistic for serial correlation in the residuals. HET is White's statistic for heteroskedasticity and is distributed as χ^2. The symbols °, ' and " denote that the test statistic differs significantly from zero at the ten, five and one percent level, respectively.

The results with domestic price gaps are presented in the upper part of Table 5.2. As can be inferred from the estimations, the traditional P^*-model is accepted for the entire time span. Here, I find that a positive price gap of 1 percent leads to a fall in the inflation rate of about 0.16 percentage points.

Surprisingly, this finding contrasts with earlier studies on the validity of this framework for Austria (see Hoeller and Poret, 1991; Tatom, 1992; Kool and Tatom, 1994). The latter studies reject a significant link between domestic price gaps and national price developments. Plausible explanations for my opposite conclusion are the use of a different method to generate the equilibrium variables, a different sample period and another frequency of the data. The regression also implies that there is a significant pass-through from domestic money growth to inflation over the full sample. However, no policy implications can be extracted from this outcome. The reason is that Austrian monetary authorities have actually never attempted to steer or control inflation by relying on monetary targeting as an intermediate strategy. Hence, Austria has never pursued a monetary policy aimed at hitting monetary targets as has been the case in Germany since the mid-1970s.

In the time interval covering the entire EMS period, the impact and significance of the domestic price gap decrease to some extent. Since 1986, the domestic price gap has, however, completely lost informative value for predicting price trends in Austria. This deteriorated suitability as an accurate indicator illustrates the blurring link between domestic monetary aggregates and national inflation rates when countries give priority to the exchange rate objective.

In the second part of Table 5.2, the results with the European price gap (GAP^f; see equation (4.13)) are shown. Over the full sample, Austrian prices do not react to economic distortions on a European scale. This picture changes in the second time interval. Now European price gaps significantly translate into price developments at the five percent level. In the last subperiod, the negative impact of the European price gaps on the inflation rate rises further from -0.15 to -0.22, while the significance level of the gap coefficient remains the same. These results are in fact the mirror-image of those with domestic price gaps. The estimations suggest that nowadays European-wide monetary conditions are more relevant for the future path of inflation in Austria. The increased importance of monetary spillover effects from other European countries is presumably caused by the European oriented focus of Austria. In this respect, its monetary philosophy as well as drastic changes in the international institutional environment, for example, the liberalization of capital flows and deregulation in the 1980s, have apparently accounted for the early monetary anchoring of Austria in Europe.

When the domestic and European gaps enter the inflation equation simultaneously (see equation (4.8)), one can again observe the shift in relative importance from domestic to European price gaps with the passage of time (see the lower part of Table 5.2). Hence, these results are in line with those where both variables are included separately. Over the full sample, both gap coefficients carry the expected negative sign, but only the national gap measure significantly affects the rate of inflation. In the entire EMS period, the predictive power of the European price gap constructed without Austrian data (that is, GAP^{f2}) improves at the cost of the domestic gap. This process continues in the last subperiod. The results pertaining to the third time interval indicate that the domestic gap even provides misleading information for price developments to come; the gap coefficient has turned positive. Conversely, the European price gap now proves to be a reliable warning signal for potential inflationary risks in Austria.

As a rough check of the usefulness of domestic and European gaps, I have performed out-of-sample forecasts. To this end, I re-run the equations for the period 1986—92 and subsequently used the estimated parameters to generate predictions for inflation in the period 1993—94. The statistical output of this exercise is documented in Table 5.3.

Table 5.3   Forecast performance of the equations with domestic and/or European price gaps over the period 1993—94

	Equation with:		
	Domestic gap	European gap (GAP^{f1})	Domestic and European gap
Root mean squared error[*]	0.56	0.50	0.52
Mean absolute error[*]	0.51	0.43	0.46
Mean absolute percentage error	98.5	88.3	93.3
Theil inequality coefficient	0.37	0.32	0.32

Note: [*] Multiplied by 100.

The forecast evaluation confirms that the insertion of a European price gap produces the best inflation predictions. Without exception the test statistics have more favourable properties in the case of the European price gap embodying the overall monetary situation in the group.

4   CONCLUDING REMARKS

Domestic money growth significantly contributes to the explanation of Austrian inflation in the period 1973—94. Since the late 1970s onwards, this has no longer been the case. Nowadays the (equilibrium) price level in Austria is largely determined by ERM-wide monetary circumstances. Thus, an excessive monetary expansion in other European countries seriously endangers price stability in Austria. Viewed in this light, targeting a European money stock in the Stage Three of EMU seems recommendable from Austria's perspective. Interestingly, these findings accord with those for Belgium and the Netherlands, which have participated in the EMS and ERM from the outset (see Chapter 4 and Groeneveld et al., 1996). Hence, the Austrian example teaches us that participation in formal exchange rate agreements is not necessarily required to build a good inflation reputation and to establish firm monetary ties with other (ERM) countries. What actually seems to matter is the commitment to follow a single-minded and transparent monetary policy, which must be supported by a broad social and political consensus and a cooperative approach in wage and price policies.

NOTES

1. This chapter is based on Groeneveld (1995).
2. As part of a bilateral agreement between Germany and the Netherlands, the current fluctuation margin of their respective currencies is 2.25 percent, whereas the formal fluctuation band of other participating currencies in the ERM is 15 percent.
3. Gnan (1994) sketches the evolution and success of Austria's 'hard currency approach'. Furthermore, he elaborates on the practical and empirical links between this strategy, the optimum currency area literature and the current process of European monetary integration.
4. In connection with recent debates on monetary integration in Europe and the move towards EMU, I feel that the approach followed by Tatom (1992) and Kool and Tatom (1994) is less appropriate in the current situation. They have concentrated exclusively on the German influence on Austrian prices. However, this strategy ignores the possibility that nominal developments in other ERM countries may also have implications for the dynamics of inflation in Austria due to the increased degree of inflation and interest convergence in Europe in the past decade. A corollary of this opinion is that European-wide monetary conditions may well exert a significant impact on German prices, too.
5. However, it must be stressed that Belgium did not publicly declare until 1990 its goal of a very narrow range of fluctuation of its currency against the German mark (Eizenga, 1994).
6. See Artis and Taylor (1994), Edison and Kole (1994), Giavazzi and Giovannini (1989) and Ungerer et al. (1986) for empirical analysis of the effect of the ERM on the behaviour of exchange rates.
7. The results of these tests are not reported here.
8. In this respect, Tatom (1992) has in fact incorrectly used a linear trend model of the level of velocity in testing the traditional P^*-model for Austria.
9. For the other ERM-countries, one can generally observe the same feature (see Chapter 3 and 4; Groeneveld et al., 1997).

6. Direct Inflation Targeting: Conceptual and Empirical Considerations

> Disinflation programs should go hand in hand with a *'once-and-for-all, widely understood and widely agreed upon, change in monetary and fiscal policy regime'*.
>
> Sargent (1983), p. 56

1 INTRODUCTION

In previous chapters, I have investigated whether a European monetary aggregate could function as a reliable additional indicator for the implementation of monetary policy in Europe in the current transitional stage of EMU. For several 'core' ERM countries this seems to be the case, since the impact of EU-wide monetary developments on national inflation appears to have risen considerably from the start of the EMS. As argued, targeting a European money stock could in a way facilitate the transition to Stage Three of EMU, where monetary policy of the common currency area will be conducted by the European Central Bank (ECB).

The ECB could also opt for a monetary strategy that has become increasingly popular in the last few years. This approach is called 'direct inflation targeting' (henceforth DIT). Recently, several industrialized countries have switched from an intermediate monetary approach to this new regime, which aims at hitting the ultimate goal of monetary policy directly. The countries include New Zealand (April 1990), Canada (February 1991), Israel (December 1991), the United Kingdom (October 1992), Sweden and Finland (in the early part of 1993).[1] The policy shift in these countries was generally considered to be an effective way for signalling the determination to achieve and maintain price stability to financial markets and the general public at a time when intermediate (nominal) anchors for monetary policy became unreliable and/or lost relevance. For New Zealand and Canada disappointment with monetary targeting has provoked this change, whereas the other countries had difficulties in maintaining fixed exchange rates. By setting explicit inflation targets these countries actually seek to enhance or, in some instances, regain the credibility of monetary policy, which in turn could reduce the costs of disinflation (Ammer and Freeman, 1994).

In this chapter, I compare from two different angles the dynamics of inflation in three DIT countries with those in neighbouring countries that have not recently changed their monetary strategies. Like Dueker and Fischer (1996), I match New Zealand with Australia, Canada with the United States and the United Kingdom with Germany. In the first approach, the data generating process of the inflation series is explored within an univariate framework using the Kalman filter technique (Section 4). With this method, I also construct proxies for inflation uncertainty. In the second set-up, I first estimate a system of interest rate and inflation equations (Section 5). These estimated models are then used to investigate the patterns of inflation and interest rates after the shift to DIT. This enables me to examine the stability of inflation and interest equations, which could be useful in assessing potential credibility effects of the change to DIT. The comparison of DIT and non-DIT countries allows me to take into account the possibility that shifts in the patterns of these variables are unrelated to the switch to DIT. The latter analysis thus basically comes down to testing the null hypothesis that this new regime has helped to bring down inflation and has consequently improved the credibility of monetary policy. If this happens to be the case, it could be a good policy option for the ECB as well. Before turning to the empirics, Section 2 first briefly explains what this new strategy implies and how it is actually implemented in New Zealand, Canada and the United Kingdom. Here, it will also become clear that this approach bears a close resemblance to other monetary strategies on several points. The concluding section merges the theoretical and empirical evidence and offers some preliminary considerations for answering the question whether monetary or inflation targeting is preferable for the ECB.

2 PRACTICAL AND THEORETICAL BACKGROUNDS

The premise of direct inflation targeting is that a clearly-specified goal of price stability may help build central bank credibility (Lane et al., 1995). In this respect, it is important to distinguish between the immediate effects taking place when a change in policy is announced, the announcement effect, and the effects occurring after agents have experienced that the announced policy change really has been pursued, the implementation effect (Christensen, 1990). This distinction is important, because a shift in policy may gain credibility only gradually rather than instanteneously. Inertial forces, such as wage contracts and financial indexation, possibly make inflation a fairly slow-moving process.[2]

The theoretical link between DIT and credibility is developed in Walsh (1995), and Persson and Tabellini (1993), who suggest that a standard

Barro—Gordon model can be extended to include inflation penalties imposed upon (or embraced by) a central bank to give it better inflation credentials.[3] However, Canzoneri, Nolan, and Yates (1995) point out that penalties in the form of an inflation contract between the government and the central bank suffer from time inconsistency problems and lack of enforceability, which may hamper the effectiveness of inflation-targeting. To resolve these problems, Green (1996) suggests that output targets are announced explicitly along with the inflation target. By targeting output at potential, incentives to trade off inflation for higher output — the source of the inflation bias — are eliminated.

Of course, announcing inflation targets as guidelines for monetary policy might, in itself, have little impact on the public's expectations. It has long been recognized that when the public lacks confidence in the ability of monetary policymakers to carry out a newly announced policy framework, (costless) disinflation is difficult to achieve (Chadha et al., 1992).[4] To boost confidence, it first must be clarified what is meant by the central concept of price stability. Indeed, many possible definitions of price stability exist. The related aspects are sometimes rather complex and technical. For instance, the target can be set in terms of the rate of change or the level of prices. Fischer (1994b) demonstrates that both options have implications for short and long-term inflation rate uncertainty. Short-term uncertainty is greater when monetary authorities adopt a target price path (implying that it attempts to neutralize past errors), while long-term uncertainty about the future price level is smaller. A disadvantage of a price-level rule is that it aims to offset the effects of supply shocks on the price level, although the optimal policy response under these circumstances is, in fact, monetary accommodation. Direct inflation targeting, by contrast, permits price-level drift and thus introduces a unit root in the price level (Fillion and Tetlow, 1993). It would also forgive — and forget — price level disturbances ensuing from supply shocks, which is the 'correct' response in the sense of incurring minimal real costs. So the case for price-level versus inflation targeting basically comes down to trading-off the benefits of price instability against the costs of output instability (Haldane and Salmon, 1995).

The specification of a quantitative inflation target involves various issues.[5] For instance, the index, target level, tolerance interval and time frame must be clearly defined.[6] In the United Kingdom the Retail Price Index is used as price index, whereas Canada and New Zealand employ the Consumer Price Index. This choice stems from the well-known advantages of these price measures: both are widely used and well understood, promptly available and rarely revised (as opposed to the GDP deflator). Regarding the tolerance margin, the countries under review apply a range for the inflation target, typically of a 2 or 3 percent points width. They have not opted for a fixed point target, because the chance of hitting it is negligible due to unpredictable shocks.[7] Because of these disturbances, even when monetary policy is consistently well-directed, there is considerable scope for persistent deviations from the point target. When adhering to such a precise objective, the cause of the likely 'failure' of monetary authorities to hit the target has to be convincingly explained to the wider public in order to avoid a loss in credibility. This will not always be an easy task. Moreover, missing the point target presumably harms the still fragile credibility of the new framework (Crockett, 1994). Obviously, the selection of an appropriate bandwidth involves a trade-off between flexibility and credibility. A wide band provides monetary authorities flexibility regarding their desired reaction to shocks, but probably creates some uncertainty concerning the determination to keep inflation in the lower part of the band, thus potentially endangering their credibility. A narrow band reduces this kind of uncertainty, but requires an almost immediate response to keep inflation in this range, which could lead to large fluctuations in short-term interest rates. Haldane and Salmon (1995) argue that, based on simulations, the range should be at least 3 percent.

A related issue concerns the long and variable lags with which monetary policy actions affect inflation (Fischer and Zurlinden, 1994). Inflation is in fact the last chain in the monetary transmission process. Aside from these lags, uncertainty about future shocks and the precise effects of changes in monetary policy instruments on the economy constitute the major problem in successfully managing a system of direct inflation targets. Mainly for this reason inflation targets are formulated for two years or more into the future. This relatively long length of the target period allows central banks some flexibility to respond to unforeseen shocks.[8] In addition, most central banks are explicitly allowed to avoid having to offset the so-called first-round effects of various (short-term) shocks over which they have no control. Under such 'exceptional' circumstances, the inflation target can be modified or may even be disregarded. Such a procedure is agreed upon in New Zealand and Canada, where a formula is provided to adjust the inflation target if supply shocks occur and/or indirect taxes are imposed (see Reserve Bank of New Zealand, 1993; Freedman, 1994). Actually, the exemption of certain types of price shocks introduces an element of arbitrariness which may jeopardize the overall credibility of the inflation-target concept (A.M. Fischer, 1993). Therefore, an accurate balance must be struck between having a genuine underlying inflation measure on the one hand, and having a measure which encapsulates the costs of inflation on the other (see Haldane, 1995).

A way for improving the overall credibility of DIT is to create transparency. This implies that the public's ability to anticipate what the monetary authorities are doing must increase.[9] To convey to economic agents a clearer understanding of the monetary authorities' reaction function, most countries on a regular basis publish an interpretative analysis of the various information variables that are used to produce an expected path for the price level (see Table 6.1).[10] Since it is recognized that these projections are surrounded by a significant degree of uncertainty, most inflation-target

Table 6.1 Direct inflation targeting in selected countries

Countries	Date of announcement[a]	Target variable[a]	Underlying inflation[a] and other caveats	Target[b]	Set by	Target horizon	Inflation report
New Zealand	March 1990	CPIU	Natural disasters	0–2% band; no explicit midpoint	Policy Target Agreement (PTA) agreed by Finance Minister and Governor	PTA for the tenure of the Governor (five years)	Monetary Policy Statement; Biannual; tabled in Parliament
Canada	February 1991	CPI	Core CPI; very large increase in oil prices or a natural disaster	midpoint 2%; ± 1% band	Finance Minister and central bank Governor	December 1993; '95–98 target; new target by end–97	Monetary Policy Report; biannual
United Kingdom	October 1992	RPIX	RPIY	1–4% band; 1-2.5% by 1997	Chancellor of the Exchequer	< 2.5% beyond 1997	Inflation report; quarterly
Sweden	January 1993	CPI	UND1 UND2	midpoint 2%; ± 1% band	Governing Board of the Bank of Sweden	'in 1995 and beyond'	Inflation (expectations) in Sweden; 3 times a year
Finland	February 1993	CPIY		2% target; no explicit band	Bank of Finland	'permanently'	no separate report
Spain	summer 1994	CPI		3.5-4% Q1-96; < 3% end-1997	Bank of Spain	medium-term objective for 1997	Inflation Report biannual

Notes:

a. RPIX = RPI excluding mortgage interest payments. CPIY = CPI excluding indirect taxes, subsidies and housing-related capital costs. CPIU = CPI excluding interest cost components, government charges, indirect taxes and subsidies and significant changes in import or export prices. Core CPI = CPI excluding food, energy and indirect taxes. RPIY = RPIX excluding indirect taxes and subsidies and interest costs. UND1 = CPI excluding indirect taxes and subsidies, interest costs and effects of depreciation after the move to a flexible exchange rate. UND2 = UND1 excluding heating oil and propellants.

b. For annual inflation unless otherwise stated.

countries have shifted — implicitly or explicitly — towards a probabilistic approach regarding monetary policy formulation, that is, a heightened focus on the distribution of inflation outcomes around the central projection.[11]

Transparency is also a condition to assess whether the central bank is accountable for hitting or missing the goal. The concept of accountability can be made operational by establishing a performance or incentive contract for the central bank (Persson and Tabellini, 1993). The general notion of accountability is that there are adverse consequences for the central bank of not meeting its pre-announced targets. It should be pointed out that the notion of accountability is virtually meaningless if monetary policy actions are dictated by political pressures. Indeed, a subservient central bank cannot be held responsible for failing to achieve the target inflation rate, because it is 'charged with trying to make trade-off compromises between a variety of objectives under the tutelage of a political master' (Goodhart and Viñals, 1994, p. 154). In this respect, it should be stressed that compared to New Zealand direct inflation targeting in Canada and the UK has been accompanied by less firm steps to give their respective central banks greater independence.

On a practical level, any attempt to control the path of the aggregate price level requires that policy makers are able to forecast inflation with some accuracy. This raises the question which candidate indicators provide reliable information about future inflation. DIT countries generally monitor several checklist variables such as money growth, credit expansion, exchange rates, the term structure of interest rates and import prices.[12] This way, the risk that a single indicator triggers an unwarranted policy response is minimized. To ensure that economic subjects do not consider monetary policy as being too eclectic, some economists recommend a formulation of a certain hierarchy in indicators and their thresholds at which policy actions will be undertaken (Fischer and Orr, 1994; Lane et al., 1995).[13]

The actual inflation targets and the main characteristics of DIT in several countries are summarized in Table 6.1. For New Zealand, which has in many respects the most elaborate and stringent program, the specific targets are set in a formal Policy Target Agreement (PTA) between the Governor and the Minister of Finance. Under the first PTA, signed in March 1990, the Reserve Bank of New Zealand aimed to achieve an annual increase in the CPI in the range of 0—2 percent by December 1992. If there was a significant change in the terms of trade, indirect taxes or government charges, or if a major natural disaster occurred, the whole agreement had to be renegotiated. Short-term targets were published by the Bank after the PTA was signed. These targets were 3.5 percent by December 1990, 1.5—3.5 percent by December 1991, and finally 0—2 percent by December 1992. In December 1990, the PTA was renegotiated, and the date for achieving 0—2 percent inflation was changed to December 1993. The current PTA was agreed upon in December 1992, and is essentially identical to the previous one. The official inflation target in

Canada is set jointly by the Bank of Canada and the Department of Finance, where changes in the 'underlying' CPI (which excludes food, energy, and temporary effects of indirect taxes) are used as an operational objective. In February 1991, it was announced that they would keep the annual inflation rate within the range of 2—4 percent by the end of 1992, within 1.5—3.5 percent by mid-1994, and within 1—3 percent by the end of 1995. In the case of the United Kingdom, inflation targets are defined on the RPI excluding mortgage interest payments and are set by the Treasury. In November 1992, the formal target range was set at a year-to-year growth rate of 1—4 percent.

In summary, the underlying idea and motivation of DIT appear to be very similar for the countries examined here. This newly designed monetary framework is expected to decrease price uncertainty through greater transparency including public monitoring of key information variables. The actual implementation of the DIT programs differs in some respects, though. Especially, the extent to which inflation targeting has been accompanied by supplementary institutional arrangements varies considerably. Some countries adopted specific frameworks for fiscal consolidation and granted the central bank greater independence to support the new regime. On the other hand, the formulation of monetary policy in DIT countries also shares many common elements. For instance, most central banks pursuing inflation targets use various information variables ('look-at-everything'). There is also a discernible intention towards greater openness and transparency in the policy process.

3   A PRELIMINARY LOOK AT THE DATA

In the empirical analysis, I use seasonally adjusted quarterly data from 1980 to 1994 on real output, prices, money and interest rates, mostly taken from the OECD Main Economic Indicators. Real output is measured as GDP in 1985 prices, while CPI is selected uniformly for all countries as the price index.[14] I use broad national monetary aggregates (*M3* or *M2*). Short-term interest rates are 3-months Treasury Bill rates in New Zealand, Australia, Canada and the US. For the UK and Germany, I use 3-month interbank rates.

Figures 6.1 to 6.3 show CPI inflation, real GDP growth and short- and long-term interest rates from 1980 through 1994 for the three pairs of countries under review. The upper left panels show that inflation has been consistently higher in New Zealand than in Australia in the early and mid—1980s on average. Over the same period, inflation in the United Kingdom clearly exceeded German inflation. The difference between Canada and the United States is less pronounced. In the late 1980s, rates of inflation in New Zealand and Canada converged to those in neighbouring non-DIT countries. For the UK, this happened in the early 1990s. Similar cross-country differences in the variability of inflation can be noted. Inflation in DIT countries has exhibited relatively large swings, whereas inflation profiles in non-DIT countries are much smoother. Again the evidence is stronger for New Zealand and the UK than for Canada.

The upper right panels show fairly synchronous business cycles in the countries under investigation, in particular in the US, the UK and Canada. Most countries faced a recession in the late 1980s and early 1990s, followed by a recovery since about 1992. Germany lags behind this pattern, due to the (asymmetric) effect of German unification in 1990. The lower panels display 3-month rates and long-term rates (approximately 10-year rates), respectively. As is evident, interest rate co-movements across countries have considerably increased since the late 1980s. The liberalization of international capital flows and deregulation of financial markets are presumably largely responsible for this. Around 1990 up to the end of 1993, interest rates show a common downward trend, with the exception of Germany, where interest rates display a transitory rise after the German unification. In the beginning of 1994, every country was faced with a turnaround in interest rate developments.

The figures also allow for a first visual inspection of the effects of direct inflation targeting. In New Zealand, both inflation and short- and long-term interest rates dropped slightly below the corresponding Australian levels around 1988, prior to New Zealand's start of DIT in 1990. Since 1990, the time paths of these variables have moved closely together across the two countries and are hardly distinguishable. The long-term interest rate in New Zealand appears to have become systematically lower that the Australian level, however. The timing of the switch in sign of these inflation and interest rate differentials raises some doubts on the impact of direct inflation targeting. It is possible, though, that anticipation effects of future policy changes have been a factor behind New Zealand's lower inflation and interest rates in the late 1980s.

Just after announcing explicit inflation targets in Canada in February 1991, the inflation gap between the US and Canada has widened quite rapidly. Since then Canadian inflation has stayed consistently below US inflation. According to Freedman (1994), this was the implicit intention of the Bank of Canada when it announced a target range for inflation of 1–3 percent by 1995 in February 1991. The relative deep recession in Canada as compared to the US may have contributed to the relative fall of inflation. Despite the strong disinflationary process in Canada, short- and long-term interest rate differentials with the US remained constant during the early 1990s. In 1994, short-term rates converge, but Canadian long-term rates remain about 2 percent higher than US rates.

As Figure 6.3 shows, UK inflation has fallen remarkably since 1990 when the United Kingdom joined the ERM. This disinflationary process coincided with an economic slowdown followed by a recession. At the same time, official rates were quickly reduced in several large steps, thereby significantly narrowing short-term interest rate differentials with Germany. After the UK's

Figure 6.1 Four macroeconomic variables for New Zealand and Australia

Annual inflation rates

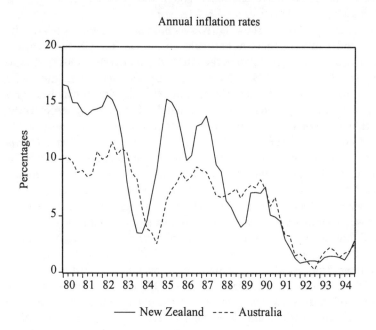

Real GDP growth

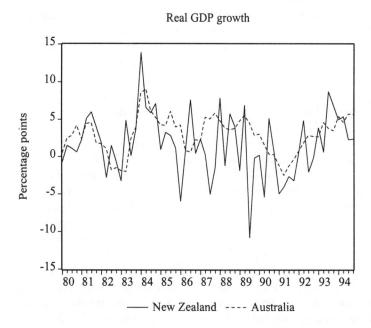

Figure 6.1 Four macroeconomic variables for New Zealand and Australia (continued)

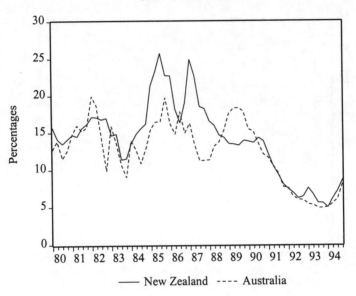

Short-term interest rates

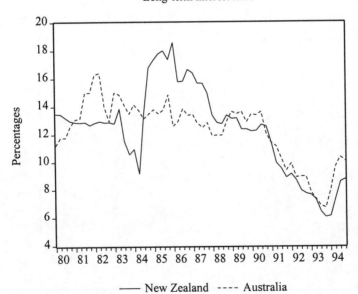

Long-term interest rates

Figure 6.2 Four macroeconomic variables for Canada and the United States

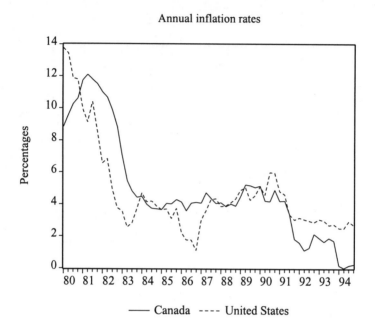

Annual inflation rates

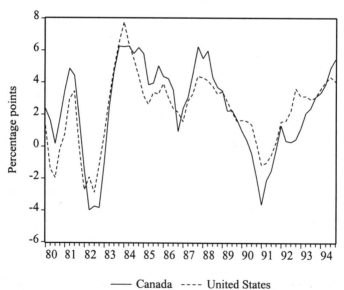

Real GDP growth

Figure 6.2 Four macroeconomic variables for Canada and the United States
(continued)

Short-term interest rates

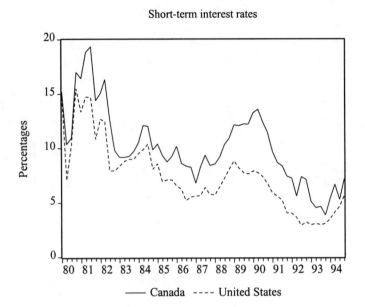

— Canada ---- United States

Long-term interest rates

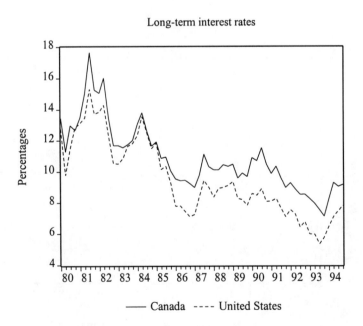

— Canada ---- United States

Figure 6.3 Four macroeconomic variables for the United Kingdom and Germany

Annual inflation rates

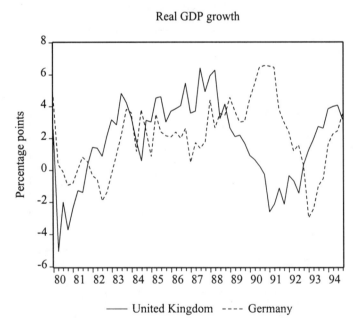

Real GDP growth

Figure 6.3 Four macroeconomic variables for the United Kingdom and Germany (continued)

Short-term interest rates

United Kingdom ---- Germany

Long-term interest rates

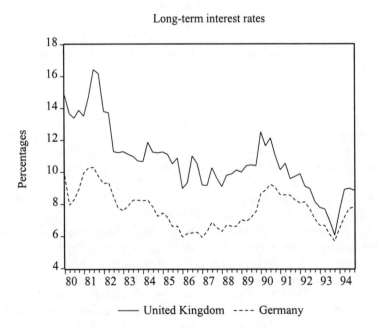

United Kingdom ---- Germany

exit from the ERM, it switched to DIT and continued the disinflationary path. From 1992 up to 1994, UK inflation has been below German inflation, partly due to the rise in German inflation after German unification in October 1990. From the inception of DIT up to early 1994, UK inflation has moved steadily toward the lower part of the target range. Thereafter, inflation has started to creep up again. Long-term interest rates are still higher in the UK than in Germany.

Evidently, an accurate evaluation of inflation targeting in the early 1990s cannot be based on visual inspection of key economic variables alone. DIT regimes were mostly implemented in a deflationary global environment, making it difficult to disentangle the contribution of targeting from the general easing of price pressures. Therefore, a more sophisticated approach is required to tackle this question. After analysing the time series characteristics of inflation, we turn to this issue in detail in Section 5.

4 THE DATA GENERATING PROCESS OF INFLATION

A considerable body of evidence establishes that the variability of prices rises with the inflation rate (Evans and Wachtel, 1993; Reagan and Stulz, 1993; Golob, 1994; Tommasi, 1994). This will distort the allocation of resources in an economy. As argued by Friedman (1977) and Okun (1971), high inflation is generally also more uncertain inflation. Whatever the cause, higher uncertainty is costly, potentially reducing investment and the welfare of savers (Huizinga, 1993).[15] The increased recognition of these notions has, in fact, led to the greater emphasis on price stability and the shift to explicit direct inflation targeting in New Zealand, Canada and the UK.

Empirical studies show that the concept of inflation uncertainty can be made operational in several ways. The variability of inflation itself, the dispersion of inflation forecasts from surveys, and estimates of the variance of inflation from time series modelling of the inflation process are frequently used as measures for inflation uncertainty. For instance, Huizinga (1993) employs univariate and bivariate ARCH models to construct proxies for inflation uncertainty, whereas Holland (1993a) derives a measure of uncertainty from out-of-sample forecasts based on a least-squares learning procedure. Arnold and den Hertog (1995) use GARCH models in examining whether differences in inflation experience or anti-inflation credentials across countries lead to differences in threshold levels of inflation below which the relationship between level and uncertainty of inflation collapses.

In the same spirit, I shall derive a measure of inflation uncertainty employing the MSKF technique. As explained in Section 3.2 of Chapter 2, this method allows for time-varying parameters and incorporates a Bayesian learning procedure. In the context of this chapter, these features seem rather appropriate since economic agents are generally assumed to behave rationally, implying that they learn quickly or gradually about a shift in monetary regime.

With the MSKF method, I generate forecasts of trend inflation one quarter ahead ($t + 1$), given all information currently available, by means of prediction equation (6.1). As soon as the actual inflation rate in $t + 1$ becomes available, the recursive residual (ϕ_t) can be computed. Depending on the size and sign of the recursive residuals, it is checked whether coefficient β requires some adjustment through the updating equation (6.2). In this updating process, old observations are discounted.

$$\pi_t = \beta_t + \epsilon_t \tag{6.1}$$

$$\beta_t = \beta_{t-1} + \mu_t \tag{6.2}$$

As is apparent from equations (6.1) and (6.2), the level of inflation is allowed to change over time, where observations of π consist of the true level in any period plus some random measurement error. β_t is a scalar state variable representing the permanent level of π. The latter is smoothed over time, because it is based on all relevant and available information at time t. Both ϵ_t and μ_t are scalar errors following independent normal distributions with zero mean and variances $\sigma^2 h$ and $\sigma^2 q$, respectively. By taking first differences of expression (6.1), it is easy to see that this simple state space model describes an IMA(1,1)-process.

When implementing the MSKF procedure, I have specified uniform initializations of the input parameters and four different parallel models, two for normal-sized errors and two for large shocks. The first one is designed to deal with transitory disturbances in the level, while the second model treats innovations as largely permanent and adjusts the parameter estimate β accordingly. The degree of persistence of shocks can be assessed by noting that:

$$\Delta\beta_t = \kappa_t \phi_t \tag{6.3}$$

where κ measures to what extent the MSKF method perceives recursive residuals to have a transitory or permanent impact on scalar β. If κ equals zero, innovations do not lead to changes in β, and the inflation process is stationary. At the other extreme ($\kappa = 1$), parameter β is fully adjusted for shocks, and inflation follows an I(1)-process. The degree of persistence may of course vary over time.

The MSKF calculations form the basis for examining whether inflation has become less uncertain, or equivalently more predictable in the course of time. To this end, the absolute value of the innovations of the models, comprising disturbances of equations (6.1) and (6.2), is taken as a proxy of conditional uncertainty. The reason is that such a proxy seems to best account for the idea that for series whose deviations from the unconditional mean can be reliably predicted, it is not fluctuations around an average value that are of concern

Figure 6.4 Inflation uncertainty

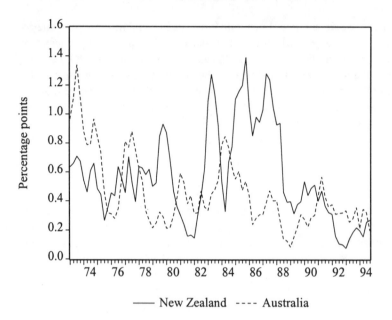

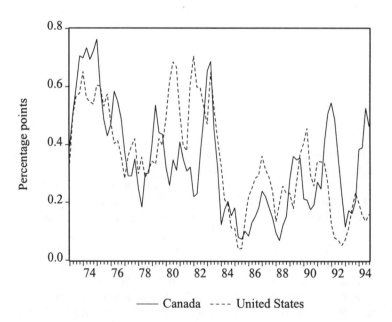

Figure 6.4 Inflation uncertainty (continued)

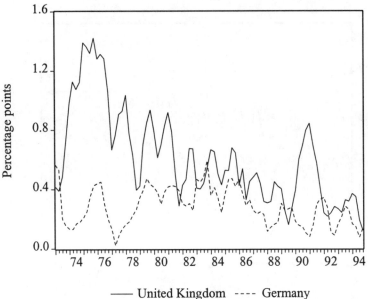

—— United Kingdom ---- Germany

but rather fluctuations around a predicted future path.

Figure 6.4 visualizes the evolution of inflation uncertainty. Uncertainty is generally estimated to be highest in periods that seem reasonable a priori. For instance, uncertainty is high in the first years of the sample period following the oil price shock of 1974. It is also relatively high in the early 1980s, probably mirroring changes in monetary policies in some countries and the effects of the second oil crisis. In New Zealand, uncertainty suddenly jumped to a very high level around 1983. The creation and subsequent lifting of capital controls in this part of the sample period are presumably partly responsible for this. Up to 1987, uncertainty remained high. Thereafter uncertainty dropped sharply. For the UK, uncertainty declined gradually since the late 1970s but suddenly peaked again in 1990. This could be associated with the sharp deceleration of actual inflation, coinciding with the UK's entry into the ERM. On the other hand, there is relatively little variation in uncertainty in Germany throughout the entire sample period.

The related aspect of persistence of innovations in the inflation process is depicted in Figure 6.5. Marked differences appear to exist across countries, which shows up in divergences in the variability as well as in the value of κ. Shocks have rather long-lived effects on inflation in the UK, the US and New Zealand, where this parameter has an average value of about 0.6. On the other hand, innovations translate to a much lesser extent into permanent shifts in the time varying parameter β for Germany. The average value of κ amounts to

Figure 6.5 Degree of inflation persistence

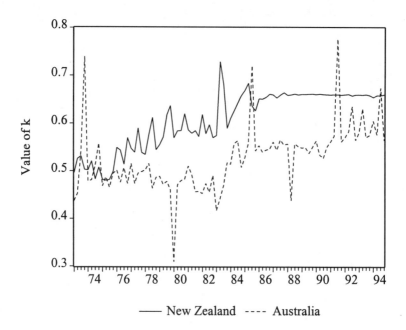

—— New Zealand ---- Australia

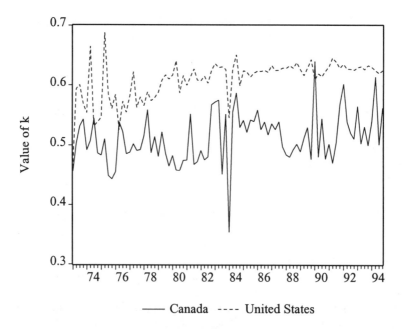

—— Canada ---- United States

Figure 6.5 Degree of inflation persistence (continued)

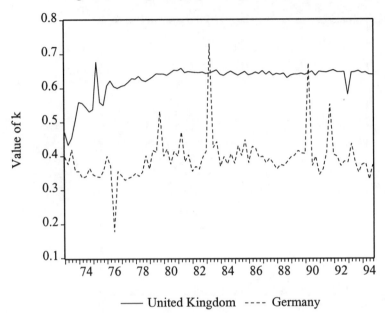

—— United Kingdom ---- Germany

0.4. Moreover, for most countries the degree of persistence hoovers around a more or less constant value throughout the entire sample. Notable exceptions are New Zealand and Australia where the value of κ has increased somewhat since 1973.

Figure 6.6 shows a scatter plot of inflation uncertainty and inflation in the six countries, along with an estimated regression line corresponding to the whole sample 1973.1—1994.4. The line is clearly upward sloping, thus pointing to a positive relationship between inflation and inflation uncertainty. In order to conduct a more formal analysis of this link, I have performed the following simple regression:

$$| \phi_t | = \alpha_0 + \alpha_1 \pi_{t-1} \tag{6.4}$$

The intercept is included to capture the constant factor in uncertainty. Table 6.2 documents the estimation results together with the average level of uncertainty and inflation in each country. Here standard errors are calculated using White's (1980) covariance matrix.

The first row confirms the picture emerging from Figure 6.6. For the group as a whole, lagged inflation significantly contributes to the explanation of inflation uncertainty. The outcomes for individual countries show that remarkable variation in the constant term exists. This coefficient ranges from 0.13 for the US to 0.29 for New Zealand. The regressions also illustrate that the significance of α_1 is usually stronger the higher the levels of inflation and

Figure 6.6 Correlation between inflation and inflation uncertainty

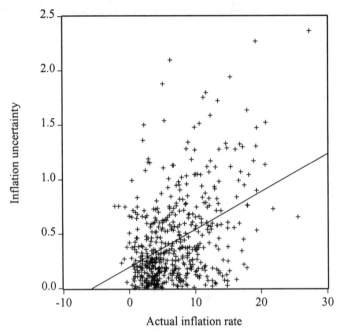

inflation uncertainty. This holds in particular for New Zealand and the UK
compared to their respective neighbours. For Canada and the US, the evidence
is less strong. Interestingly, lagged inflation does not possess explanatory
power for inflation uncertainty in Germany. In case of the UK, a rise in the
inflation rate of one percentage point produces the strongest rise in inflation

Table 6.2 Inflation uncertainty and inflation (sample 1973.1–1994.4)

	π^a	$|\phi|^a$	α_0	$\alpha_1 \pi_{t-1}$	SE	DW
All countries	6.8	0.43	0.18 (7.3")	3.57 (8.5")	0.36	1.60
New Zealand	9.5	0.57	0.29 (4.3")	2.90 (4.0")	0.49	1.61
Australia	7.9	0.45	0.27 (3.8")	2.05 (2.2')	0.35	1.35
Canada	6.0	0.34	0.21 (3.6")	2.13 (2.4')	0.26	1.35
United States	5.7	0.35	0.13 (2.1')	3.77 (3.4")	0.29	2.04
United Kingdom	8.5	0.61	0.25 (3.2")	4.22 (4.0")	0.43	1.87
Germany	3.5	0.27	0.23 (6.1")	1.29 (1.4)	0.21	1.74

Notes: π^a stands for average inflation and $|\phi|^a$ represents average inflation uncertainty.
Heteroskedasticity consistent t-values are shown behind the estimated coefficients. SE is the
standard error of the regression. DW is the Durbin Watson statistic. The symbols ' and " denote
significance at the five and one percent level, respectively.

uncertainty (0.0422). This seems a rather small impact, but one has to realize that the effects may not be negligible in real terms.[16]

Taken together, these results hint that neither DIT countries nor non-DIT countries have similar time series characteristics of inflation or 'inflation uncertainty histories'. However, inflation uncertainty is on average much higher in DIT countries. The regressions are in conformity with earlier empirical work, suggesting that the positive relationship between uncertainty and the level of inflation is stronger in countries with higher inflation (Evans, 1991; Holland, 1993b, among others). Moreover, the estimations corroborate the findings of Ball (1992) and Arnold and den Hertog (1995). I also find indications that there appear to be threshold levels of inflation below which the link between the inflation rate and inflation uncertainty becomes less strong or even breaks down.

5 INFLATION AND INTEREST RATE DYNAMICS

The obvious purpose of the introduction of direct inflation targets in a number of countries has been to increase the credibility of the monetary authorities' commitment to low inflation. If successful, inflation targeting could lead to a relatively fast — and painless — decline of both inflation expectations and actual inflation and, consequently, to lower nominal interest rates. To the extent that nominal interest rates contained a risk premium due to inflation uncertainty prior to the inflation targeting period, real interest rates might show a decline as well. Therefore both inflation and interest dynamics will be subject to structural changes if inflation targeting is effective.

Up to now, only limited empirical evidence is available concerning the effectiveness of DIT. Haldane and Salmon (1995) perform simulation experiments with a small macroeconomic model of the UK to address the desirability of direct inflation targeting. They conclude that either direct inflation or nominal GDP targeting is superior to intermediate monetary targeting, provided that some positive weight is given to output stabilization. Dueker and Fischer (1996) compare the inflation performance of DIT countries with that in neighbouring non-DIT countries using a Markov-switching model. Their results are ambiguous and do not allow a straightforward assessment of how instrumental the inflation targets have been in the observed inflation reduction in DIT countries. Freeman and Willis (1995) apply a simple practical procedure developed by Svensson (1993) in attempting to evaluate empirically the credibility of inflation targeting in DIT countries. Using long-term interest data to estimate changes in long-term real interest rates and taking spillovers from international markets and cyclical effects into consideration, they conclude that the credibility of direct inflation targeting regimes has on balance deteriorated during the recent period of economic recovery, that is, the past year and a half.

To empirically examine possible credibility effects of inflation targeting on the time path of actual inflation and interest rates, I modify and apply a procedure used by Blanchard (1984) and Kremers (1990).[17] I first estimate a reduced-form model of inflation and interest rates over the pre-reform period. Subsequently, dynamic out-of-sample forecasts are constructed for the postreform period and compared to actual inflation and interest rate outcomes. Benchmark results are obtained by performing the same exercises for neighbouring non-DIT countries. In this way, I take into account the possibility that breaks in inflation or interest rate patterns are mainly caused by international economic factors rather than the shift to DIT. If the models for DIT countries generate inaccurate forecasts compared to those for non-DIT countries, this can be interpreted as a sign that the policy shift has been effective in changing inflation and interest rate dynamics in DIT countries. To check the robustness of our results, I also estimate the reduced-form model over the whole sample period and explicitly test for a structural break in the relations at the time of the switch to DIT.

Before estimating the models, the order of integration of the variables included must be identified. To this end, I conduct standard augmented Dickey Fuller tests where higher order autoregressive lags are introduced to generate a white-noise error process. The results are reported in Table 6.3. The test statistics suggest that the logarithmic levels of prices, output, money, and interest rates are nonstationary. The growth rates of the latter three variables appear to be stationary. For the change in prices, the results are ambiguous and point to the possibility of nonstationarity.

Based on the information contained in Table 6.3, I specify the two reduced-form equations with the change in inflation ($\Delta \pi$) and the change in the nominal interest rate (Δi) as dependent variables. Equations (6.5) and (6.6) comprise the benchmark model.

$$\Delta \pi_t = \alpha + \gamma \pi_{t-1} + \sum_{j=1}^{4} \delta_j \Delta \pi_{t-j} + \sum_{j=0}^{4} \zeta_j \Delta y_{t-j} + \sum_{j=0}^{4} \eta_j \Delta m_{t-j} + \sum_{j=1}^{4} \theta_j \Delta i_{t-j} \qquad (6.5)$$

$$\Delta i_t = \vartheta + \xi i_{t-1} + \sum_{j=1}^{4} \kappa_j \Delta i_{t-j} + \sum_{j=0}^{4} \lambda_j \Delta y_{t-j} + \sum_{j=0}^{4} \mu_j \Delta m_{t-j} + \sum_{j=1}^{4} \nu_j \Delta \pi_{t-j} \qquad (6.6)$$

where Δ denotes the difference operator. Initially, both equations are assumed to have the following set of explanatory variables: current and up to four quarters lagged growth rates of money (m) and output (y), and one to four quarters lagged changes in inflation and interest rates.[18] Moreover, since Table 6.3 suggests that inflation rates and nominal short-term interest rates are stationary in some countries, the inflation equation contains the one-quarter lagged inflation level, while the interest equation contains the one-quarter lagged interest rate level.

Table 6.3 ADF unit root tests

variable	CPI	y	m	i
		Log levels		
New Zealand	−2.5 (c, 5)	−2.2 (t, 1)	−2.5 (t, 7)	−0.9 (n, 1)
Australia	−2.6 (c, 4)	−3.0 (t, 4)	2.9 (n, 1)	−2.4 (c, 4)
Canada	−2.6 (t, 1)	−2.0 (t, 1)	0.9 (n, 5)	−3.1 (t, 3)
United States	−3.1 (t, 1)	−2.5 (t, 1)	0.4 (t, 1)	−2.9 (t, 5)
United Kingdom	−1.7 (c, 1)	−2.9 (t, 5)	−1.9 (t, 5)	−2.5' (c, 6)
Germany	−3.1 (t, 3)	−2.4 (t, 1)	−2.6 (t, 1)	−3.0' (c, 5)
		Growth rates		
variable	CPI	y	m	i
New Zealand	−2.7 (t, 4)	−8.3' (n, 1)	−2.0' (n, 0)	−6.0' (n, 0)
Australia	−3.5' (t, 3)	−8.2' (c, 0)	−6.6' (c, 0)	−3.4' (n, 5)
Canada	−2.5 (t, 6)	−3.3' (n, 0)	−2.0' (n, 1)	−7.7' (n, 0)
United States	−3.2' (c, 0)	−3.8' (n, 0)	−3.2' (t, 4)	−10.3' (n, 0)
United Kingdom	−3.7' (c, 7)	−2.2' (n, 1)	−2.2 (t, 4)	−6.8' (n, 0)
Germany	−1.3 (n, 2)	−3.9' (n, 0)	−4.3' (c, 0)	−5.5' (n, 0)

Notes: CPI is the consumer price index, *y* denotes real GDP, *m* is the money stock, and *i* stands for the short-term interest rate. The entries show the relevant test statistic. The character in parentheses indicates the insertion of an intercept only, *c*, or a constant and a trend, *t*. A specification without an intercept and a trend is indicated as (*n*,..). The figure in parentheses shows the number of lagged dependent variables included. The symbol ′ means that the statistic differs significantly from zero at the five percent level.

Although I do not develop a complete model of the economy underlying these relations, these equations may be interpreted as a dynamic version of reduced form equations resulting from a simple and rather standard aggregate supply-demand model with a goods and a money market. Hence, the 'theoretical foundation' of this model contrasts with the P^*-model used in previous chapters, where the money supply is assumed to determine the equilibrium price level. However, the former approach is more in line with the main characteristics and backgrounds of DIT. First, it represents the different status of the money supply under DIT. Money growth is not considered to be the main driving force of changes in inflation, but merely acts as one of the leading indicators in the policy process. Second, shocks to the price level are not neutralized under DIT, but persist infinitely. Hence, no attempt is made to return to a certain equilibrium price level after shocks have occurred. Third, DIT countries follow a so-called 'checklist approach'. They explicitly use various information variables — yield curves, money supply, import prices — together with forecasts from econometric models when taking policy steps. After some time, the public is informed why policy actions were undertaken or postponed and which indicators have played a crucial role in the policy choice. From a presentational perspective, this differs from an intermediate monetary strategy where monetary policy primarily concentrates on the — medium term — development of a particular economic variable (for example, monetary aggregates, exchange rates). In practice, a larger set of indicator variables is used in DIT countries. However, unreported results show that the use of a different set of information variables does not change the overall picture. Moreover, experiments with different subsets of information indicators pointed to the existence of significant correlation between these variables, thus supporting the inclusion of only a few information variables in the regressions.

Since inflation and interest rates are usually assumed to interact through the conduct of monetary policy, the error terms of the two equations are possibly correlated, rendering OLS estimation inappropriate. To ensure consistent and (asymptotically) efficient parameter estimates, I therefore apply the iteratively seemingly unrelated regression (SUR) method.[19] SUR involves generalized least-squares estimation and achieves an improvement in efficiency by taking into account the fact that cross-equation error correlations may not be zero. The residuals are iteratively recalculated and the residual covariance matrix is updated until convergence is achieved. This technique is asymptotically full information maximum likelihood (FIML).

For all countries, estimation starts in 1980.1 and ends one quarter before the announcement and start of DIT. For neighbouring countries that did not switch to DIT the same end date is used. Consequently, the end-points differ across countries. For New Zealand (and Australia) the end point is 1989.4, for Canada (and the United States) it is 1990.4, while for the United Kingdom (and Germany) it is 1992.2. Experiments with longer time spans, for example, starting in 1973.1, produced unsatisfactory results. Using Chow breakpoint tests, significant structural breaks were detected in the early 1980s in most relations. This would make the latter models rather inappropriate for forecasting purposes. It is noteworthy that these breaks more or less coincide with major changes in monetary policy regimes in most countries.[20]

I start the estimation of our system of equations with the full model. Subsequently, I delete those terms that were insignificant at the 10 percent level using the 'general-to-specific' modelling approach. No a priori restrictions are imposed on the sign and magnitude of the parameters. These final parsimonious models will then be used to generate out-of-sample forecasts. This is done by running a dynamic simulation of the estimated system, where the iterative Gauss-Seidel algorithm is employed. In the simulation, realized output and money growth are used. For inflation and interest rates, on the other hand, the model's own forecasts of inflation and interest rates serve as input for the construction of subsequent predictions.[21]

The final estimation results are presented in Tables 6.4 to 6.6. The rows show the estimated equations results together with a set of diagnostic

Table 6.4 Estimated inflation and interest rate models for New Zealand and Australia

New Zealand

$$\Delta\pi = 2.26 - 0.15\,\pi_{-1} + 0.35\,\Delta\pi_{-1} - 0.53\,\Delta\pi_{-4} - 0.06\,\Delta m_{-4} + .56\,\Delta i_{-3}$$
$$(2.0')\quad(1.8°)\quad(2.6")\quad(3.7")\quad(2.3')\quad(2.5')$$

	R^2	SER	DW	Q(8)	ARCH	BP	Sample
	0.77	1.69	2.0	3.1	5.7	6.1	80.1–89.4
						(85.1)	

$$\Delta i = -0.17\,\Delta i_{-2} + 0.04\,\Delta y_{-1} + 0.07\,\Delta y_{-2} + 0.05\,\Delta y_{-3} - 0.03\,\Delta m + .04\,\Delta m_{-1}$$
$$(1.6°)\quad(3.0")\quad(4.3")\quad(3.6")\quad(3.0")\quad(3.2")$$
$$-0.03\,\Delta m_{-4} + 0.12\,\Delta\pi_{-1} + 0.29\,\Delta\pi_{-2} + 0.12\,\Delta\pi_{-3}$$
$$(2.7")\quad(2.1')\quad(5.3")\quad(1.9°)$$

	R^2	SER	DW	Q(8)	ARCH	BP	Sample
	0.91	1.22	2.1	8.6	5.0	12.9	80.1–89.4
						(85.1)	

Australia

$$\Delta\pi = 3.00 - 0.47\,\pi_{-1} + 0.39\,\Delta\pi_{-3} - 0.15\,\Delta y + 0.08\,\Delta i_{-1}$$
$$(2.4')\quad(5.2")\quad(3.3")\quad(3.8")\quad(2.0')$$

	R^2	SER	DW	Q(8)	ARCH	BP	Sample
	0.70	1.40	1.7	11.2	2.6	8.1	80.1–89.4
						(85.1)	

$$\Delta i = 5.19 - 0.48\,i_{-1} - 0.18\,\Delta i_{-3} - 0.19\,\Delta y + 0.22\,\Delta y_{-2} + 0.13\,\Delta m_{-1}$$
$$(4.2")\quad(5.8")\quad(1.9°)\quad(4.9")\quad(5.1")\quad(2.9")$$
$$+ 0.74\,\Delta\pi_{-2}$$
$$(6.1")$$

	R^2	SER	DW	Q(8)	ARCH	BP	Sample
	0.75	1.48	1.6	10.5	2.6	5.1	80.1–89.4
						(85.1)	

Notes: The model is estimated with the Seemingly Unrelated Regression technique. The absolute t–values are recorded below the estimated coefficients in parentheses. SER is the Standard Error of the Regression. DW is the Durbin Watson statistic. Q(8) is the Box–Pierce statistic for serial correlation in the residuals. The reported statistic is the likelihood ratio. ARCH is the test statistic for fourth order Auto Regressive Conditional Heteroskedasticity and has an asymptotic χ^2 distribution with four degrees of freedom. BP is the Chow-test for a breakpoint in the relationship at the date indicated in parenthesis. The symbols °, ' and " denote that the statistic under consideration is significantly different from zero at the ten, five and one percent level, respectively.

Table 6.5 Estimated inflation and interest rate models for Canada and the United States

		R^2	SER	DW	Q(8)	ARCH	BP	Sample
Canada	$\Delta\pi = -0.20\ \pi_{-1}\ -0.17\ \Delta\pi_{-4}\ 0.10\ \Delta y_{-1}\ -0.13\ \Delta y_{-2}\ 0.09\ \Delta y_{-4}\ 0.09\ \Delta m_{-3}$	0.90	1.01	1.8	8.4	3.0	12.6	80.1—90.4
	$\quad\ \ (3.8")\quad\ (1.6°)\qquad\ (2.4')\qquad\ (2.9')\qquad\ (2.5')\qquad\ (2.8")$						(85.3)	
	$\qquad\ .15\ \Delta i_{-3}$							
	$\qquad\ (1.7°)$							
	$\Delta i = -0.03\ i_{-1}\ 0.15\ \Delta i_{-1}\ -0.25\ \Delta i_{-2}\ 0.20\ \Delta i_{-3}\ -0.32\ \Delta i_{-4}\ 0.04\ \Delta y_{-1}$	0.91	1.02	1.9	2.5	4.1	10.3	80.1—90.4
	$\quad\ \ (2.1')\quad\ (1.7°)\quad\ (2.7")\qquad\ (2.2')\qquad\ (3.2")\qquad\ (3.5")$						(85.3)	
	$-0.10\ \Delta y_{-2}\ 0.08\ \Delta y_{-4}\ 0.30\ \Delta\pi_{-1}\ 0.36\ \Delta\pi_{-4}$							
	$\ \ (2.1')\qquad\ (2.0')\qquad\ (2.6')\qquad\ (2.9')$							
United States	$\Delta\pi = 2.02\ -0.53\ \pi_{-1}\ .45\ \Delta\pi_{-2}\ -0.25\ \Delta\pi_{-3}\ 0.32\ \Delta y\ -0.28\ \Delta y_{-1}$	0.92	1.03	2.4	12.8	1.1	5.3	80.1—90.4
	$\quad\ \ (3.3")\ (6.4")\qquad\ (3.5")\qquad\ (2.3')\qquad\ (6.7")\quad\ (4.6")$						(85.3)	
	$-0.24\ \Delta y_{-2}\ .32\ \Delta m_{-1}\ .82\ \Delta i_{-1}\ .92\ \Delta i_{-2}\ .60\ \Delta i_{-3}$							
	$\ \ (3.1")\qquad\ (5.9")\qquad\ (5.9")\qquad\ (4.7")\qquad\ (4.2")$							
	$\Delta i = .28\ \Delta i_{-2}\ .40\ \Delta i_{-3}\ .29\ \Delta y\ -0.22\ \Delta y_{-2}\ .17\ \Delta m_{-1}\ -0.18\ \Delta m_{-4}$	0.92	0.88	1.9	3.0	5.0	9.7	80.1—90.4
	$\quad\ \ (2.7")\quad\ (4.6°)\quad\ (6.4°)\quad\ (4.3")\qquad\ (3.5")\qquad\ (4.2")$						(85.3)	
	$-0.20\ \Delta\pi_{-1}\ 0.34\ \Delta\pi_{-2}\ 0.34\ \Delta\pi_{-3}$							
	$\ \ (2.7")\qquad\ (3.5")\qquad\ (3.2")$							

Notes: For an explanation of the abbreviations and symbols see Table 6.4.

Table 6.6 Estimated inflation and interest rate models for the United Kingdom and Germany[a]

	R^2	SER	DW	Q(8)	ARCH	BP	Sample
United Kingdom							
$\Delta\pi = -0.31\,\pi_{-1}\;-0.15\,\Delta y_{-3}\;0.24\,\Delta m_{-2}\;-0.11\,\Delta m_{-3}\;0.09\,\Delta i_{-1}$	0.72	2.00	2.1	3.5	2.3	2.1	80.1–92.2
$\qquad(4.9")\qquad(1.9°)\qquad(4.9")\qquad(1.9°)\qquad(2.0')$						(86.2)	
$\Delta i = -0.07\,i_{-1}\;-0.32\,\Delta i_{-2}\;0.05\,\Delta m\;0.25\,\Delta\pi_{-2}\;0.12\,\Delta\pi_{-3}$	0.80	1.12	2.0	11.8	1.0	3.5	80.1–92.2
$\qquad(2.1')\qquad(1.7°)\qquad(2.7")\qquad(2.2')\qquad(3.2")$						(86.2)	
Germany[b]							
$\Delta\pi = -0.71\,\Delta\pi_{-1}\;-0.58\,\Delta\pi_{-2}\;-0.32\,\Delta\pi_{-4}\;-0.17\,\Delta y\;0.15\,\Delta y_{-2}\;0.40\,\Delta m_{-1}$	0.68	1.33	1.6	5.3	1.7	6.3	80.1–92.2
$\qquad(6.5")\qquad(4.8")\qquad(3.4")\qquad(3.0")\qquad(2.9")\qquad(1.8°)$						(86.2)	
$\qquad-0.43\,\Delta m_{-2}\;0.69\,\Delta i_{-1}$							
$\qquad(1.9°)\qquad(2.7")$							
$\Delta i = 0.54\,\Delta i_{-1}\;0.36\,\Delta m_{-1}\;-0.38\,\Delta m_{-2}\;0.17\,\Delta\pi_{-2}$	0.94	0.65	1.8	3.7	2.0	16.0°	80.1–92.2
$\qquad(4.5")\qquad(3.3")\qquad(3.4°)\qquad(3.1")$						(86.2)	

Notes:
a. For an explanation of the abbreviations and symbols see Table 6.4.
b. The German data only apply to West Germany.

statistics. Generally speaking, the models fit the data reasonably good. In most instances, both real and monetary variables exert a significant influence on price and interest rate developments. Furthermore, lags of changes in interest rates enter the inflation equations with a positive sign and vice versa. The German, US and Canadian models appear to track the actual data best, while the specifications for New Zealand and the UK have the largest standard errors of the regression. The residuals appear to have quite acceptable properties as well. Box-Pierce Q-tests suggest that the errors are uncorrelated, implying that the models do not systematically under- or overpredict inflation. ARCH test statistics indicate that the null hypothesis of homoskedasticity cannot be rejected. According to the BP statistics, stability of the estimated equations cannot be rejected either.

The estimated systems of equations are used to generate dynamic out-of-sample forecasts. This way, I can analyse the behaviour of prices and interest rates after the adoption of DIT conditional on the development of their proximate determinants. That is, this approach tries to separate the impact of these economic factors from the potential effects of DIT. In addition, by comparing the results for DIT countries with those for non-DIT countries the outcomes can be put in a more complete perspective. Under our null hypothesis that DIT has affected the dynamic structure of the models, one would expect the forecasting accuracy of the models for DIT countries to be worse than the predictive power of the non-DIT countries' equations. In particular, if DIT indeed contributes to the credibility of disinflation programs, systematic overpredictions of inflation and interest rates are to be expected. To the extent that an increase in credibility lowers the required real interest rate, overpredictions of the latter variable are also expected. The resulting forecast evaluation measures are listed in Table 6.7.

In this table, most out-of-sample test statistics are expressed relative to their in-sample counterparts to correct for differences in the statistical fit of the underlying models across countries. This holds for the *RMSE*, *MAE*, and *U*-statistic. For instance, the *RMSE* value for New Zealand inflation of 3.8 implies that the out-of-sample *RMSE* is 3.8 times the in-sample *RMSE*. The out-of-sample mean errors are given in absolute terms, however.

In general, out-of-sample forecasts are quite inaccurate relative to in-sample performance. *RMSE*, *MAE*, and *U* increase dramatically in most cases. Main exceptions are the inflation forecasts for Germany and the UK, which even outperform the in-sample outcomes. Systematic overpredictions of interest rates are observed across all countries, most prominently so in New Zealand and Australia. In the latter two countries, inflation forecasts also far exceed realized inflation. In the other four countries, the systematic bias in inflation predictions is limited.

Figures 6.7 to 6.12 provide a graphical illustration of the out-of-sample forecast performance for the three pairs of countries. Predicted and actual inflation and nominal interest rates (in levels) are displayed for the post-reform

Table 6.7 Forecast evaluation of inflation and interest rates

		Inflation				Interest rate			
	T	RMSE	MAE	U	ME	RMSE	MAE	U	ME
New Zealand	20	3.8	4.8	7.0	−8.5	5.8	6.5	9.0	−4.8
Australia	20	4.4	5.2	6.4	−5.4	4.0	4.5	4.8	−4.2
Canada	16	2.3	2.3	5.9	−1.6	2.9	3.4	4.0	−2.3
United States	16	2.3	2.4	4.4	−0.2	1.7	2.1	3.5	−1.2
UK	10	0.8	0.8	2.7	0.2	2.0	2.4	3.8	−2.0
Germany	10	0.9	0.7	0.7	−0.3	5.1	5.8	4.8	−2.9

Notes: T denotes the number of quarters in the simulation period. *RMSE* stands for the root mean square error. *MAE* is the mean absolute error. *U* is Theil's inequality coefficient. The values of the latter three variables are normalized. For instance, *RMSE* is the *RMSE* of the out-of-sample simulation errors divided by the *RMSE* of the in-sample residuals. A value of *RMSE*, *MAE* and *U* close one indicates that the underlying estimated equation has not changed to a large extent in the simulation period. *ME* is the mean simulation error. For New Zealand and Australia inflation and interest rates are simulated over the period 1990.1—1994.4. In case of Canada and the US, both variables are forecast over the period 1991.1—1994.4. Price and interest rate developments in the UK and Germany are simulated over the period 1992.3—1994.4.

period, together with the implied time paths of real interest rates.

When looking at the results for each country pair in more detail, one can observe that the actual inflation performance appears to be much better in both New Zealand and Australia than projected on the basis of the pre-reform model. Be that as it may, the value of the mean error indicates that inflation is to a much larger degree overestimated in New Zealand. Over the period 1990 up to 1995, predicted inflation lies on average about 8.5 and 5.4 percentage points higher than actual inflation in New Zealand and Australia, respectively. This difference could be (partly) attributable to the shift to DIT, and thus offers some evidence for the null hypothesis. On the other hand, nominal interest rates are overestimated to more or less the same extent in both countries; also the divergence between actual and forecasted interest rates starts earlier in Australia (late 1990) than in New Zealand (mid-1991). Finally, implied real interest rates are underpredicted in New Zealand for most of the period 1990—94, whereas an overprediction was hypothesized. In Australia, actual and predicted real rates show little systematic divergence. Overall, only the relatively large overprediction in New Zealand's inflation supports the null hypothesis. The other comparative evidence of New Zealand versus Australia is much more ambiguous.

For the second country pair, differences in forecast error statistics are less pronounced. The Canadian system of equations appears to forecast actual inflation and interest rate movements just somewhat less precise than the American one. In addition, I find that inflation is to some extent overpredicted

Figure 6.7 Actual and simulated inflation and interest rates for New Zealand

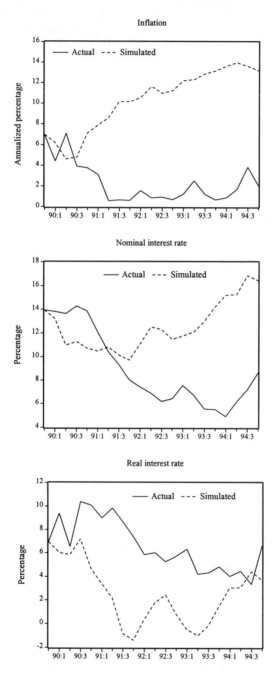

Figure 6.8 Actual and simulated inflation and interest rates for Australia

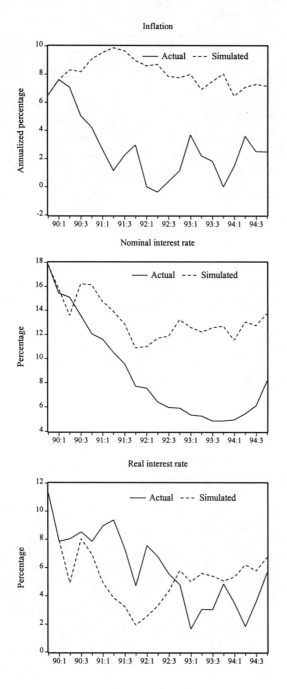

Inflation Patterns and Monetary Policy

Figure 6.9 Actual and simulated inflation and interest rates for Canada

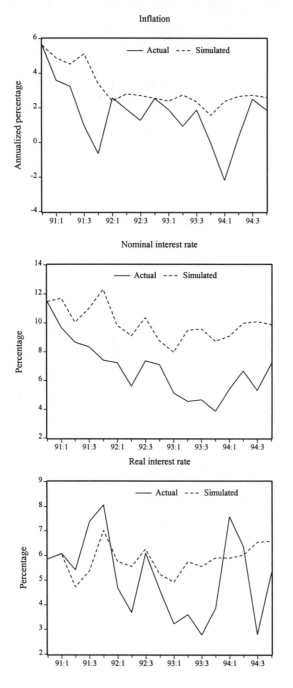

*Figure 6.10 Actual and simulated inflation and interest rates for the
United States*

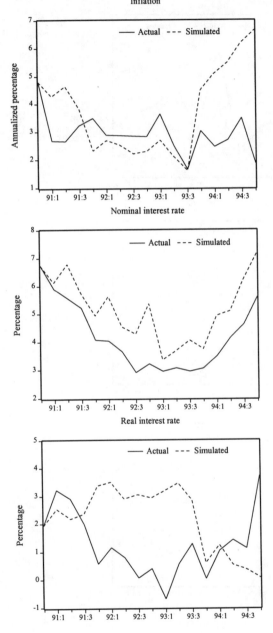

Figure 6.11 Actual and simulated inflation and interest rates for the United Kingdom

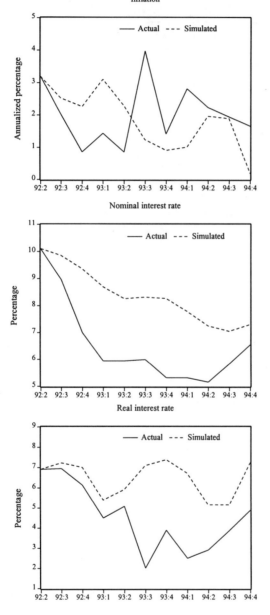

Figure 6.12 Actual and simulated inflation and interest rates for Germany

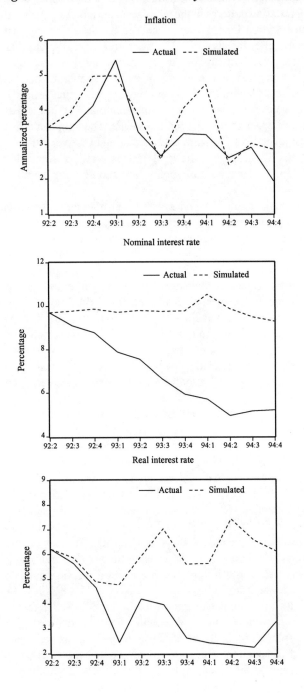

in Canada, whereas the estimated model for the US seems on balance quite capable in explaining inflation patterns in the simulation period. As Figure 6.9 shows, the Canadian inflation bias is mainly caused by the relatively fast disinflation immediately after the start of DIT. After mid-1991, the bias has almost completely disappeared. In case of the US, one would have expected a more favourable inflation performance during most of the simulation period. It is just around 1993 that the forecasted values exceed the actual inflation rates. Based on these projections, one can only conclude that DIT has had at best a favourable initial impact on disinflation in Canada. The long-run effect appears minimal. Moreover, no significant overprediction of the real interest rate occurs in Canada. By contrast, the real interest rate is somewhat overestimated in the US. Under the null hypothesis it should have been the other way round.

For the last country pair, I find that, on average, out-of-sample forecasts remain on track in both countries (see Figure 6.11 and 6.12). In Germany, the correspondence between forecasts and realizations is very close for the whole post-reform period. For the UK, initial overpredictions in 1992–93 are compensated by underpredictions in 1993–94. In this respect, the UK's experience is quite similar to the Canadian one. Immediately after the start of DIT, disinflation is faster than projected. However, this gain disappears in about a year or two. Neither *RMSE* nor the *MAE* point to a structural change in inflation dynamics in Germany and the UK. Actually, the predictive performance is quite good. Both in Germany and the UK, nominal interest rates are consistently overpredicted, leading to real interest rate overpredictions. Opposite to my null hypothesis, these effects are larger in Germany than in the UK.

To test the robustness of the above findings, I have also performed tests on the stability of the system of equations for each country. Therefore, I have re-estimated the models for each country over the full sample period 1980–94. The optimal specifications are again obtained through the general-to-specific approach outlined above. Subsequently, I also include the explanatory variables multiplied by a dummy that equals unity prior to the start of DIT and zero thereafter. Hence, the significant variables are included twice in the specifications before the shift to DIT. Under the null hypothesis that no structural breaks have occurred, the regression coefficients on the added explanatory variables should be jointly insignificantly different from zero. This restriction is tested both for each equation and for the system as a whole. The results are reported in Table 6.8.

For New Zealand, the inflation equation shows a structural break at the 10 percent level, but stability of the interest equation cannot be rejected. The system as a whole displays instability at the 10 percent level as well. For Australia, each individual equation exhibits a structural break and stability of the system is even rejected at the 5 percent level. Surprisingly, instability is

Table 6.8 Stability of the systems

	System		$\Delta\pi$		Δi	
	χ^2	Prob	χ^2	Prob	χ^2	Prob
New Zealand	22.8	0.08	13.1	0.06	9.9	0.26
Australia	52.8	0.00	23.1	0.00	29.9	0.02
Canada	39.9	0.00	19.9	0.03	21.1	0.01
United States	30.4	0.05	21.3	0.02	10.8	0.25
United Kingdom	11.5	0.64	7.4	0.39	5.8	0.57
Germany	7.7	0.87	2.6	0.90	4.5	0.73

Notes: Chi-squared statistics (χ^2) are used to test the hypothesis that the coefficients of the added variables are jointly zero. Prob denotes the probability of rejecting this hypothesis. The breakpoints are 1989.4 for New Zealand and Australia, 1990.4 for Canada and the US, and 1992.2 for the UK and Germany.

thus more pronounced in the non-DIT country than in the DIT country. Comparing Canada and the US, one can observe structural instability in Canada in both each equation and the overall system. In case of the US, the inflation relationship is unstable, but the interest rate equation is not. The entire system is, however, unstable as well. Here, the equations of the DIT country indeed show the greatest instability. Finally, no signs of instability in the relationships are found for the UK and Germany.

Although it is perhaps still too early to assess the full consequences of the adoption of explicit inflation targets (McCallum, 1995), my results are clearly somewhat disappointing for the proponents of inflation targeting. Both the simulations and the tests on structural instability do not convincingly hint that the switch to DIT has affected the path of inflation, though it should be noted that these methods provide just crude tests of the credibility hypothesis. The cross-country examination reveals that in case of New Zealand inflation is severely overpredicted from the start of DIT onward,[22] but the same is true for Australia, albeit to a lesser extent. In the other two DIT countries, Canada and the UK, actual inflation initially declines faster than projected on the basis of the estimated system over the pre-reform period. However, no permanent effects seem to exist. This could stem from the fact that DIT was not backed by substantial reforms on other fronts in the latter countries (for example, central bank independence, fiscal austerity) as opposed to New Zealand. Nominal interest rates are on the other hand systematically overpredicted in all countries. Apparently, worldwide changes in economic and financial structures have offered scope for a looser monetary policy stance. Finally, the hypothesized overprediction of real interest rates due to an increase in credibility and a resulting drop in risk premium after the start of direct inflation targeting, is only discernible in Germany and the UK, and to some extent in the US. In New Zealand, on the other hand, the real rate is significantly under-estimated. Fortunately, these observations appear to be robust to variations in the model specifications.

6 WHAT MONETARY STRATEGY FOR THE ECB: SOME PRELIMINARY THOUGHTS

As discussed in Section 2, the factors ultimately determining the degree of success of either monetary or direct inflation targeting can be clearly identified and are well-established in the economic literature. This means that the ECB will be faced with many identical conceptual and practical issues when adhering to either monetary or inflation targets. For example, in both cases it seems advisable to inform the public on a regular basis about the main backgrounds of monetary policy actions in a general fashion, thus increasing transparancy and credibility. Moreover, national central banks in the EU also agree that, irrespective of the choice of the target variable, the ECB should monitor various indicators which can provide useful information for future price developments. This may call for a ranking of indicators in final policy decisions. The use of target zones and the medium term orientation of monetary policy are also beyond dispute. Therefore, one should not exaggerate the differences between monetary and inflation targeting. In this connection, Von Hagen (1995) argues that the Bundesbank in fact uses implicit inflation targets when setting its monetary targets.

Despite the similarities between monetary and direct inflation targeting, one cannot jump to the conclusion that it does not really matter which target is ultimately chosen. The final selection should be based on the relative scores of each alternative on various criteria. Following Cukierman (1995), the ideal target satisfies four conditions. The objective should be easy to control, highly visible (or transparant) to the public, highly correlated with the final objective in case of an intermediate target, observable at short intervals and should not interfere with the achievement of other economic goals. Obviously, no target meets all these requirements simultaneously. Therefore the ultimate choice will by definition be governed by some normative elements.

Let me now briefly apply these conditions for monetary and inflation targets. To start with, monetary targets, and narrow monetary aggregates in particular, are in principle more controllable by the monetary authorities. As documented in numerous studies, financial innovations and related changes in the relationship between money and prices tend to reduce the attractiveness and effectiveness of monetary targeting. Inflation targets on the other hand may have a visibility advantage because inflation is a more widely understood concept. The major disadvantage of the direct approach is its relative vulnerability to expansionary pressures on central banks to (temporarily) reduce interest rates and achieve various real objectives. This danger is potentially greater in periods where the inflation target is attained. This dilemma is less likely to occur in case of monetary targets, since the actual execution of this approach is more exclusively concentrated in the domain of monetary policy makers. The latter strategy may make it easier for central banks to shield themselves from political pressures and to argue why further monetary easing would threaten the realization of their intermediate targets. It could thus be more difficult to resist the temptation to release the monetary brakes when adhering to an inflation targeting framework. Another complicating factor is that the effects of monetary policy on inflation are less easy to quantify in the short run, and even in the medium term due to long and variable lags in the monetary policy process (Issing, 1994). An additional argument in favour of monetary targeting is that the Bundesbank has relied rather successfully on this monetary framework for more than twenty years now. The continuation of this approach in Stage Three of EMU could imply the transfer of some degree of credibility to the ECB.

From a presentational viewpoint, monetary targeting seems thus somewhat more preferable than direct inflation targeting. Here, I do realize that such a strategy may be complicated by the changeover to a common currency, which could result in substantial changes in liquidity preferences in the union. Moreover, the actual inflation outcome is of course the only thing that counts. A continuously low and stable inflation rate helps to build credibility whereas a lasting bad inflation performance destroys it.

NOTES

1. A detailed overview of the practical and conceptual features of direct inflation targeting in each of these countries is provided in Leiderman and Svensson (1995). Australia has just recently become a direct inflation-targeting country. However, compared to New Zealand, the Australian monetary framework is rather informal and untransparant.
2. These factors constitute the major costs of disinflation. The vast literature on this subject is surveyed in Blanchard (1990).
3. See Canzoneri (1985) and Rogoff (1985) for earlier work in this direction.
4. Agénor and Taylor (1992) list various sources for the lack of confidence in a new (fiscal or monetary) policy.
5. See, for example, Goodhart and Viñals (1994) and Svensson (1995).
6. Of course, the quantification of the objective, the horizon over which the target is to be hit, the choice between a point target or a range and the width of such a target band are also very important operational features of monetary targeting.
7. Note that countries pursuing intermediate targets generally apply target zones for the same reasons.
8. Actually, the medium term orientation of monetary targeting is inspired by the same considerations.
9. New Zealand is — as yet — the only direct inflation targeting country pursuing the contractual solution to this inflation bias problem.
10. The Reserve Bank of New Zealand must publish an official statement that reviews progress towards price stability every six months, and the Bank's Governor is regularly questioned in parliament on inflation performance and prospects. The Bank of England publishes a

quarterly Inflation Report containing an analysis of how the various determinants of inflation interact to generate the expected course of inflation. Moreover, the minutes of monthly meetings between the Bank's Governor and the Treasury are made public within about six weeks.

11. A different strand in the economic literature emphasizes that central banks should not be too explicit about the parameters in their reaction functions (Stein, 1989; Garfinkel and Oh, 1995). If the public perfectly knows what kind of new information will trigger a policy response, the effectiveness of monetary policy could be undermined by pre-emptive behaviour.

12. On this point, the direct approach also has clear similarities to an intermediate strategy. For example, the Bundesbank has never pursued its monetary growth targets in a dogmatic manner, but also constantly monitors a wide range of key economic variables containing information on future price developments (Goos, 1994).

13. In this respect, one also has to bear in mind that the correlation between inflation and indicators may exhibit structural breaks. Assuming for a moment that this will not occur, what should be done if prices are forecast to exceed the target path? Theoretically, the optimal policy response should depend on quantitative knowledge about the impact of the policy instrument on inflation. Here a potential problem is that the link between monetary policy instruments and future inflation can also vary substantially over time and is therefore difficult to estimate, see Cecchetti (1995).

14. Note that inflation targets in the UK are formulated in terms of the RPI. I assume that the RPI and CPI are sufficiently related to justify the use of the CPI.

15. For a survey of the costs of inflation see Driffill et al. (1990) and S. Fischer (1994a).

16. A logical extension would be to investigate the impact of inflation uncertainty on the real economy. This subject is beyond the scope of this chapter and is left for future research.

17. Kremers (1990) uses this approach to evaluate the credibility effects of disinflation through the adoption of a fixed exchange rate with respect to a low-inflation country. Alternative approaches can be found in Ball (1995). In general, credibility effects of disinflation programs are difficult to uncover, as elaborated by Agénor and Taylor (1992).

18. See Tallman (1995) for a description of alternative forecasting models of inflation.

19. Groeneveld et al. (1998a) have repeated the computational exercise with the Two Stage Least Squares estimation technique. Moreover, they have also added the one-period lagged level of the interest rate in the inflation equation and the one-period lagged inflation rate in the interest rate expression. The results presented in the main text appear to be fairly insensitive to these changes.

20. For the US, Söderlind (1995) also ascribes instabilities in the inflation and interest rate equations around 1980 to a shift in the monetary policy regime. In 1979 the Fed signalled a tough anti-inflationary stance by switching to the money stock as the only intermediate target. In 1982 the Fed resumed interest rate targeting.

21. To check the robustness of our results, I have also performed out-of-sample simulations based on uniform models incorporating three lags of each explanatory variable. Moreover, models were also estimated with long-term interest rates. Unreported regressions show that the outcomes are insensitive to these variations in the model specifications.

22. Gerlach (1993) found that the introduction of DIT has not influenced the inflation equations in New Zealand and Canada. This opposite finding probably results from the use of a shorter sample period (1981.1—1993.1) and a less comprehensive inflation model.

7.   About the Ins and Outs

The convergence criteria are not there to help countries to converge smoothly into the union. They are to be interpreted as road-blocks preventing the high-inflation countries from entering the union.

De Grauwe (1996), p.11

1 INTRODUCTION

As argued in previous chapters, either monetary or direct inflation targeting is an appropriate policy option for the European Central Bank. For various reasons, an exchange rate objective is unsuitable. However, European countries that do not immediately qualify for participation in EMU or do not want to join EMU are expected to peg to the euro.[1] The consensus among monetary policy makers is that absence of some form of monetary coordination between the euro area and the countries with a derogation in Stage Three of EMU could lead to excessive exchange rate volatility, thus undermining the Single Market.[2] In the worst scenario, 'competitive depreciations' are expected to lead eventually to the introduction of some kind of trade barrier (see Persson and Tabellini, 1996). A reformed version of the old ERM is seen as a remedy against these potential threats.[3]

To determine which countries are actually eligible for participation in EMU from the outset, the Maastricht Treaty contains so-called convergence requirements.[4] If countries fail to meet these criteria, they will, in principle, not be allowed to join EMU. Here, I do realize that this decision will also be governed by political considerations.

Given the current focus on this issue, this chapter attempts to shed light on the evolution of economic convergence in Europe and to identify potential candidates of the initial EMU group on purely economic grounds. Hence, I won't elaborate on the use and rationale of the convergence targets.[5] In the analysis, all present member states of the European Union and Switzerland are put to the test.

In the literature, several approaches are proposed to empirically explore economic convergence. These alternatives are highlighted in Section 2. Aside from the inclusion of a large group of European countries, this chapter also deviates from most of the existing literature in other respects. First, I pay attention to the evolution of convergence since 1979 through 1995. Second, my research deals with monetary as well as real convergence. To this end, I look at a number of variables. The data set comprises variables for which targets are formulated in the Maastricht Treaty, that is, public debt and deficit ratios, inflation and interest rates. This set is augmented with variables that are generally considered important for judging the homogeneity of a 'virtuous' monetary union (for example, Gros and Thygesen, 1992; de Grauwe, 1996), that is, the current account balance as a percentage of GDP, economic growth and unemployment rates. By focusing on a wide range of economic indicators, I obtain a fairly complete picture of national economies. A preliminary assessment of the above variables is provided in Section 3. Another difference with earlier work is that I use two different techniques to measure the degree of convergence in Europe. In Section 4.1, I compute an overall indicator of convergence, following the procedure of Gros and Thygesen (1992). Section 4.2 attempts to construct homogenous groups of countries for each economic characteristic by employing cluster analysis. These results will subsequently be used to assign numerical values to countries belonging to a particular group. This way, I can investigate whether the countries' relative positions with respect to certain economic factors have significant effects on national long-term interest rates. In the concluding section, I seek to answer the question what degree of nominal and real convergence is desirable and/or necessary to ensure the solidity of a monetary union.

2 CONVERGENCE IN EUROPE: A BRIEF REVIEW OF THE LITERATURE

Essentially, three ways of approaching the question of convergence can be distinguished in the literature. In the first approach, patterns of raw figures are compared across countries. In this setup, Germany generally functions as the benchmark country, because it has quickly become the anchor of the EMS due to its superior inflation track record.[6] A large fraction of the empirical work concentrates on inflation and/or interest rate convergence (see Biltoft and Boersch, 1992; Bini Smaghi, 1994; Weber, 1992). Others primarily pay attention to the effect of the ERM on exchange rates (see for instance Artis and Taylor, 1988 and 1994; Sapir and Sekkat, 1995). A strong empirical finding of this research is that it is difficult to attribute inflation convergence to the existence or participation in the ERM (see also Padoa-Schioppa, 1988). Indeed, inflation has come down remarkably in most industrialized countries in the course of the 1980s. Collins (1988) claims that this phenomenon mirrors the worldwide change in attitudes towards inflation. On the other hand, it has become well established that the EMS has been successful in limiting exchange rate volatility up to 1992/93 (von Hagen and Neumann,

1994).

In the second approach, suggested by de Grauwe and Gros (1991), an overall barometer of convergence is constructed. This indicator provides summary information about the macroeconomic environment in individual countries. Gros and Thygesen (1992) apply this method in the context of the process towards EMU, but only report the outcomes for 1991. They ask what actions are needed in individual countries to reach a reasonable degree of convergence. Their simple measure of convergence incorporates the inflation performance and the deficit and debt relative to GDP as referred to in the convergence criteria. To prevent the index from being dominated by the latter measure, national debt ratios are normalized by first subtracting the EU mean debt-to-GDP ratio and then dividing the result by ten. This standardized variable indicates what budgetary adjustment is required to bring national debt ratios to the EU average over a period of ten years. Since the authors feel that there will be efforts to place the main convergence criteria in a broader macroeconomic framework, two additional variables are included in the indicator; the current account balance in terms of GDP and the unemployment rate. All these variables can be added because they are all dimensionless, that is, they are ratios or rates of change. According to their calculations, Germany, the Netherlands, France and Denmark are a rather homogenous group in terms of the EMU indicator, which ranges from 11.6 for the Netherlands to 12.8 for Germany. The other countries belong to the second tier, with indexes varying between 16.4 for the United Kingdom and 30.2 for Italy. Greece stands alone with a value of about 52. Of course, the aggregate indicator obtained this way does not capture the exact qualifications of the Maastricht targets. First, the indicator uses an absolute standard in all respects rather than the relative inflation measure stipulated in the Treaty's criterion. Second, the addition of five variables implies that a deficient performance in one field can in fact be compensated by a favourable performance in an other area. Finally, not every variable included belongs to the set of EMU criteria.

In the third, less frequently applied alternative, the degree of convergence is studied by subdividing European countries with similar characteristics into homogenous groups. Koedijk and Kool (1992, 1994), van Poeck and van Gompel (1994), and Jacquemin and Sapir (1996) use cluster or principal components analysis for the identification of EMS countries that share either equal economic, technological or demographic structures. In the first two studies, the analysis concentrates on inflation and interest rate convergence in the EMS. To this end, inflation and interest rate clusters are formed for each year since the inception of the EMS. Both studies find that convergence of both variables was apparent, although convergence was neither very rapid, nor monotonic nor identical across countries. Another finding is that it appears to be more difficult to enter the low interest rate group than the low inflation cluster. Moreover, the EMS appears to have gradually evolved into a system with Germany acting as a (Stackelberg) leader.

Jacquemin and Sapir (1996) investigate whether a hard core of EU countries comprising Belgium, France, Germany, Luxembourg and the Netherlands emerges naturally as the most coherent one among all the combinations of the member states. The analysis is carried out on the basis of twelve indicators containing information about the economic structure (for example, exports, population, R&D expenditures) in 1992 and 1993. The statistical technique permits to single out K groups of homogenous units from a set of $N > K$ units. Instead of creating clusters of countries in a twelve-dimension space, they work with a more limited number of axes corresponding to two or three principal components. Their central result is that two groups of countries can be distinguished. A 'southern' group (including Greece, Ireland, Portugal and Spain) and a 'northern' group (comprising all other EU countries). Hence, a fundamental dichotomy exists between the central states and peripheral countries, despite the EU structural funds which redistribute resources in favour of poorer member states. Italy's position between the North and South category is, however, highly unstable.

This chapter builds on the second and third approach. Both variants will be modified and extended in several directions. To start with, I include all present EU member states and Switzerland in my research. Furthermore, I provide a more complete picture of convergence by studying its evolution from 1979 up to and including 1995. Contrary to most other studies, the analysis also focuses on monetary as well as real convergence. Before turning to this topic, the next section briefly discusses the development of the macroeconomic variables under consideration.

3 SOME STYLIZED FACTS

In the analysis, I use annual data from 1979 through 1995. These data are collected from *OECD* and *Eurostat*. The data set comprises the Maastricht convergence criteria as well as variables that are often regarded equally important for assessing the homogeneity and viability of a monetary union. The variables include the current account (CA), government budget deficit (DF) and government debt (DR), all as a percentage of nominal GDP. All inflation figures (INF) are based on changes in consumer price indices. Long-term interest rates (LI) refer to government bonds with a maturity of 10 years, while the short-term rates (SI) are three-month interbank rates. Unemployment (UN) is expressed in terms of the total labour force. Economic growth (EG) is measured as the annual change of real GDP. The countries under investigation are Austria (AU), Belgium (BE), Denmark (DE), Finland (FI), France (FR), Germany (GE), Greece (GR), Ireland (IE), Italy (IT), the Netherlands (NL), Portugal (PO), Spain (SP), Sweden (SW), Switzerland (CH) and the United Kingdom (UK).[7] For Germany, the data pertain to West Germany until 1991 and to unified Germany for the period 1992–95.

Table 7.1 shows the average value of these variables over three periods. The entire sample is broken down into two subperiods. As a breakpoint, I have chosen 1986. This date more or less marked the beginning of the 'hard' EMS (Giavazzi and Spaventa, 1990). The early EMS period is one of frequent realignments of central parities. In the first part of the sample, the degree of financial market integration was probably also smaller. After January 1987 no further realignment occurred up to 1992 (von Hagen and Neumann, 1994) and several non-EMS countries actually started to shadow the German mark.

On the whole, I observe large variations in both the level and development of the real economic variables across countries. Some economies take extreme positions on several fronts simultaneously in a particular time span. For instance, Ireland has combined a fairly large current account deficit with a high public debt, growth and unemployment rate over the complete sample. Another feature is that real variables in particular have different means in the two subperiods. This is exemplified by the column labelled UN which uncovers one of the major weaknesses of most Western European economies. Unemployment has been creeping up and has also become more persistent. In 1995, seven countries had unemployment rates in double digits. The labour market conditions are especially poor in Spain and Finland. As is apparent from the second column, every country has run government budget deficits over the entire time span, except for Finland. The increased priority attached to fiscal consolidation has, however, only resulted in lower deficits in the second subsample in seven countries, particularly in Ireland, Portugal, Belgium and Denmark. On the other hand, seven countries were rather unsuccessful in their consolidation efforts. Within this group, Greece and France experienced the largest deterioration in fiscal positions, while the Finnish government budget balance turned negative. The other element of government finances, that is, the debt-to-GDP ratio, has clearly risen in most countries. Notable exceptions are Switzerland and the United Kingdom. Switzerland has managed to keep the debt ratio just below 17 percent, whereas the UK has been able to bring this ratio down by 10 percentages points to 44 percent in the second subperiod. On the other hand, the public debt burden already required substantial corrections in the case of Belgium and Ireland in the early 1980s. Around the mid-1980s, public finances have also become a major problem for Italy and Greece. In both countries, the debt accumulated by about 40 percentage points to 106 and 92 percent of GDP, respectively.

As opposed to the real variables, the monetary data display more similar movements over time as the right side of the table illustrates. The latter variables clearly exhibit a common downward trend in all cases. Inflation has dropped in every country considered, albeit to varying degrees. In the second subsample, only Greece still experiences double-digit inflation figures. Since

Table 7.1 Some key macroeconomic variables

	Sample	CA	DF	DR	EG	UN	INF	LI	SI
		CA	*DF*	Real variables *DR*	*EG*	*UN*	Monetary variables *INF*	*LI*	*SI*
AU	79—95	−0.4	−3.2	53.2	2.3	4.2	3.6	8.0	7.0
	79—86	−0.6	−2.8	44.4	1.9	3.1	4.5	8.6	7.4
	87—95	−0.3	−3.5	61.1	2.6	5.2	2.8	7.5	6.6
BE	79—95	1.2	−8.0	119.4	1.9	11.0	4.1	9.7	9.7
	79—86	−1.4	−9.9	104.0	1.5	11.1	6.0	11.4	11.8
	87—95	3.4	−6.3	133.1	2.2	10.9	2.4	8.3	7.8
CH	79—95	4.7	−0.4	16.7	1.6	1.4	3.4	4.9	5.3
	79—86	3.7	−0.3	16.7	2.1	0.6	3.7	4.6	4.9
	87—95	5.7	−0.6	16.7	1.2	2.1	3.1	5.2	5.6
DE	79—95	−1.4	−2.6	62.4	2.0	9.5	5.4	12.5	11.1
	79—86	−3.8	−3.9	57.5	2.5	8.7	8.2	16.2	13.2
	87—95	0.7	−1.4	66.8	1.5	10.2	2.9	9.2	9.3
FI	79—95	−1.9	0.7	24.9	2.4	7.8	5.8	11.5	11.5
	79—86	−1.4	2.9	14.5	3.7	5.3	8.0	12.2	12.9
	87—95	−2.3	−1.2	34.1	1.3	10.1	3.7	10.8	10.2
FR	79—95	−0.2	−2.7	33.3	2.0	9.4	5.8	10.4	10.0
	79—86	−0.5	−2.1	26.1	1.9	8.3	9.4	12.6	11.7
	87—95	−0.0	−3.2	39.7	2.1	10.5	2.7	8.5	8.5
GE	79—95	1.2	−2.4	42.2	2.3	7.1	3.1	7.5	7.0
	79—86	0.9	−2.4	37.8	1.7	6.4	3.6	8.0	7.4
	87—95	1.3	−2.4	46.1	2.8	7.8	2.8	7.2	6.6
GR	79—95	−3.4	−10.7	71.8	1.6	7.1	17.9	19.1	18.8
	79—86	−4.9	−8.6	49.5	1.7	5.7	21.3	18.9	17.3
	87—95	−2.1	−12.6	91.7	1.5	8.4	14.9	19.3	20.0

Table 7.1 Some key macroeconomic variables (continued)

		Real variables					Monetary variables		
	Sample	CA	DF	DR	EG	UN	INF	LI	SI
IE	79—95	−2.2	−7.1	95.6	3.8	13.7	7.2	11.7	11.9
	79—86	−8.0	−11.5	91.4	2.3	12.4	12.2	14.6	14.8
	87—95	3.0	−3.2	99.4	5.1	14.8	2.8	9.1	9.4
IT	79—95	−0.5	−10.2	89.0	2.2	8.8	9.4	13.6	13.5
	79—86	−0.7	−10.8	69.6	2.5	7.4	14.1	15.9	15.7
	87—95	−0.4	−9.8	106.2	2.0	10.1	5.3	11.7	11.6
NL	79—95	2.8	−4.6	69.9	2.1	7.2	2.9	8.0	7.3
	79—86	2.4	−5.2	59.7	1.6	7.6	4.0	8.9	8.0
	87—95	3.2	−4.1	78.9	2.6	6.7	2.0	7.3	6.7
PO	79—95	−2.3	−6.8	65.1	2.7	6.8	14.7	20.3	16.0
	79—86	−4.6	−9.0	60.1	2.5	8.1	21.1	23.9	19.2
	87—95	−0.3	−5.0	69.6	3.0	5.6	9.0	17.1	14.1
SP	79—95	−1.2	−4.7	41.1	2.3	18.2	8.9	13.4	13.9
	79—86	−0.5	−4.6	30.0	1.5	16.5	12.7	14.9	15.4
	87—95	−1.8	−4.8	51.0	2.9	19.8	5.5	12.1	12.6
SW	79—95	−1.4	−3.3	57.7	1.6	3.6	6.9	11.4	11.0
	79—86	−1.7	−4.1	53.7	2.1	2.7	8.8	12.1	12.1
	87—95	−1.1	−2.5	61.2	1.1	4.3	5.3	10.7	10.4
UK	79—95	−0.6	−3.5	48.7	2.0	8.6	6.6	10.6	10.4
	79—86	0.9	−3.3	54.0	1.9	8.8	8.8	12.1	11.8
	87—95	−2.0	−3.6	44.0	2.0	8.4	4.7	9.3	9.3

Notes: The data are from OECD and Eurostat. I have used comparable national figures, unless otherwise indicated. *CA* is the current account balance in terms of GDP; *DF* denotes the government deficit as a percentage of GDP; *DR* is the public debt expressed in terms of GDP; *EG* is the growth rate of real GDP; *UN* is the unemployment rate in percent; *INF* is the change in the CPI, excluding interest costs of mortgages; *LI* is the 10-year interest rate; *SI* represents the 3-month interbank or Treasury Bill rate. The German figures refer to West Germany up to 1992 and to unified Germany thereafter.

inflationary pressures have also strongly abated in non-EMS countries, it is likely that common factors have been at work. In this respect, the increased recognition of the costs of inflation have probably played an important role. The fall in inflation has, however, not been accompanied by an equal decrease in short-term and long-term interest rates in some countries, implying that their real interest rates have gone up. Financial markets are possibly still not entirely convinced of the sincerity of policy makers to pursue disinflation policies in some countries. On the other hand, this phenomenon could also largely reflect major remaining differences in the liquidity and openness of national capital markets.

In the following section, the variables just described will be used to examine the issue of economic convergence in a more sophisticated way.

4 AN EMPIRICAL ANALYSIS OF CONVERGENCE IN EUROPE

4.1   A Thermometer for Convergence

In this subsection, I repeat the computational exercise of Gros and Thygesen (1992). As outlined above, their convergence indicator encompasses five major macroeconomic variables. These factors are summed and measure the overall health of an economy. In their perception, a high value of the index means that the country needs a great deal of adjustment before it is a 'virtuous' candidate of a monetary union characterized by price stability, a balanced budget, full employment and a balanced external current account. The indicator, *IND*, is computed as follows:

$$IND_{i,t} = -CA_{i,t} - DF_{i,t} + \frac{DR_{i,t} - DR_{eu,t}}{10} + INF_{i,t} + UN_{i,t}, \quad (7.1)$$

where the subscripts i and t denote country i and time t, respectively. The weighting of the variables incorporated in this indicator is obviously subjective. Also note that the current account and government budget balances expressed as a percentage of GDP enter the equation with a negative sign. That is, surpluses lower the value of the indicator, whereas deficits push the indicator upward. Furthermore, I also apply the same scaling procedure for the debt-to-GDP ratios to dampen their weight in the overall indicator. The European debt ratio is simply the unweighted average of the national ratios:

$$DR_{eu,t} = \frac{\sum_{i=1}^{15} DR_{i,t}}{15} \quad (7.2)$$

Before turning to the hierarchical ranking of countries over time, I first briefly pay attention to the time path of the calculated indices for individual countries. Figure 7.1 plots these indicators along with the overall 'European' indicator, which is computed as the unweighted average of the national indicators and acts as a benchmark. The European index peaked in 1982 around 27.5, while the 'European economy' displayed the smallest disequilibria in 1988 when the indicator stood at approximately 15. Since then, the European barometer has stayed below 20.

The first panel of Figure 7.1 depicts the barometer for three relatively small and open economies. Within this group, Belgium is the only country where the indicator has moved permanently above the European average. This can be largely ascribed to its large public debt burden. Due to remarkable improvements in other economic areas, the Belgian indicator has gradually approached the Austrian index. Leaving aside the 'outlier' Switzerland, the Dutch economy has been the healthiest of all the other European economies since 1993. The indicators of the three biggest founding fathers of the ERM drawn in the second panel show that Italy, whose index has recently reached its lowest value of 27, is still far away from the group of around average performing countries. This can be blamed on its fiscal accounts in particular. Up to the early 1990s, the German economy has consistently outperformed the French one. Thereafter, the overall macroeconomic performance of both countries almost coincide. This can be explained by the adverse economic effects following German unification. This event led to a large fiscal deficit, higher inflation and a current account deficit.

Compared to other countries, the indicators of the 'southern' European countries do not show a very smooth development over time. Overall, the indices fluctuate rather wildly and lay well above the European average. Greece and Spain in particular can be put in one category because they still require substantial adjustments in almost every field of economic policy. From the mid-1980s onward, Portugal obviously does not belong to this club anymore. By contrast, the 'Nordic' countries were generally not far from fitting into a virtuous monetary union up to the late 1980s. They seemed to have their economies in order. In 1991, the Swedish and Finnish indicators suddenly edged upward. The sharp worsening in the fiscal sphere is mainly responsible for this. For Finland, the increasing legion of jobless people has played an important role as well.

The final panel of Figure 7.1 emphasizes Switzerland's special position. Actually, Switzerland is a class of its own due to its large current account surplus and a debt/GDP ratio far below the European average, which render its convergence indicator negative since 1982. In addition, the macroeconomic track record of Ireland catches the eye. In the first few years of the sample, Ireland was by far the worst case with a value of 60 in 1981. This picture is completely reversed in the 1990s. Since 1992, Ireland has not only economically outperformed the United Kingdom, but is also ranked second after the Netherlands.

Figure 7.1 Convergence indicators for 15 countries

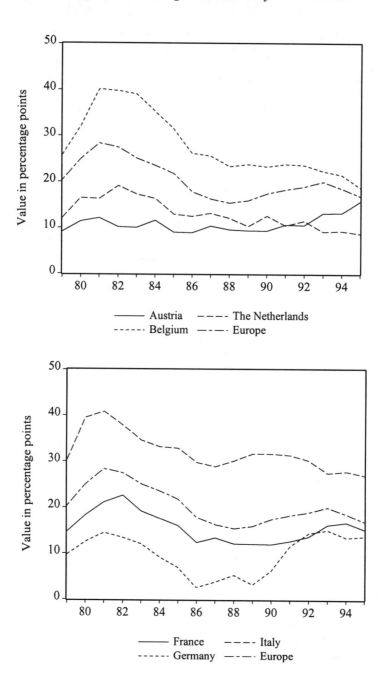

Figure 7.1 Convergence indicators for 15 countries (continued)

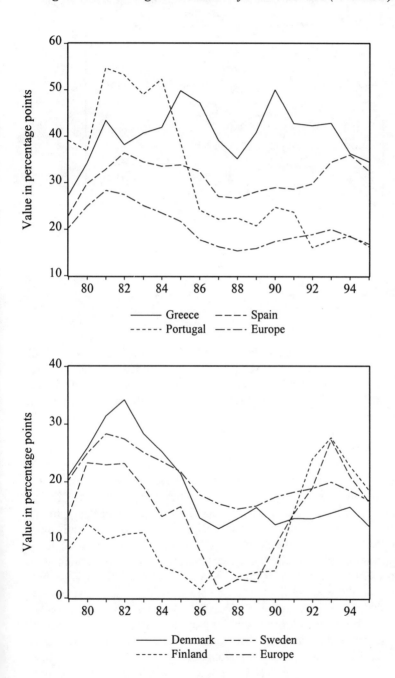

Figure 7.1 Convergence indicators for 15 countries (continued)

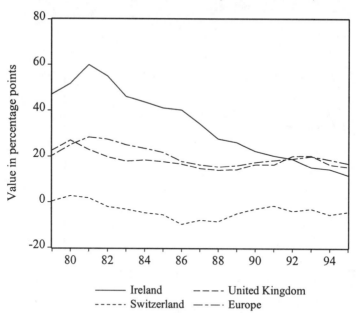

Admittedly, the indicators can only be a suggestive measure of convergence. Nevertheless, it allows for an easy classification of the countries into groups. This is done in Figure 7.2, where each country's relative position is visualized every five years. The left panels of this figure show the seven healthiest countries, whereas the remaining countries appear in the right panels. For obvious reasons, Switzerland is deleted from our sample.

Interestingly, the composition of the first and second tier has not drastically altered over time. Austria, France, Germany and the Netherlands have always been part of the 'core' group. Overall, these countries have always had quite similar economic characteristics. Denmark and the United Kingdom have regularly traded places in the first and second category. In this connection, the hurdles to an early participation in EMU are apparently more political than economic in the case of the UK. Especially in terms of its fiscal position, the UK can certainly join the first group. The Spanish situation remains relatively problematic since Spain appears to be lacking firm integration in the single market. The exceptionally high unemployment rate is a sign that Spain has not as yet finished the process of adjusting to foreign competition. It may therefore be unwise to join the monetary union from the beginning. Portugal has succeeded in eliminating a large part of its economic imbalances; its indicator came down from about 55 in 1982 to a mere 16 in 1995. As a consequence, Portugal has attained a much better starting position in terms of inflation, unemployment and fiscal accounts than its big neighbour. In the case of Belgium, Greece and Italy, worse public finances are predominantly responsible for the high values of the indicators. This is also the reason why Belgium — which is generally believed to be an initial member of the monetary union — has never been able to acquire a place in the vanguard.

An optimist could say that the overall picture is less gloomy because the distance between the best and worst performing countries has diminished remarkably with the passage of time. Since the beginning of the sample the differential has narrowed about 15 percentage points to 26 in 1995. An examination of the determinants of the indicators reveals, however, that this convergence can be mainly ascribed to narrowing inflation gaps since 1990. Differences in the other economic fields have hardly disappeared over time.

4.2   Cluster Analysis

Compared to the previous approach, cluster analysis constitutes a more sophisticated and formal way to address the issue of convergence. In practice, many techniques are in use for performing cluster analysis (see Everitt, 1993). However, most of them have one thought in common. This basic idea is that the extent to which two groups are to be regarded as separate clusters depends on the distance between their means as compared to the mean distance within the clusters. This is a statistical criterion bearing a formal resemblance to the test of homogeneity of classes used in the analysis of variance (Kendall, 1980).

I have chosen Ward's minimum variance method. This technique is an agglomerative hierarchical clustering procedure, and is well suited for my purposes.[8] It proceeds by a series of successive fusions of q members into a number of classes. The first partition consists of q single-member 'clusters', the last partition consists of a single group containing all q members. At each step in Ward's approach, a union of every possible pair of clusters is considered and the two clusters whose fusion results in the minimum increase in 'information loss' are merged. Here, information loss is defined in terms of an error sum-of-squares criterion. More technically, Ward's method involves the minimization of the sum of squared Euclidean distances between individual observations and their cluster mean. It joins clusters to maximize the likelihood at each level of the hierarchy under the assumptions that a multivariate normal mixture, equal spherical covariance matrices and equal sampling probabilities exist. I have run Ward's algorithm for the variables included in Table 7.1 using the SAS package.

Table 7.2 contains the key results of the cluster analysis every five years. Here, the Root-Mean-Square Standard Deviation (*RMSSD*) and the Euclidean mean square root of distances between all observations (*EUCL*), or equivalently the Root-Mean-Square Distance, are presented along with the number of clusters discovered (*NC*). The *RMSSD* and *EUCL* are defined as:

Figure 7.2 Homogenous groups of countries

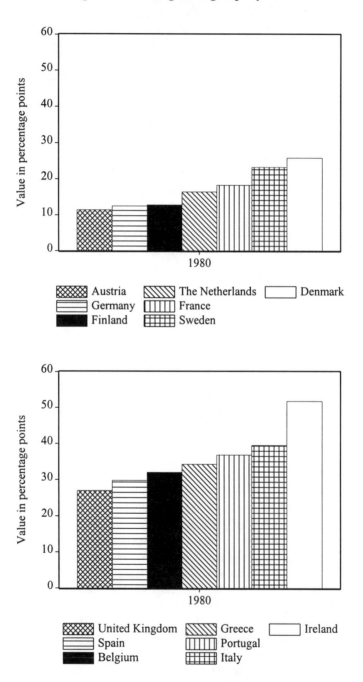

Figure 7.2 Homogenous groups of countries (continued)

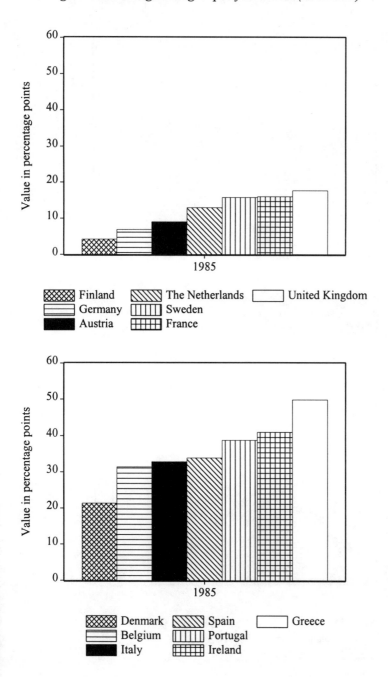

Figure 7.2 Homogenous groups of countries (continued)

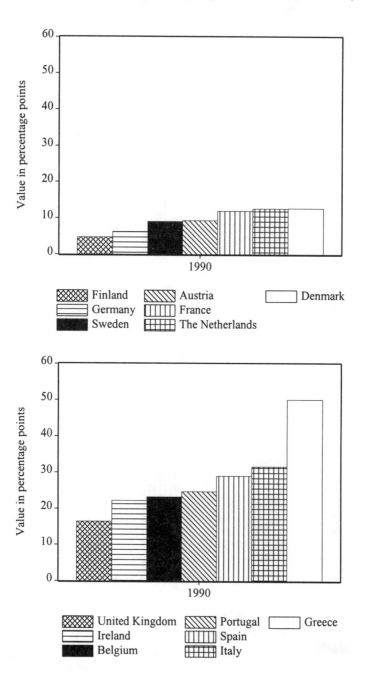

Figure 7.2 Homogenous groups of countries (continued)

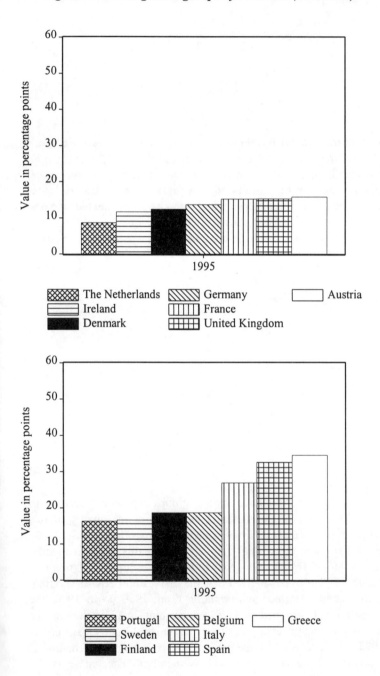

$$RMSSD = \sqrt{\frac{\sum_{i=1}^{n}(x_i - \bar{x})^2}{n-1}} \qquad (7.3)$$

$$EUCL = \sqrt{\frac{\sum_{j<i}\|x_i - x_j\|^2}{n(n-1)/2}} \qquad (7.4)$$

where n denotes the number of countries, x is the economic variable under consideration and the subscripts i and j stand for country i and j, respectively. *EUCL* can in fact be interpreted as a crude overall measure of convergence. The appropriate number of clusters for the data is based on the most commonly applied clustering criteria, which are also implemented in SAS. Everitt (1993, p. 91) asserts that these criteria arise from considering the following three matrices which can be computed from a partition of the data.

$$T = \frac{1}{n}\sum_{i=1}^{g}\sum_{j=1}^{n_i}(x_{ij} - \bar{x})(x_{ij} - \bar{x})' \qquad (7.5)$$

$$W = \frac{1}{n-g}\sum_{i=1}^{g}\sum_{j=1}^{n_i}(x_{ij} - \bar{x}_j)(x_{ij} - \bar{x}_i)' \qquad (7.6)$$

$$B = \sum_{i=1}^{g}n_i(\bar{x}_i - \bar{x})(\bar{x}_i - \bar{x})' \qquad (7.7)$$

These matrices represent respectively, total dispersion, within-group dispersion and between-group deviation, and meet the following condition:

$$T = W + B \qquad (7.8)$$

Each classification of q countries into g groups can be captured in an index, $f(q, g)$. The value of this index is indicative of the quality of this particular clustering. In this case, I have selected the partition corresponding to the minimum value of the within-group sum-of-squares, or, equivalently, the maximum value of the between-group term as the criterion for grouping.

From Table 7.2, it can be inferred that the dispersion between inflation rates has just recently declined substantially. From 1980 up to 1990, the *EUCL* for inflation only dropped by 4 percentage points to 23. In the last five years of the sample, this distance measure decreased by 13 percentage points to 9.9 in 1995. This accords with the general notion that a marked degree of inflation convergence has taken place across countries in recent years. To date, the levels of inflation in Europe are low by historical standards. The emergence of a common approach to monetary policy making with a clear

Table 7.2 *General outcomes of the cluster analysis*

Year	1980			1985			1990			1995		
	RMSSD	EUCL	NC	RMSSD	EUCL	NC	RMSSD	EUCL	NC	RMSSD	EUCL	NC
CA	2.2	12.0	5	2.6	14.3	5	2.2	12.3	5	2.4	13.1	5
DF	3.4	18.4	5	3.9	21.6	5	4.2	23.1	5	1.8	9.7	5
DR	15.3	83.9	4	23.0	125.9	5	25.5	139.6	5	22.9	125.6	5
EG	1.6	8.9	4	0.7	3.8	4	1.7	9.3	4	1.3	7.2	4
INF	4.9	26.8	4	4.7	25.7	4	4.2	23.0	4	1.8	9.9	3
SI	2.8	14.6	5	3.5	19.1	5	2.7	14.9	4	2.8	15.2	4
UN	2.3	12.5	4	4.1	22.4	4	5.2	17.6	4	3.7	20.5	4

Notes: RMSSD denotes the Root-Mean-Square Standard Deviation; *EUCL* is the Euclidean mean square root of distances between all observations; *NC* represents the number of clusters detected. For an explanation of the abbreviations of the economic variables in the first column the reader is referred to Table 7.1.

orientation towards price stability has contributed to this favourable outcome. On the other hand, one can observe that the real sides of national economies exhibit less signs of convergence, except for the national deficits in terms of GDP. Interestingly, the latter feature presumably partly reflects recent efforts to bring goverment deficits more in line with the Maastricht criterion. Indeed, the degree of fiscal discipline varied widely across countries in the larger part of the sample. The distance measure reveals a growing divergence of national deficits until the early 1990s. By that time, national governments started worrying about the sustainability of the large public deficits and opted for budgetary consolidation. These changed attitudes have led to a remarkable decline in both *RMSSD* and *EUCL*. In the first part of the 1980s, the dissimilarity measure for the debt ratio jumped by 40 percentages points to 126. In the final year of the sample, *EUCL* still stood at this level. For unemployment, an identical pattern emerges. In the early 1980s, national unemployment rates were relatively close to each other, with an *EUCL* of 12.5. Subsequently, the distance measure rapidly increased to more than 22, and has almost permanently stayed above 20 afterwards. However, the evolution of dispersion is clearly influenced by the contribution of Spain, one of the very high unemployment countries (see also Viñals and Jimeno, 1996). The Spanish unemployment rate shot up sharply in the early 1980s (and again in 1992–93) and has doubled that of the other countries since the mid-1980s. When Spain is excluded, I find a smaller increase in unemployment dispersion up to the late 1980s, and a weak downward trend since then. The fourth row shows that economic growth rates were quite similar in the mid-1980s. Thereafter, the gap between national growth figures first widened, but narrowed again in the course of the 1990s. In effect, business cycles have become only marginally more synchronous.

The columns labeled *NC* in Table 7.2 suggest that for each macroeconomic variable three to five distinct clusters can be discerned. A closer look at the partitions reveals some interesting things. To start with, the clusters have been subject to drastic changes. Table 7.3 reports the countries forming the various groups. Especially for the real variables, countries frequently switch from one cluster to another. In addition, no clear tendency towards greater concentration of countries in a particular cluster is visible over the years. This finding supports the earlier observation that real convergence still leaves much to be desired. Some countries have permanently brought up the rear. For the years recorded in the table, Greece has never entered an *A*-cluster, while Spain belonged to a first tier just once, namely in 1980 regarding its debt-to-GDP-ratio. By contrast, Switzerland has been very successful and always occupied good positions in many economic fields simultaneously. Another noteworthy feature is that a clear-cut distinction between European countries often referred to as the 'core' or the (geographic) 'periphery' cannot be made. For instance, some 'core' countries (for example, Belgium and France) have unemployment rates which are higher than in some countries generally put in the peripheral group (for example, Greece and Portugal). Hence, the typical notion of these terms does not seem to apply to real convergence.

Concerning the monetary variables, the story is completely different. For inflation, the first cluster has become densely populated in the 1990s. This result is in line with the findings of Koedijk and Kool (1992) and van Poeck and van Gompel (1994). Four countries have almost permanently belonged to the first club, that is, Austria, Germany, the Netherlands and Switzerland. Since 1994, eleven countries are members of cluster A with inflation rates of 3 percent or lower, thus coming close to what is generally considered as a reasonable degree of price stability. This group consists of countries with different monetary policy strategies. Among them, we have Germany which adheres to monetary targeting. There are also countries in the first category where monetary policy is predominantly guided by exchange rate considerations as a result of their participation in the ERM. Apparently, the latter countries have not exploited the widening of fluctuation margins to 15 percent in the ERM in 1993 to run a significantly looser monetary policy than Germany and have, as a result, realized comparable inflation rates. By contrast, the turbulence on the European exchange markets in 1992 motivated — or some would probably say forced — the UK, Sweden and Finland to switch to a regime of direct inflation targeting (see Chapter 6). This policy turnaround has not resulted in noticeable differences in inflation performance compared to European countries with intermediate monetary strategies. The inflation track record of two other ERM members, Portugal and Spain, has remained relatively poor. The above considerations suggest that mere participation in a formal exchange rate arrangement is neither a sufficient nor necessary condition to reach a reasonable degree of inflation convergence.[9] This does not mean that exchange rate targeting cannot work as a disciplinary device for countries still suffering from a low anti-inflation reputation.

For short-term interest rates, a fairly similar picture emerges. In the beginning of the period, nine countries fell into category D and E, but most of them have managed to move to a lower interest rate group with the passage of time. In the last year of the sample, the clusters A and B comprise exactly the same countries as group A for inflation, with the exception of Sweden. Apparently, several countries are still unable to enter the lowest interest rate group although this would be justified on their recent inflation performance. This feature probably mirrors the opinion of financial markets that the latter countries have not — as yet — reached the same degree of credibility of countries with a long-standing tradition of low inflation, for example, Germany. For countries which have been relatively inflation prone in the past, monetary policy has to be somewhat tighter for some time since credibility is certainly not built overnight.

I shall now look at the overall economic performance of individual countries. This will be done by assigning zero points to countries belonging to cluster A in a particular economic field (for example, the lowest inflation,

Table 7.3 Composition of clusters in four selected years

		1980	1985	1990	1995
CA	A	UK	CH	CH GE NL	CH BE IE
	B	NL FR CH	BE GE NL PO SP UK	AU BE DE IE	NL FI
	C	GE AU SP IT FI	AU FI FR IT SW	FR IT PO	DE FR IT SW
	D	BE GR DE PO SW	DE IE	SP SW UK	GE PO SP UK
	E	IE	GR	FI GR	AU GR
DF	A	FI	FI	FI SW	CH DE IE
	B	CH FR	CH GE	CH	GE NL
	C	AU GE GR SP	AU DE FR NL SW UK	AU DE FR GE IE UK	BE FR
	D	DE NL SW UK	IE PO SP	BE NL PO SP	AU FI PO SP UK
	E	BE IE IT PO	BE IT GR	IT GR	GR IT SW
DR	A	CH FI FR SP	CH FI FR	CH FI	CH
	B	AU DE GE DR SW	AU GE SP UK	FR GE SP SW UK	FI FR GE UK
	C	IT NL PO UK	DE GR NL SW	AU DE PO	AU DE PO SP
	D	BE IE	IT PO	GR NL	IE NL SW
	E		BE IE	BE IE IT	BE IT GR
EG	A	BE CH FI IT PO	CH DE UK	GE IE	IE
	B	AU IE	AU FI GR IE IT NL PO SP	AU BE NL PO SP	DE FI IT PO SP SW UK
	C	FR GE GR NL SP SW	FR GE SW	CH DE FR IT SW	AU BE FR GE GR NL
	D	DE UK	BE	FI GR UK	CH

Table 7.3 Composition of clusters in four selected years (continued)

		1980	1985	1990	1995
INF	*A*	AU BE CH GE NL	AU CH GE NL	AU BE DE FR GE IE NL	AU BE CH DE FI FR GE IE NL SW UK
	B	DE FI FR SW	BE DE FI FR IE UK	CH FI IT SP UK	IT PO SP
	C	IE PO SP UK	IT SP SW	PO SW	GR
	D	GR IT	GR PO	GR	
SI	*A*	CH	AU CH GE NL	AU CH GE NL	AU BE CH GE NL
	B	AU GE NL	BE DE FR	BE DE FR IE IT	DE IE FI FR UK
	C	FR SW	IE FI SP UK	FI SP SW UK	PO SP SW
	D	BE FI UK	IT SW	GR PO	IT GR
	E	DE GR IE IT PO SP	GR PO		
UN	*A*	AU CH SW	AU CH FI SW	AU CH FI PO SW	AU CH NL PO SW UK
	B	GE GR NL	DE GE GR IT NL PO	GE GR NL UK	DE GE GR
	C	FI IT UK	BE FR UK	BE DE FR IT	BE FR IE IT
	D	BE DE FR IE PO SP	IE SP	IE SP	FI SP

Notes: The variables in the first column are explained below Table 7.1. The second column refers to the clusters discovered. Cluster *A* contains the best performing countries, category *B* comprises the first best performing countries, and so on. The clusters are formed on the basis of Ward's minimum variance method as programmed in the SAS package.

highest current account surplus). The countries in the second tier (cluster *B*) get one point, and so on. Since I use seven variables, the number of points can thus lie between 0 and 28. Subsequently, I add the individual scores, which gives me an alternative ordering of countries. The economically healthiest nation is the country that has earned the least penalty points. Note that this classification has an advantage over the barometer of convergence discussed in Section 4.1, because it is insensitive to extreme values of economic variables. This index also embodies a broader set of macroeconomic variables.

In the next step, the overall indicator index serves as input for Ward's clustering algorithm to separate the countries into distinct groups. Table 7.4 records the clusters according to the total penalty points. As in Figure 7.2, Switzerland is excluded from the sample, because it has always collected by far the fewest points. In 1985, the value of its indicator just amounted to one. Of all countries, Ireland holds the 'record' with an index of 22 points in 1986. Since then, its economy has clearly improved. This cannot be concluded for Spain, Italy and Greece, whose indicators still hover between 15 and 20. As a consequence, Italy — one of the initiators of the EMS — is nearly always

Table 7.4 Classification of European countries based on their overall economic health

Cluster	1980	1985	1990	1995
A	Austria, Finland, Germany, France, Netherlands, Sweden	Austria, Finland, Germany, Netherlands	Germany, Austria, Netherlands	Ireland, Denmark, Netherlands, Germany
B	Spain, United Kingdom, Belgium, Greece	United Kingdom, Denmark, France	Denmark, Finland, France, Sweden, Ireland	United Kingdom, Belgium, Finland, France
C	Italy, Denmark, Portugal	Spain, Sweden	Belgium, Portugal, United Kingdom	Austria, Portugal, Sweden
D	Ireland	Belgium, Italy, Portugal, Ireland	Spain, Italy	Spain, Italy
E		Greece	Greece	Greece

Notes: Cluster *A* contains the healthiest economies (that is, highest growth rate, lowest unemployment rate), category *B* comprises the first best performing countries, and so on.

categorized in cluster *D*. Germany and the Netherlands have always been members of the first tier, with indices never exceeding 10 points. This feature also demonstrates how close the Netherlands are economically integrated with Germany. Up to the early 1990s, Austria has also occupied a favourable position. In the past few years, it fell back to the third category due to worsening current account and government balances. France and Belgium have almost continuously belonged to the second or even third group. Their overall economic performance has generally been comparable to that of the United Kingdom, which has stipulated for an opt-out clause in the Treaty. Taken together, the first cluster has never contained more than six countries and has only included this number of countries in the early 1980s.

5 ECONOMIC PERFORMANCE AND LONG-TERM INTEREST RATES

As a further extension, I now investigate whether the relative score of the countries in a particular economic area has a significant impact on the level of nominal or real long-term interest rates. This analysis could provide insights into the possible effects of national economic characteristics that may cause interest rate differentials within a monetary union or that could even exert an upward pressure on long-term interest rates throughout the union. Moreover, it could also tell us something about the credibility of European economic convergence (see Groeneveld et al., 1998b). In advance, it should be stressed that this investigation is of a partial nature. I only explore the correlation between these variables and interest rates and do not pay attention to other possible interdependencies between these variables.

Table 7.5 Correlation matrix of indices

Index	CA	DF	DR	EG	INF	SI	UN
CA	1.00						
DF	0.30	1.00					
DR	0.08	0.59	1.00				
EG	−0.00	0.08	−0.08	1.00			
INF	0.41	0.35	0.07	0.04	1.00		
SI	0.43	0.38	0.12	−0.02	0.69	1.00	
UN	0.05	0.35	0.28	−0.06	0.06	0.32	1.00

Notes: The abbreviations are explained below Table 7.1.

In the regressions, I use the numerical values given to the various clusters as explanatory variables. Preliminary testing pointed to the existence of a marked degree of correlation between several indices. This is confirmed by the correlation matrix presented in Table 7.5. Inflation and short-term interest rate indices appear to be strongly linked with a correlation coefficient of almost 0.7. Not surprisingly, the countries' positions regarding both fiscal variables also show a clear correspondence with a correlation coefficient of about 0.6. The other indices display a substantially lower degree of correlation. To minimize the risk of multicollinearity, I have dropped the indices for short-term interest rates and the government deficit ratio from the estimation equation. In practice, the empirical results prove to be insensitive to the inclusion of either the debt ratio or the deficit ratio.

As a starting point, I pool all cross-country and time series data and carry out OLS regression on the entire data set. These regressions function as benchmark specifications. Subsequently, I experiment with different subsets of pool members to obtain an indication of the robustness of the baseline results. Only the most salient outcomes of the latter exercise will be touched upon. Moreover, it is well-established in the literature that the level of national interest rates is determined by common worldwide factors as well as country-specific factors (for example, Barro and Sala-i-Martin, 1990; Koedijk et al., 1994; Orr et al., 1995). As a proxy for the common elements in interest rates across EU countries, I include time-varying intercepts in the pooled regressions (see also Knot, 1995). The country-specific factors are represented by my constructed indices. All in all the estimation equations look like:

$$LI_{i,t} = C_t + \alpha_j INDEX_{j,i,t} \tag{7.9}$$

LI stands for the nominal or real long-run interest rate, *C* is the time-varying intercept and *INDEX* represents the assigned numerical value of the cluster in which country *i* belongs at time *t* with respect to economic variable *j*. The value of this term ranges between zero and four. Initially, I included five indices denoting various economic variables (*CA, DR, EG, INF* and *UN*) in the equation. In the estimations, I have not imposed a priori restrictions on the signs of the coefficients. Theoretically, the move from a 'good' to a 'bad' cluster could equally well translate into higher or lower nominal or real interest rates in some cases. In addition, one indicator reflecting the overall health of the economies, that is, embodying all five variables simultaneously, is regressed on long-term interest rates. This index is derived from the outcomes tabulated in Table 7.4. The real interest rates are simply proxied by subtracting the actual inflation rates from the nominal interest rates.

From column A of Table 7.6, it can be inferred that the overall fit of the equation with the nominal interest rate as dependent variable is quite good. The time-dependent intercepts plotted in Figure 7.3 point to structural changes in the impact of common factors on nominal interest rates in the first years of the sample.[10] In 1981, the constant term reached the highest value of 9.6.

Table 7.6 Pooled regression results (sample 1979–95)

	Nominal interest rate		Real interest rate	
	Coefficient (t-value)		Coefficient (t-value)	
	A	B	C	D
Current account	0.49 (3.4")		0.51 (3.5")	
Debt ratio	0.54 (4.3")		0.42 (3.3")	
Economic growth	−0.21 (1.6°)		−0.39 (2.5′)	
Inflation	2.92 (17.8")		−1.85 (10.3")	
Unemployment	0.34 (2.4′)		0.33 (2.4′)	
Overall index		1.00 (13.1")		0.02 (0.3)
$\bar{R}^2$	0.77	0.46	0.56	0.29
SER	2.26	3.44	2.31	2.64
DW	0.73	0.35	0.56	0.51
Panel observations	255		255	

Notes: SER is the standard error of the regression; DW is the Durbin Watson statistic. The absolute t-value is shown behind the coefficients in parentheses. The symbols °, ′, " represent significance at the ten, five and one percent level, respectively.

Thereafter, the intercept averaged 5.8. It also turns out that every indicator contributes significantly to the explanation of interest rates. As expected, I find a positive coefficient for inflation. The value of this parameter is quite high; interest rates in countries in neighbouring clusters differ by 2.9 percentage points. The indices for the current account balance, debt ratio and unemployment also enter the equation with positive signs. The move to a worse current account cluster shows up in an increase in nominal interest rates of about 0.5 percentage point. Persistent imbalances between savings and investment at national levels thus influence country-specific risk premia on interest rates. Furthermore, higher public indebtedness has an upward effect on nominal interest rates. Entering a lower debt cluster leads to a fall in the nominal interest rate of about 0.5 percentage point. The coefficient of the unemployment index is also significantly different from zero, with a value close to 0.3. A possible explanation for this positive parameter is that financial markets know that policy makers care much about unemployment. An increase in the unemployment rate will generally prompt politicians to do

Figure 7.3 Evolution of time-varying intercepts

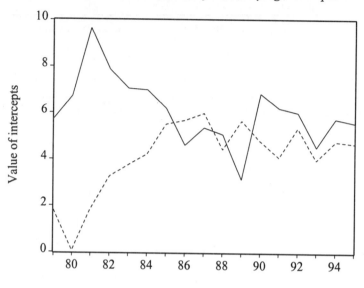

— Nominal interest rate equation   ---- Real interest rate equation

something about it. Aside from taking budgetary steps, the easing of monetary policy is an option to temporarily stimulate economic activity and to reduce unemployment, at the risk of generating higher inflation (expectations). Financial markets are aware of these political trade-offs and consequently demand higher risk premia in nominal interest rates in countries belonging to a high unemployment cluster. Economic growth indices are negatively correlated with interest rates. This negative sign is consistent with theory, since low growth rates, reflected in the high values of the indices, are largely attributable to an aggregate decline in consumption ratios or falling demands for investment funds. These factors represent a potential source of downward pressure on interest rates.

Column B shows that nominal interest rates clearly depend on the general economic situation in individual countries. Compared to nations belonging to the second cluster, countries in the highest group are experiencing 1.0 percentage point lower nominal rates. Since the five variables encompassed in the overall index do not exert a similar impact on interest rates, the R^2 and SER have less favourable properties relative to the equation incorporating all indices separately.

The estimation results with real long-term interest rates are reported in columns C and D of Table 7.6. As in the nominal interest rate equation, the time-varying intercepts hint at structural breaks in the pattern of real interest rates around 1980 (see Figure 7.3). In the first three years of the sample, the value of the intercept just averaged 1.2, while the constant term amounted to 4.7 in the remaining years. As is evident from the value of the R^2 and SER, real interest rates are more difficult to explain by the same indices than nominal interest rates. On the other hand, the sign of most coefficients is generally the same as those in the nominal interest rate equation, although their values are somewhat different in some instances. The coefficient of the inflation index is the only exception to this general pattern. Actually, this should not come as a surprise, considering the findings of other empirical work and the method used to proxy real interest rates. Most studies find that real interest rates are negatively linked to actual inflation. This means that no one-to-one relationship exists between the nominal interest rate and the inflation rate, because economic agents generally do not fully and immediately adjust their inflation expectations to actual inflation. This explains why the inflation parameter differs significantly negative from zero.[11] Apart from this difference, the estimations still indicate that countries with public debt problems are confronted with country-specific credit or default risks in their real interest rates. The final column shows that the overall index has no explanatory power. Obviously, the different effects of the separate indices on real interest interest cannot be appropriately captured in a single indicator measuring the overall health of national economies.

To check for the robustness of the benchmark results, I also run regressions with all possible combinations of explanatory variables. In all instances, I never obtained different results regarding the significance, sign and magnitude of the coefficients of individual indices. The baseline outcomes also appear to be fairly insensitive to the inclusion of a particular country in the pool. Unreported regressions indicate that only the presence of the 'outlier' Switzerland influences the size and significance of the parameters for economic growth, inflation and joblessness somewhat.

An interesting follow-up is to carry out the same exercise with different sets of pool members. Such an investigation allows to determine the robustness of my benchmark results. Of course, one can construct numerous combinations of countries. To keep the presentation surveyable, I mainly concentrate on the exploration of two country groups. In group I, I put countries that are generally expected to join EMU from the outset and have (un)officially joined the ERM for a long time, that is, Austria, Belgium, France, Germany, Ireland, Italy, the Netherlands and the United Kingdom. The inclusion of Italy and the UK may be somewhat disputable on different grounds. First, the Italian economy differs significantly from the other economies comprising group I in many respects. The Italian economy has also generally exhibited the worse overall performance within this group (see Table 7.4). However, Italy is a founding member of the EMS which could make it politically difficult to keep Italy outside the union. Actually, the UK's participation in the ERM did not last very long and it is also doubtful whether the UK takes part in EMU. Nevertheless, I have decided to include the UK in group I because it fits well into this group from an economic viewpoint. Below, I shall verify whether the presence of Italy and the UK has a noticeable impact on the results. Group II consists of the remaining countries, that is, Denmark, Finland, Greece, Portugal, Spain and Sweden. As discussed earlier, Switzerland is a special case. Therefore, I have omitted this country from the sample.

In the regressions, I follow the same procedure as in Table 7.6. The pooled regression results with time-varying intercepts are shown in the left part of Table 7.7. To begin with, the overall fit of the equations is much better in the case of group I than of group II. Statistically speaking, the regressions for the assumed EMU group also outperform the benchmark equations documented in Table 7.6. This suggests that the relationship between interest rates and the indices is more homogenous in group I. Thus, the composition of the country groups seems to matter. Regarding individual indices, striking dissimilarities exist between the estimations for both groups. First, the large coefficients for the current account index for group II imply that its external disequilibria prompt financial markets to demand much higher risk premia in both nominal and real interest rates. On the other hand, it can be expected that the current account balance will lose relevance for the determination of long-term interest rates in group I with the establishment of EMU. The reason is that a large fraction of the imports and exports of these countries will remain inside this virtuous union. Other remarkable differences concern the magnitude of the parameters for the debt ratio and unemployment. The move to a higher public indebtedness or unemployment cluster shows up in a much stronger rise in both nominal and real interest rates in category II. The countries in group II may thus expect larger economic gains in the long run when they decide to undertake substantial fiscal adjustments. Concerning the relative scores on the inflation front in both country groupings, a formal Wald test leads to the rejection of the hypothesis that the inflation index coefficients in the nominal interest rate equations are significantly different in both groups. By contrast, I find that this parameter is about one percentage point lower in the equation of group II. Apparently, a decrease in inflation in category II, which encompasses countries with relatively bad inflation histories, is deemed less credible by economic agents. An improvement in inflation performance leads to a less pronounced downward revision of inflation expectations and thus higher real interest rates for countries categorized in group II. Finally, the index for economic growth does not possess explanatory power in the equations for both groups.

As a final exercise, I have experimented with the composition of the two groups described above. That is, I have transferred one country at a time from its initial group to the other category. These experiments yield a few additional insights. The most prominent finding is that the regressions discussed above obscure the special position of Italy as the right panel of Table 7.7 illustrates. The statistical characteristics of the equations for both

Table 7.7 *Pooled regression for different country groupings (sample 1979—95)*

Countries	Nominal interest rates		Real interest rates		Nominal interest rates		Real interest rates	
	AU BE FR IE IT GE NL UK	DE FI GR PO SP SW	AU BE FR IE IT GE NL UK	DE FI GR PO SP SW	AU BE FR IE GE NL UK	DE FI GR IT PO SP SW	AU BE FR IE GE NL UK	DE FI GR IT PO SP SW
	A	B	C	D	E	F	G	H
	Coefficient (t-value)		Coefficient (t-value)		Coefficient (t-value)		Coefficient (t-value)	
Current account	0.26 (2.6")	0.78 (2.2')	0.26 (2.2')	0.60 (1.5)	0.30 (3.9")	0.86 (2.6)	0.23 (2.3')	0.65 (1.9°)
Debt ratio	0.33 (3.8")	0.97 (3.0")	0.31 (3.1")	0.82 (2.3')	0.19 (2.6')	0.46 (1.9)	0.05 (0.7)	0.54 (2.1')
Economic growth	−0.07 (0.6)	0.04 (0.2)	0.02 (0.2)	−0.03 (0.1)	−0.22 (2.4')	0.25 (0.9)	−0.18 (1.9°)	0.10 (0.4)
Inflation	2.53 (15.7")	2.44 (6.7")	−1.72 (9.1")	−2.78 (6.8")	2.05 (12.5")	2.54 (7.6")	−2.18 (10.6")	−2.73 (7.7")
Unemployment	0.37 (3.3")	0.69 (2.9")	0.29 (2.2')	0.70 (2.6')	0.58 (6.3")	0.55 (2.5')	0.50 (4.4")	0.59 (2.5')
$\bar{R}^2$	0.86	0.61	0.68	0.54	0.89	0.61	0.73	0.59
SER	1.10	2.40	1.29	2.68	0.83	2.34	1.04	2.47
DW	1.16	0.86	0.74	0.68	1.16	0.84	1.11	0.68
Panel observations	136	102	136	102	119	119	119	119

Notes: SER is the standard error of the regression; DW is the Durbin Watson statistic. The absolute t-value is shown behind the coefficients in parentheses. The symbols °, ' and " represent significance at the ten, five and one percent level, respectively.

categories improve as a result of the move of Italy to group II. The elimination of Italy leads to a nearly halving of the coefficient for the debt ratio index — which also becomes slightly less significant — in the nominal interest rate equation, while the statistical link between this index and the real interest rate even breaks down completely (column G). From column E and G, one can also conclude that the economic growth term starts to exercise a significantly negative effect, whereas the parameter of the inflation index drops by 0.5 percentage point to approximately 2. Naturally, the transfer of Italy to the second group also leaves its mark on the estimation results (columns F and H). In conclusion, Italy appears to dominate the outcomes in group I, especially regarding the effects of public debt positions on interest rates.[12] The shift of Belgium, which has an equally unattractive fiscal history, from group I to category II hardly affects the estimations. This can be interpreted to mean that financial markets consider its public debt a less serious problem. As a corrolary, the classification of Belgium in group I is more justified than the inclusion of Italy in this group. In general, the move of other countries from one group to the other leads to a deterioration of the explanatory power of the regressions. In the case of the UK, the consequences for the size of the coefficients are negligible, too. Only the index for the current account becomes less significant and its parameter decreases in magnitude in the equation for group I excluding the UK compared to the estimation for group I including the UK, while the opposite is true for the regressions for group II.

6 SUMMARY AND SOME POLICY CONSIDERATIONS

This chapter has focused on a topic that is currently heavily debated within the European union. It concerns the evolution and degree of economic and monetary convergence in the EU. The question of convergence has obviously gained importance since the formulation of the Maastricht Treaty in 1991. This document contains criteria which will be used to determine which countries are eligible for participation in EMU from the outset. Aside from the variables assigned as convergence targets, this chapter has analysed the development of other key macroeconomic variables that are generally considered to be equally important to assess the viability of a monetary union.

A striking finding of my empirical analysis is that the distinction of all current EU countries and Switzerland in terms of their nominal performance has blurred over time. Particularly in the 1990s, there has been a remarkable convergence in inflation across European countries. The increased recognition of the costs of inflation and the progress towards greater central bank independence are often regarded as the key factors underlying this phenomenon.[13] Interestingly, the overall disinflation process does not appear to be accompanied by an identical narrowing of the credibility gap of monetary policy in all countries. The cluster analysis conveys that some countries in the lowest inflation cluster still encounter higher short-term interest rates than other countries belonging to the same inflation group (see Table 7.3).

On the other hand, the 'EMU' barometers as well as formal clustering techniques hardly point to real convergence in the EU over time. Indeed, fiscal and current account positions still vary greatly across countries, while the composition of the country clusters with respect to economic growth looks completely different every year. Besides, persistent large cross-country disparities of unemployment rates point to the existence of barriers to labour mobility within Europe, including language and cultural differences (Bini Smaghi and Vori, 1993). An exception to this overall picture is the path of fiscal deficits in the last years of the sample. Probably due to the adoption of the Maastricht Treaty, there has been a remarkable convergence of fiscal deficit ratios in the 1990s.

The latter observations do not answer the fundamental question whether lack of real convergence impedes a smooth functioning of a monetary union. First of all, one has to realize that it is an illusion to expect that real convergence will ever become complete. This consideration possibly requires some qualification for countries with dramatically high unemployment rates (for example, Spain) and for convergence in the fiscal field.[14] The pooled regressions show that unemployment exercises a positive influence on both nominal and real interest rates. If countries with extremely high unemployment rates are permitted to join EMU, they could exert an upward effect on — risk premia in — interest rates throughout the union. An exceptionally high unemployment rate also indicates that a country lacks firm integration in the Single Market and has not as yet finished the process of adjusting to foreign competition. Such a country should therefore postpone participation in a currency union for its own sake, too. In addition, I think that a certain level of fiscal convergence between potential union members is recommendable. The estimations suggest that countries with sound fiscal positions experience substantially lower interest rates. This finding is consistent with other empirical studies on the determination of interest rates (see Knot, 1996; Orr et al., 1996) and argues in favour of a further improvement of fiscal positions in Europe. The eventual participation of countries with high public deficits or debt ratios carries the risk of putting upward pressure on interest rates throughout the union. For example, the estimations show that the statistical relationship between debt ratio indices and interest rates in the generally expected core EMU is fully attributable to the presence of Italy. Apart from this aspect, fiscal retrenchment would also create or restore some leeway for fiscal policy to perform the desired stabilization function in the face of adverse shocks in some member states in the future, given that the exchange rate is no longer available to cushion asymmetric disturbances (see, for example, Masson, 1996; Pauer, 1996).

All in all, the majority of EU countries would qualify for participation in a 'virtuous' monetary union regarding the convergence requirement of a high degree of price stability. However, some countries should definitely have to wait a little while before entering the union, because the credibility of their monetary policies appears to be less well-established than that of the other countries. In my opinion, the presence of a long-standing anti-inflation reputation should be given a large weight in assessing the eligibility of a particular country to join EMU. Regarding the state of real convergence, I feel that potential union members should only have broadly comparable economic characteristics (except for fiscal balances).

NOTES

1. Obstfeld and Rogoff (1995) offer a survey of various aspects of attempting a unilateral peg of the exchange rate.
2. Baldwin and Seghezza (1996) provide an overview of the literature on the relation between European integration and growth.
3. At the time of writing, the precise modalities of this new mechanism still have to take shape. However, it is certain that it will not have exactly the same characteristics of the old ERM, which has proven rather unsuccessful in fostering a zone of monetary stability in Europe in 1992 and 1993 (see Eichengreen and Wyplosz, 1993).
4. The four main criteria for the transition to EMU are a high degree of price stability, sustainability of the government financial position, observance of normal fluctuation margins in the EMS for at least two years without devaluation, and evidence of durability of convergence reflected in long-term interest rates (Article 109 j).
5. Buiter et al. (1993) and de Grauwe (1996) sharply criticize these criteria. Particularly, the condition that government deficits should not exceed 3 percent of GDP, and gross public debt should be below 60 percent of GDP or declining at a sufficiently rapid pace is highly questioned. Von Hagen and Lutz (1996) emphasize that the fiscal and inflation criteria may not be mutually consistent.
6. The issue of German dominance (or asymmetry) in the EMS is investigated in de Grauwe (1989), Fratianni and von Hagen (1992), Henry and Weidmann (1994) and Herz and Röger (1992), among others.
7. Due to a lack of data Luxemburg is excluded from my sample.
8. See Milligan (1981) for a review of simulation studies comparing various methods of cluster analysis.
9. In a survey of recent empirical cross-country literature, Quirk (1994) also concludes that there is little unambiguous association of the choice of exchange regime with macroeconomic performance, inflation in particular.
10. This feature is consistent with other empirical work on interest rates. For instance, Cumby and Mishkin (1986) offer evidence of a major shift in the underlying stochastic nature of interest rate movements in Europe around 1980.
11. A positive correlation between inflation rates or clusters and real interest rates could theoretically exist if higher inflation rates go hand in hand with higher uncertainty, which would in turn add risk premia in the real rates (see Section 4 of Chapter 6). Obviously, the indices are inaccurate proxies for inflation uncertainty.
12. Note that these findings are in line with those of Jacquemin and Sapir (1996), who find that Italy's position between the core and peripherical group is unstable.

13. These universal elements make it difficult to isolate the contribution of the ERM to inflation convergence among its members (see Section 2).

14. As Viñals and Jimeno (1996) rightly stress, the currently high unemployment rates in Europe are mainly caused by common European factors with a structural nature. Evidently, monetary policy cannot be used to eliminate these structural causes of unemployment. Thus, divergent unemployment rates should — in principle — not constitute a problem to achieve consensus in the ESCB about the appropriate stance of monetary policy.

8. Summary and Concluding Remarks

The convergence achieved during the transition to Stage Three and possibly the adoption of certain strategies and tactics in the conduct of monetary policy should help the ESCB to inherit the credibility of successful central banks in the Community. Yet, the credibility of the ESCB will ultimately depend on its effectiveness in delivering price stability.

Monticelli and Viñals (1993), p. 26

1 SUMMARY

In the 1990s, European monetary policy makers have been, and still are, faced with many challenging issues. In this respect, the process towards EMU obviously comes to mind. According to the agreed time schedule, the monetary policy for the EMU area will be delegated to the European System of Central Banks in January 1999. To ensure a smooth functioning of EMU, numerous hurdles have to be overcome. For instance, national money market instruments and national monetary statistics have to be harmonized in advance and decisions have to be made regarding the distribution of seigniorage of the ESCB among national central banks (see Groeneveld and Visser, 1997).

As discussed in the introductory Chapter 1, another remarkable feature of the 1990s was the significant drop in inflation in many industrialized countries. Nowadays, most Western countries are close to what is considered to be a reasonable degree of price stability. The increasing orientation of monetary policy towards price stability is generally held largely responsible for this. This policy shift reflects the notion that high and variable inflation impedes an efficient allocation of resources in an economy. To enable central banks to perform their tasks adequately, most countries granted their central banks more independence to pursue anti-inflationary policies. This implies, among other things, that central banks are free to choose the monetary strategy to reach price stability. As a logical consequence of these developments, the future ESCB is also given a clear mandate to fight inflation in the euro area and is equipped with a significant degree of institutional and functional autonomy. How the ESCB will actually seek to attain low and stable inflation, is still an open question and one of the major issues for the years to come.

Against these backgrounds, this book focuses on the dynamics of inflation in connection with the monetary strategies of central banks in various countries. To this end, Chapter 2 outlines the theoretical model used to explore the link between monetary aggregates and inflation in a number of European countries. This concept is called P^* and is related to a strategy of monetary targeting. The essence of this model is that a deviation between the actual and the equilibrium price level — the price gap — indicates the short-run direction of the price level, and consequently inflation. In this volume, I have proxied the equilibrium price level with the multi-state Kalman filter method developed by Kool (1989).

Subsequently, it is investigated empirically whether national price movements in a number of European countries are predominantly driven by national or European-wide monetary factors (Chapters 3, 4 and 5). The picture emerging from Chapter 3 underlines that national price movements in four initial ERM members (that is, Belgium, France, Germany and the Netherlands) are significantly correlated with domestic monetary and real disturbances, so that the P^*-framework has predictive and analytical relevance. These empirical findings cannot be translated into monetary policy recommendations in all cases, because Belgium, France and the Netherlands attempt to maintain a fixed value of their currencies vis-à-vis the German mark. Under these circumstances, internal monetary developments become highly endogenous and, consequently, almost unmanageable for the monetary authorities. For Germany as the anchor country of the ERM, the results suggest that the Bundesbank has been right not abandon its monetary policy philosophy of monetary targeting in the past decade, as movements in $M3$ seem to have a significant impact on inflation and play an important role in the determination of the price level.

However, the significant strides toward both economic and monetary integration within the European Union may have rendered domestic price developments more sensitive to European instead of domestic monetary developments with the passage of time. This hypothesis is tested on the basis of an extended version of the original P^*-model in Chapter 4. The empirical outcomes point to increasing monetary interdependencies in the four countries mentioned above. In the longest possible estimation period (1973.1–1992.4), European imbalances are generally not relevant for predicting inflation in individual countries. For the non-anchor countries, the information content of European monetary developments for future domestic inflation trends has gradually increased since the inception of the EMS in 1979, whereas the explanatory power of national monetary aggregates has eroded considerably. Since the early 1980s, local monetary developments do not translate into national price movements at all. For Austria, a former shadow member of the ERM, I obtain comparable results. The Austrian example also shows that participation in formal exchange rate arrangements is not necessarily required to establish firm monetary ties with other (ERM) countries. In the case of Germany, I find that the domestic price gaps still exercise a significant effect on German inflation in the 1980s. Although Germany keeps a certain degree of monetary independence, the estimations show that monetary conditions in Germany's immediate neighbours increasingly matter for inflation in Germany. This points to the need for more attention for the development of aggregate European monetary conditions, and closer coordination of monetary policies. This way, the transition to Stage Three of EMU could be smoother as well, provided that the ESCB would also primarily base its policy decisions on the development of European monetary aggregates.

Aside from monetary targeting, the ESCB can also opt for a direct inflation targeting strategy. The practical features and empirical achievements of this relatively new policy option are detailed in Chapter 6. In the empirical part, I compare from different angles the dynamics of inflation in three direct inflation-targeting countries with those in neighbouring countries that have not recently changed their monetary strategies. Like Dueker and Fischer (1995), I match New Zealand with Australia, Canada with the United States and the United Kingdom with Germany; in all cases the former adopted explicit inflation targets in the course of the 1990s. Although it is perhaps still too early to assess the full consequences of the formulation of inflation targets (McCallum, 1995), my results are somewhat disappointing for the proponents of direct inflation targeting. Both the simulations and tests on structural instability in inflation and interest rate equations do not convincingly hint that the switch to direct inflation targeting has affected the path of inflation and interest rates.

The last section of Chapter 6 merges the theoretical and empirical evidence of the preceding chapters and offers some preliminary thoughts for answering the question whether monetary or direct inflation targeting is recommendable for the ESCB. Having established that the ESCB will be faced with many identical conceptual and practical issues when adhering to either monetary or inflation targets, I argue that one cannot simply jump to the conclusion that it does not really matter which strategy is ultimately chosen and that the selection will be governed by some normative elements. All things considered, monetary targeting seems — as yet — somewhat more preferable than inflation targeting. The reason is that inflation is the last chain in the monetary transmission mechanism. In other words, the impact of monetary policy measures on monetary aggregates is in principle easier to identify. A more pragmatic argument to slightly favour monetary targeting is that the Bundesbank has relied relatively successfully on monetary targeting for more than twenty years. As a result, the continuation of this monetary strategy in Stage Three could allow some degree of credibility to be inherited by the ESCB.

In the run up to Stage Three of EMU, the question which countries will be subjected to the monetary policy set by the ESCB became more and more urgent. Formally, the convergence criteria as formulated in the Maastricht Treaty should be employed to determine the composition of EMU. Since the issue of credibility of European economic convergence is extremely important (see Groeneveld et al., 1998b), Chapter 7 is devoted to the evolution of both economic and monetary convergence among all current EU members and Switzerland since 1979. A striking finding is that the distinctions among all present EU countries and Switzerland in terms of nominal performance has blurred over time. Particularly in the 1990s, there has been a remarkable convergence in inflation profiles and dynamics across European countries. Interestingly, the overall fall in inflation does not seem to be accompanied by an identical narrowing of the credibility gap of monetary policy in all countries. My results convey that some countries in the lowest inflation cluster are still marked by higher short-term interest rates than other countries belonging to the same inflation group. As opposed to nominal developments, 'EMU' barometers as well as formal clustering techniques hardly point to real convergence across my set of countries over time. By using pooled regression techniques, I also find that the composition of the countries' groups matters for the relationships between real and nominal variables and interest rates. Overall, countries with less sound fiscal positions and exceptionally high unemployment rates experience substantially higher nominal and real interest rates (see also Orr et al., 1996).

2 CONCLUDING REMARKS

Economic research usually does not provide definite answers, but only tries to clarify certain phenomena. In the context of this book, this remark particularly holds for the selection of an appropriate monetary strategy for the ESCB. Admittedly, the analysis only offers weak preliminary support for monetary targeting by the ESCB. The actual use of a European money supply as indicator or intermediate target can, in fact, destabilize a previously stable relationship between prices and European monetary aggregates (Lucas, 1976). Moreover, the European money stock has to prove its usefulness for monetary purposes in practice. This requires frequent evaluations of the stability of money demand functions and of the information content of monetary variables for future price movements. Naturally, the credibility of the actual inflation outcome is the only thing that counts, irrespective of the monetary strategy chosen by the ESCB.

Which European countries give up their national monetary autonomy was unknown at the time of writing this book. Regarding the convergence requirement of a high degree of price stability, the majority of EU countries would, however, qualify for participation in EMU. It remains to be seen whether the apparently identical inflation preferences across European countries will continue to exist in EMU, though. In this respect, the reaction function of the ESCB will undoubtedly trigger a large body of research in the coming years.

In this volume, I also touch upon various topics that surely deserve further research. For example, the question how to cope with possible asymmetric shocks in EMU needs closer examination. In this respect, it should be explored whether accurate alternative adjustment mechanisms exist to cushion these idiosyncratic disturbances, given that the exchange rate is no longer available (Masson, 1996). Here, one could think of the deregulation of national labour markets and the removal of physical, mental and fiscal barriers for people to move to other countries. Another issue that will undoubtedly trigger numerous academic and policy studies concerns the relationship between the inside and outside countries. Here, questions have to addressed whether the envisaged monetary coordination framework (that is, ERM-II) suffices to safeguard the Single Market and to promote the necessary economic convergence between the ins and the outs. Finally, the introduction of the euro will have a large impact on financial markets and financial structures, thus providing food for many directions of new research.

References

Adams, C. and D.T. Coe (1990), 'A Systems Approach to Estimating the Natural Rate of Unemployment and Potential Output for the United States', *IMF Staff Papers*, **37** (2), 232–93.

Agénor, P.R. and M.P. Taylor (1992), 'Testing for Credibility Effects', *IMF Staff Papers*, **39** (3), 545–71.

Alesina, A. (1988), 'Macroeconomics and Politics', in *NBER Macroeconomics Annual*, pp. 17-52, Cambridge 1988.

Alesina, A. and V. Grilli (1993), 'On the Feasibility of a One or Multi-Speed European Monetary Union', *Economics and Politics*, **5** (2), 145–65.

Ammer, J. and R.T. Freeman (1994), 'Inflation targeting in the 1990s: The experiences of New Zealand, Canada and the United Kingdom', *International Finance Discussion Paper*, (473), Board of Governors of the Federal Reserve System.

Angeloni, I., C. Cottarelli and A. Levy (1991), 'Cross-Border Deposits and Monetary Aggregates in the Transition to EMU', *IMF Working Paper* 91/114.

Argy, V. (1992), 'The Equilibrium Rate of Inflation with Discretion and Some Reputation', Banca Nazionale del Lavoro, *Quarterly Review*, **182**, 329–47.

Arnold, I.J.M. (1994), 'The Myth of a Stable European Money Demand', *Open Economies Review*, **5**, 249–59.

Arnold, I.J.M. and R.G.J. den Hertog (1995), 'European Time-Series Relationships between Inflation and Inflation Uncertainty: In Search of Threshold Levels', *De Economist*, **143** (4), 495–519.

Artis, M.J. and D. Nachane (1990), 'Wages and Prices in Europe: A Test of the German Leadership Hypothesis', *Weltwirtschaftliches Archiv*, **126** (1), 59–77.

Artis, M.J. and M. Taylor (1988), 'Exchange Rates, Interest Rates, Capital Controls and the European Monetary System: Assessing the Track Record', in F. Giavazzi, S. Micossi and M. Miller (eds), *The European Monetary System*, Cambridge University Press.

Artis, M.J. and M.P. Taylor (1994), 'The Stabilizing Effect of the ERM on Exchange Rates and Interest Rates: Some Nonparametric Tests', *IMF Staff Papers*, **41** (1), 123–47.

Artis, M.J, R.C. Bladen-Hovell and W. Zhang (1993), 'A European Money Demand', in P.R. Masson and M. Taylor (eds), *Policy Issues in the Operation of Currency Unions*, Cambridge University Press.

Artus, P., S. Avouyi-Dovi, E. Bleuze and F. Lecointe (1991), 'Transmission of U.S. monetary policy to Europe and asymmetry in the European monetary system', *European Economic Review*, **35**, 1369–84.

Baldwin, R.E. and E. Seghezza (1996), 'Growth and European Integration: Towards an Empirical Assessment', *CEPR*, Discussion Paper Series, No. 1393.

Ball, L. (1992), 'Why Does High Inflation Raise Inflation Uncertainty', *Journal of Monetary Economics*, **29**, 371–88.

Ball, L. (1995), 'Disinflation with imperfect credibility', *Journal of Monetary Economics*, **35**, 5–23.

Bank of England, *Inflation Report and Quarterly Bulletin* (various issues).

Banque de France (1996), '27 January 1996 Monetary Policy Council Meeting Defining France's Monetary Policy', Press Release.

Bank of Japan (1990), 'A Study of Potential Pressure on Prices: Application of P* to the Japanese Economy', *Special Paper*, (186).

Barro, R.J. (1989), 'Interest-Rate Targeting', *Journal of Monetary Economics*, **23**, 3–30.

Barro. R.J. and D.B. Gordon (1983), 'Rules, Discretion and Reputation in a Model of Monetary Policy', *Journal of Monetary Economics*, **12**, 101–21.

Barro, R.J. and X. Sala-i-Martin (1990), 'World Real Interest Rates', in *NBER Macroeconomics Annual*, pp. 15–74.

Baumol, W.J. (1952), 'The transactions demand for cash: An inventory theoretic approach', *Quarterly Journal of Economics*, **66**, 545–58.

Bayoumi, T. (1992), 'The Effect of the ERM on Participating Economies', *IMF Staff Papers*, **39** (2), 330–56.

Bayoumi, T. and B. Eichengreen (1993), 'Shocking Aspects of European Monetary Unification', in F. Giavazzi and F. Torres (eds), *The Transition to Economic and Monetary Union in Europe*, pp. 193–240, Cambridge University Press, Cambridge.

Bayoumi, T. and B. Eichengreen (1994a), 'Macroeconomic Adjustment under Bretton Woods and the Post-Bretton-Woods Float: An Impulse-Response Analysis', *The Economic Journal*, **104** (425), 813–27.

Bayoumi, T. and B. Eichengreen (1994b), 'One Money or Many? Analyzing the Prospects for Monetary Unification in Various Parts of the World', *Princeton Studies in International Finance*, (76).

Bayoumi, T. and P.B. Kenen (1993), 'How Useful is an EC-wide Monetary Aggregate as an Intermediate Target for Europe?', *Review of International Economics* I(3), 209–20.

Bayoumi, T. and A. Thomas (1994), 'Relative Prices and Economic Adjustment in the US and EU: A Real Story About European Monetary Union', *CEPR*, Discussion Paper Series, No. 988.

Baxter, M. and A.C. Stockman (1989), 'Business Cycles and the Exchange Rate Regime: Some International Evidence', *Journal of Monetary Economics*, **23** (3), 377–400.

Beaudry, P. and G. Koop (1993), 'Do recessions permanently change output?', *Journal of Monetary Economics,* **31**, 149–63.

Bekx, P. and G. Tullio (1989), 'A Note on the European Monetary System and the Determination of the DM–Dollar Exchange Rate', *Cahiers economiques de Bruxelles*, (123), 329–43.

Belgische Vereniging der Banken (1988), 'Monetary Policy in Belgium: Instruments and application', *Aspects and Documents*, No. 81.

Bernanke, B., and I. Mihov (1996), 'What Does the Bundesbank Target?', paper presented at the *International Seminar on Macroeconomics*.

Bernanke, B. and F. Mishkin (1992), 'Central Bank Behaviour and the Strategy of Monetary Policy: Observations from six Industrialized Countries, in *NBER Macroeconomics Annual 1992*, pp. 185–238.

Bergeijk, P.A.G. van, R.C.G. Haffner and P.M. Waasdorp (1993), 'Measuring the Speed of the Invisible Hand: The Macroeconomic Costs of Price Rigidity', *Kyklos*, **46** (4), 529–44.

Berk, J.M. and C.C.A. Winder (1994), 'Price Movements in the Netherlands and Germany and the Guilder-Dmark Peg', *De Economist*, **142** (1), 63–74.

Bertocchi, G. and M. Spagat (1994), 'Learning, experimentation, and monetary policy', *Journal of Monetary Economics*, **32**, 169–83.

Biltoft, K. and C. Boersch (1992), 'Interest Rate Causality and Asymmetry in the EMS', *Open Economies Review*, (3), 297–306.

Bini Smaghi, L. (1994), 'EMS Discipline: Did it Contribute to Inflation Convergence?', Banca Nazionale del Lavoro, *Quarterly Review*, **189**, 187–97.

Bini Smaghi, L. and P. del Giovane (1992), 'Convergence of Inflation, Prerequisite for EMU', Banca d'Italia, *Temi di discussione*, No. 186.

Bini Smaghi, L. and S. Vori (1993), 'Rating the EC as an Optimal Currency Area', *Temi di discussione*, No. 187.

Blanchard, O.J. (1984), 'The Lucas Critique and the Volcker Deflation', *American Economic Review*, **74**, 211–15.

Blanchard, O.J. (1990), 'Why does Money Affect output? A Survey', in B.M. Friedman and F.H. Hahn (eds), *Handbook of Monetary Economics*, vol. II, North Holland Publishing Company, pp. 797–835.

Blanchard, O.J. and P.A. Muet (1993), 'Competitiveness through disinflation: an assessment of the French macroeconomic strategy', *Economic Policy*, **16**, 11–56.

Bomhoff, E.J. (1991), 'Stability of Velocity in the Major Industrial Countries: A Kalman Filter Approach', *IMF Staff Papers*, **38** (3), 626–42.

Bordo, M.D. (1993), 'The Gold Standard, Bretton Woods and Other Monetary Rimes: A Historical Appraisal', *The Federal Bank of St. Louis Review*, **75** (2), 123–99.

Bordo, M.D. and L. Jonung (1987), 'The long-run behavior of the velocity of circulation: The international evidence', *Cambridge University Press*, Cambridge.

Boughton, J.M. (1992), 'International Comparisons of Money Demand: A Review Essay', *Open Economies Review*, **3**, 323–43.

Braun, S.N. (1990), 'Estimation of Current Quarterly Gross National Product by Pooling Preliminary Labor Market Data', *Journal of Business and Economic Statistics*, **8** (2), 293–304.

Brown, R.L., J. Durbin and J.M. Evans (1975), 'Techniques for Testing the Constancy of Regression Relationships over Time', *Journal of the Royal Statistical Society*, series B, (37), pp. 149–63.

Bruneel, D. (1992), 'La Monnaie', *La Revue Banque Editeur*, Paris.

Buiter, W.H., G. Corsetti and N. Roubini (1993), 'Sense and Nonsense in the Treaty of Maastricht', *Economic Policy*, **16**, CEPR, London.

Bullard, J.B. (1994), 'Measures of Money and the Quantity Theory', *Federal Reserve Bank of St. Louis Review*, **76** (1), 19–30.

Butter, F.A.G. den and M.M.G. Fase (1981), 'The demand for money in EEC-Countries', *Journal of Monetary Economics*, **8**, 201–30.

Campbell, J.Y. and P. Perron (1991), 'Pitfalls and Opportunities: What Macroeconomists Should Know about Unit Roots', in *NBER Macroeconomics Annual 1991*, pp. 141—219.

Canzeroni, M.B. (1985), 'Monetary Policy Games and the Role of Private Information', *American Economic Review*, **75**, 1056—70.

Canzeroni, M.B., C. Nolan, and A. Yates (1995), 'Mechanisms for Achieving Monetary Stability', *Bank of England*, Working Paper.

Caporale, G.M. and N. Pittis (1993), 'Common Stochastic Trends and Inflation Convergence in the EMS', *Weltwirtschaftliches Archiv*, **129** (2), 207—15.

Cassard, M., T.D. Lane and P.R. Masson (1994), 'ERM Money Supplies and the Transition to EMU', *IMF Working Paper* 94/1.

Cecchetti, S.G. (1995), 'Inflation Indicators and Inflation Policy', *NBER,* Working Paper, No. 5161.

Cesar, H., J. de Haan and J. Jacobs (1990), 'Monetary targeting in the Netherlands: an application of co-integration tests', *Applied Economics*, **22**, 1537—48.

Chadha, B., P.R. Masson and G. Meredith (1992), 'Models of Inflation and the Costs of Disinflation', *IMF Staff Papers*, **39** (2), 395—431.

Christiano, L.J. (1989), 'P^*: Not the Inflation Forecaster's Holy Grail', *Federal Reserve Bank of Minneapolis, Quarterly Review*, pp. 3—18.

Christiano, L.J. and M. Eichenbaum (1989), 'Unit roots in real GNP: Do we know, and do we care?', *NBER*, Working Paper, No. 3130.

Christensen, M. (1990), 'Policy Credibility and the Lucas Critique-Some New Tests', in P. Artus, Y. Barroux and G. McKenzie (eds), *Monetary and Financial Models*, Dordrecht, Kluwer Academic Publishers.

Clarida, R. and M. Gertler (1996), 'How the Bundesbank Conducts Monetary Policy', *NBER*, Working Paper, No. 5581.

Collins, S.M. (1988), 'Inflation and the European Monetary System', in F. Giavazzi, S. Micossi and M. Miller (eds), *The European Monetary System*, Cambridge University Press, Cambridge, pp. 112—39.

Collins, S.M. and F. Giavazzi (1993), 'Attitudes toward Inflation and the Viability of Fixed Exchange Rates: Evidence from the EMS', in M. Bordo and B. Eichengreen (eds), *A Retrospective on the Bretton Woods System*, University of Chicago Press, Chicago, pp. 547—86.

Committee of Governors of the Central Banks of the Member States of the European Economic Community, *Press Communiqué*, September 1987.

Cooley, T.F. and S.F. LeRoy (1981), 'Identification and Estimation of Money Demand', *American Economic Review*, **71** (5), 825—44.

Crockett, A.D. (1994), 'Rules versus Discretion in Monetary Policy', in J.A.H. de Beaufort Wijnholds, S.C.W. Eijffinger and L.H. Hoogduin (eds), *A Framework for Monetary Stability*, Dordrecht, Kluwer Academic Publishers, pp. 165—84.

Cukierman, A. (1995), 'Targeting Monetary Aggregates and Inflation in Europe', paper presented at the International Conference on Future European Monetary Policy on 30 November/1 December 1995, Kronberg/Ts.-Germany.

Cumby, R.E. and F.S. Mishkin (1986), 'The International Linkage of Real Interest Rates: The European—US Connection', *Journal of International Money and Finance*, **5**, 5—23.

Davidson, R. and J.G. MacKinnon (1981), 'Several Tests for Model Specification in the Presence of Alternative Hypothesis', *Econometrica*, **49** (3), 781—93.

De Nederlandsche Bank, *Annual Report*, various issues.

Deutsche Bundesbank (1992), 'The Relationship between the Money Stock and Price Developments in Germany', *Monatsbericht*, **44** (1), 20–9 (in German).

Deutsche Bundesbank (1995), 'Money demand and Currency Substitution in Europe', *Monatsbericht*, **47** (1), 33–49 (in German).

Dickey, D.A. and W.A. Fuller (1979), 'Distribution of the Estimators for Autoregressive Time-Series with a Unit Root', *Journal of the American Statistical Association*, **74** (366), 427–31.

Dickey, D.A. and W.A. Fuller (1981), 'Likelihood Ratio Statistics for Autoregressive Time Series with a Unit Root', *Econometrica*, **49** (4), 1057–72.

Dickey, D.A. and S.G. Pantula (1987), 'Determining the order of differencing in autoregressive processes', *Journal of Business and Economic Statistics*, **5**, 455–62.

Diebold, F.X. and G.D. Rudebusch (1989), 'Long Memory and Persistence in Aggregate Output', *Journal of Monetary Economics*, **24**, 189–209.

Driffill, J., G.E. Mizon and A. Ulph (1990), 'Costs of Inflation', in B.M. Friedman and F.H. Hahn (eds), *Handbook of Monetary Economics*, Vol. II, North Holland Publishing Company, pp. 1013–66.

Dueker, M.J. (1993a), 'Can Nominal GDP Targeting Rules Stabilize the Economy?', *Federal Reserve Bank of St. Louis Review*, **75** (3), 15–29.

Dueker, M.J. and A.M. Fischer (1996), 'Do Inflation Targets Redefine Central Bank Inflation Preferences? Results from an Indicator Model', in J.A.J. Alders, K. Koedijk, C. Kool and C. Winder (eds), *Monetary Policy in a Converging Europe*, Kluwer Academic Publishers, pp. 21–38.

Dunnen, E. den (1979), 'Postwar monetary policy', *De Economist*, **127** (1), 21–57.

Dwyer, G.P. (1993), 'Rules and Discretion in Monetary Policy', *Federal Reserve Bank of St. Louis Review*, **75** (3), 3–13.

Ebrill, L.P. and S.M. Fries (1991), 'Broad Money Growth and Inflation in the United States', *IMF Staff Papers*, **38** (4), 736–50.

Economic Unit (1991), *Report on Harmonisation of Broad Monetary Aggregates*, Committee of Governors of the Central Banks of the Member States of the European Economic Community.

Economic Unit (1993), *Cross-border holdings and EC-wide monetary relationships*, Committee of Governors of the Central Banks of the Member States of the European Economic Community.

Edison, H.J. and L.S. Kole (1994), 'European Monetary Arrangements: Implications for the Dollar, Exchange Rate Variability and Credibility', Board of Governors of the Federal Reserve System, *International Finance Discussion Papers*, No. 468.

Ees, H. van, H. Garretsen and E. Sterken (1993), 'On the scope for monetary policy in a small open economy with fixed exchange rates and capital market imperfections', paper presented at the conference of the European Economic Association, Helsinki.

Ees, H. van, E. Sterken, D. Wansink and A.A.T. Wesseling (1989), 'Consequences of financial innovation in the Netherlands', in J. de Haan and L.H. Hoogduin (eds), *The implications of financial innovation and integration for monetary policy*, Nederlands Instituut voor het Bank- en Effectenbedrijf (in Dutch).

Eichengreen, B. (1993), 'Three perspectives on the Bretton Woods System', in M. Bordo and B. Eichengreen (eds), *A Retrospective on the Bretton Woods System*, University of Chicago Press, Chicago, pp. 621–58.

Eichengreen, B. (1993a), 'European Monetary Unification', *Journal of Economic Literature*, **31**, 1321—57.

Eichengreen, B. (1993b), 'The Endogeneity of Exchange Rate Regimes', *NBER*, Working Paper, No. 4361.

Eichengreen, B. and C. Wyplosz (1993), 'The Unstable EMS', *Brookings Papers on Economic Activity*, (1), 51—143.

Eizenga, W. (1994), 'The National Bank of Belgium and Monetary Policy', Société Universitaire Européenne de Recherches Financières Tilburg, *Papers on Monetary and Policy and Financial Systems*, No. 17.

Emerson, M., D. Gros, A. Italianer, J. Pisani-Ferry and H. Reichenbach (1992), *One Market, One Money: An Evaluation of the Potential Benefits and Costs of Forming an Economic and Monetary Union*, Oxford University Press.

Engle, R.F. and C.W.J. Granger (1987), 'Co-integration and Error Correction: Representation, Estimation and Testing', *Econometrica*, **55** (2), 251—76.

European Monetary Institute (1997), *The Single Monetary Policy in Stage Three: Elements of the Monetary Policy Strategy of the ESCB*, Frankfurt am Main.

Evans, M. (1991), 'Discovering the Link between Inflation Rates and Inflation Uncertainty', *Journal of Money, Credit, and Banking*, **23** (2), 169—84.

Evans, M. and P. Wachtel (1993), 'Inflation Regimes and the Sources of Inflation Uncertainty', *Journal of Money, Credit, and Banking*, **25** (3), 475—511.

Everitt, B.S. (1993), '*Cluster Analysis*', third edition, Edward Arnold.

Falk, M. and N. Funke (1995), 'The Stability of Money Demand in Germany and in the EMS: Impact of German Unification', *Weltwirtschaftliches Archiv*, **131**, 470—88.

Fase, M.M.G. (1985), 'Monetary Control: the Dutch Experience', in C. van Ewijk and J.J. Klant (eds), *Monetary Conditions for Economic Recovery*, Martinus Nijhoff, Dordrecht.

Fase, M.M.G. (1994), 'In Search for Stability: An Empirical Appraisal of the Demand for Money in the G7 and EC Countries', *De Economist*, **142** (4), 421—54.

Fase, M.M.G. and C.C.A. Winder (1993), 'The Demand for Money in the Netherlands and the other EC Countries', *De Economist*, **141** (4), 471—96.

Fase, M.M.G. and C.C.A. Winder (1997), 'Wealth and the Demand for Money in the European Union', *DNB Staff Reports*, No. 6.

Fillion, J.F. and R. Tetlow (1993), 'Zero-Inflation or Price-Level Targeting? Some Answers from Stochastic Simulation on a Small Open-Economy Macro Model', in *Economic Behaviour and Policy Choice Under Price Stability*.

Fischer, A.M. (1993), 'Inflation Targeting: The New Zealand and Canadian Cases', *Cato Journal*, **13** (1), 11—27.

Fischer, A.M. and M. Zurlinden (1994), 'Geldpolitik mit formellen Inflationszielen: eine Übersicht', *Quartalsheft Scheizerische Nationalbank*, **12** (1), 65—76.

Fischer, A.M. and A.B. Orr (1994), 'Monetary Policy Credibility and Price Uncertainty: The New Zealand Experience of Inflation Targeting', *OECD Economic Studies*, **22**, 155—79.

Fischer, S. (1994a), 'The Costs and Benefits of Disinflation', in J.A.H. de Beaufort Wijnholds, S.C.W. Eijffinger and L.H. Hoogduin (eds), *A Framework for Monetary Stability*, Dordrecht, Kluwer Academic Publishers, pp. 31—42.

Fischer, S. (1994b), 'Modern Central Banking', in *The Future of Central Banking*, The Tercentenary Symposium of the Bank of England, Cambridge University Press, pp. 262–308.

Fisher, I. (1911), *The Purchasing Power of Money*, John Wiley, New York.

Fisher, G.R. and M. McAleer (1981), 'Alternative Procedures and Associated Tests of Significance for Non-Nested Hypothesis', *Journal of Econometrics*, **16**, 103–19.

Fratianni, M. and J. von Hagen (1992), *The European Monetary System and European Monetary Union*, Westview Press, London.

Freedman, C. (1994), 'Formal Targets for Inflation Reduction: The Canadian Experience', in J.A.H. de Beaufort Wijnholds, S.C.W. Eijffinger and L.H. Hoogduin (eds), *A Framework for Monetary Stability*, Dordrecht, Kluwer Academic Publishers, pp. 17–30.

Freeman, R.T. and J.L. Willis (1995), 'Targeting Inflation in the 1990s: Recent Challenges', paper presented at the Western Economic Association International Conference, San Diego, California.

Friedman, M. (1956), 'The quantity theory of money: a restatement', in M. Friedman, *Studies in the Quantity Theory of Money*, The University of Chicago Press, Chicago.

Friedman, M. (1977), 'Nobel lecture: Inflation and Unemployment', *Journal of Political Economy*, **85**, 451–72.

Friedman, B.M. (1994), 'Intermediate Targets versus Information Variables as Operating Guides for Monetary Policy', in J.A.H. de Beaufort Wijnholds, S.C.W. Eijffinger and L.H. Hoogduin (eds), *A Framework for Monetary Stability*, Kluwer Academic Publishers, pp. 109–33.

Fuller, W.A. (1976), *Introduction to Statistical Time Series*, John Wiley, New York.

Funke, M. and S. Hall (1994), 'Is the Bundesbank Different from Other Central Banks: A Study Based on P*', *Empirical Economics*, **19**, 691–707.

Galy, M. (1992), 'Implementation of Monetary Policy in EMS Countries Participating in the Exchange Rate Mechanism', *IMF Working Paper* 92/87.

Gardner, E.H. and W.R.M. Perraudin (1993), 'Asymmetry in the ERM: A Case Study of French and German Interest Rates Before and After German Unification', *IMF Staff Papers*, **40** (2), 427–50.

Garganas, N.C. (1993), 'The Implications of a Single European Currency and Monetary Policy: Prospects and Policy Issues', *Centre for European Policy Studies*, Working Document No. 77.

Garfinkel, M.R. and S. Oh (1995), 'When and how much to talk Credibility and Flexibility with Private Information', *Journal of Monetary Economics*, **35** (2), 341–57.

Gerlach, S. (1993), 'Inflation Targets and Monetary Policy', *BIS*, mimeo.

Gerlach, S. (1994), 'German Unification and the Demand for German M3', *BIS*, Working Paper No. 21.

Giavazzi, F. and A. Giovannini (1989), *Limiting Exchange Rate Flexibility: The European Monetary System*, MIT Press, Cambridge, Massachusetts.

Giavazzi, F. and L. Spaventa (1990), 'The "New" EMS', in P. de Grauwe and L. Papademos (eds), *The European Monetary System in the 1990s*, Longman, London/New York, pp. 65–85.

Giovannini, A. (1990), 'The Transition to European Monetary Union', *Essays in International Finance*, No. 178.

Giovannini, A. (1993), 'Bretton Woods and its Precursors: Rules Versus Discretion in the History of International Monetary Regimes', in M. Bordo and B. Eichengreen (eds), *A Retrospective on the Bretton Woods System*, University of Chicago Press, Chicago, pp. 109—54.

Giovannini, A. and B. Turtelboom (1992), 'Currency Substitution', *NBER*, Working Paper, No. 4232.

Gnan, E. (1994), 'Austria's Hard Currency Policy and European Monetary Integration', *De Pecunia*, **6** (3).

Golob, J.E. (1994), 'Does Inflation Uncertainty Increase with Inflation?', *Federal Reserve Bank of Kansas City Economic Review*, (3), pp. 27—38.

Goodhart, C. (1989), 'The conduct of monetary policy', *The Economic Journal*, **99**, 293—346.

Goodhart, C. and J. Viñals (1994), 'Strategy and Tactics of Monetary Policy: Examples from Europe and the Antipodes', *mimeo*.

Goos, B. (1994), 'German Monetary Policy and the Role of the Bundesbank in the ERM', *Economic and Financial Review*, **1** (1), 3—11.

Grauwe, P. de (1989), 'Is the European Monetary System a DM-zone?', *NBER*, Working Paper, No. 297.

Grauwe, P. de (1994a), 'Monetary Policies in the EMS: Lessons from the Great Recession of 1991—3', *CEPR*, Discussion Paper Series, No. 1047.

Grauwe, P. de (1994b), 'Towards EMU without the EMS', *Economic Policy*, pp. 147—85.

Grauwe, P. de (1996), The Economics of Convergence: Towards Monetary Union in Europe', *Weltwirtschaftliches Archiv*, **132** (1), 1—27.

Grauwe, P. de and D. Gros (1991), 'Convergence and Divergence in the Community's Economy on the Eve of Economic and Monetary Union', in P. Ludlow (eds), *Setting EC Priorities*, Brussels and CEPS.

Grauwe, P. de and W. Vanhaverbeke (1991), 'Is Europe an Optimum Currency Area? Evidence from Regional Data', *CEPR*, Discussion Paper Series, No. 555.

Green, J.H. (1996), 'Inflation Targeting: Theory and Policy Implications', *IMF Working Paper*, WP/96/35.

Grilli, V., D. Masciandaro and G. Tabellini (1991), 'Political and Monetary Institutions and Public Finance Policies in the Industrial Countries', *Economic Policy*, **13**, 341—92.

Groeneveld, J.M. (1995), 'Monetary Spill-Over Effects in the ERM: The Case of Austria, a Former Shadow Member', *Oesterreichische Nationalbank*, Working Paper 20, Vienna.

Groeneveld, J.M., K.G. Koedijk and C.J.M. Kool (1996), 'Monetary Interdependencies in the Core ERM Countries: The P*-approach', in J.A.J. Alders, K. Koedijk, C. Kool and C. Winder (eds), *Monetary Policy in a Converging Europe*, Kluwer Academic Publishers, pp. 39—60.

Groeneveld, J.M., K.G. Koedijk and C.J.M. Kool (1997), 'Money, Prices and the Transition to EMU, Banca Nazionale del Lavoro, *Quarterly Review*, **205**, pp. 481—504.

Groeneveld, J.M., K.G. Koedijk and C.J.M. Kool (1998a), 'Inflation Dynamics and Monetary Strategies: Evidence from six Industrialized Countries', *Open Economies Review*, **9**, pp. 21—38.

Groeneveld, J.M., K.G. Koedijk and C.J.M. Kool (1998b), 'Credibility of European Economic Convergence', *Weltwirtschaftliches Archiv*, forthcoming.

Groeneveld, J.M. and A. Visser (1997), 'Seignoriage, Electronic Money and Financial Independence of Central Banks', Banca Nazionale del Lavoro, *Quarterly Review*, **200**, 69—88.

Gros, D. and N. Thygesen (1992), *European Monetary Integration: From the European Monetary System to European Monetary Union*, Longmans, London.

Haan, J. de and L.H. Hoogduin (1987), 'Shift of emphasis in monetary policy', *Economische Statistische Berichten*, pp. 1068—72 (in Dutch).

Haan, L. de, C.G. Koedijk and J.E.J. de Vrijer (1992), *The rise in liquidity holdings in the 1980s*, De Nederlandsche Bank, Monetaire monografieën, **12**, (in Dutch).

Hagen, J. von (1993), 'Monetary union, money demand, and money supply: A review of the German monetary union', *European Economic Review*, **37**, 803—36.

Hagen, J. von (1995), 'Inflation and Monetary Targeting in Germany', in L. Leiderman and L.E.O. Svensson (eds), *Inflation Targets*, CEPR, London, pp. 107—21.

Hagen, J. von and S. Lutz (1996), 'Fiscal and Monetary Policy on the Way to EMU', *Open Economies Review*, **7** (4), 299—325.

Hagen, J. von and M.J.M. Neumann (1994), 'Real Exchange Rates within and between Currency Areas: How far away is EMU?', *The Review of Economics and Statistics*, **76** (2), 236—44.

Haldane, A.G. (1991), 'The exchange rate mechanism of the European monetary system: a review of the literature', *Quarterly Bulletin of the Bank of England*, **31** (1), 73—82.

Haldane, A. (1995), 'Inflation targets', *Bank of England Quarterly Bulletin*, August 1995, pp. 250—59.

Haldane, A. and C.K. Salmon (1995), 'Three issues on Inflation Targets: Some United Kingdom Evidence', Bank of England, *mimeo*.

Hall, S.G. and A. Milne (1994), 'The Relevance of P-star Analysis to UK Monetary Policy', *The Economic Journal*, **104**, 597—604.

Hallman, J.J., R.D. Porter and D.H. Small (1989), 'M2 per Unit of Potential GNP as an Anchor for the Price Level', *Board of Governors of the Federal Reserve System, Washington D.C.*, April 1989.

Hallman, J.J., R.D. Porter and D.H. Small (1991), 'Is the price level tied to the M2 Monetary Aggregate in the long run?', *American Economic Review*, **81** (4), 841—58.

Hamilton, J.D. (1989), 'A New Approach to the Economic Analysis of Non-Stationary Time Series and the Business Cycles', *Econometrica*, **57**, 357—84.

Harvey, A.C. (1991), *Forecasting, structural time series models and the Kalman filter*, Cambridge University Press.

Hein, S.E. and P.T.W.M. Veugelers (1983), 'Predicting Velocity Growth: A Time Series Perspective', *Federal Reserve Bank of St. Louis Review*, **65** (4), 34—43.

Henry, J. and J. Weidmann (1994), 'Asymmetry in the EMS revisited: Evidence from the causality analysis of daily Eurorates', *Rheinische Friedrich-Wilhelms-Universität Bonn*, Discussion Paper No. B-280.

Herz, B. and W. Röger (1992), 'The EMS is a greater Deutsche mark area', *European Economic Review*, **36**, 1413—25.

Hochreiter, E. and G. Winckler (1995), 'The advantages of tying Austria's hands: The success of the hard currency strategy', *European Journal of Political Economy*, **11**, 83—111.

Hoeller, P. and P. Poret (1991), 'Is P-star a good indicator of inflationary pressure in OECD countries?', *OECD Economic Studies*, No. 17.

Holland, S. (1993a), 'Comment on: Inflation Regimes and the Sources of Inflation Uncertainty', *Journal of Money, Credit, and Banking*, **25** (3), 514—20.

Holland, S. (1993b), 'Uncertain Effects of Money and the Link between the Inflation Rate and Inflation Uncertainty', *Economic Inquiry*, **31**, 39—51.

Huizinga, J. (1993), 'Inflation Uncertainty, Relative Price Uncertainty, and Investment in U.S. Manufacturing', *Journal of Money, Credit, and Banking*, **25** (3), 522—49.

Humphrey, T.M. (1989), 'Precursors of the P-Star Model', *Federal Reserve Bank of Richmand Economic Review*, **75** (4), 3—9.

Icard, A. (1991), 'Economic Policy Coherence and the Fight against Inflation — The French and European Experience', paper presented at the *Fifth International Conference of the Institute for Monetary and Economic Studies of the Bank of Japan* held at 24—25 October 1991 in Tokyo.

Icard, A. (1994), 'Monetary Policy and Exchange Rates: The French Experience', in J.A.H. de Beaufort Wijnholds, S.W.C. Eijffinger and L.H. Hoogduin (eds), *A Framework for Monetary Stability*, Kluwer Academic Publishers, pp. 239—56.

International Monetary Fund (1994), 'Background information to the staff report on the 1994 article IV consultation for Germany'.

International Monetary Fund, *World Economic Outlook*, various issues.

Ireland, P.N. (1994), 'Money and Growth: An Alternative Approach', *American Economic Review*, **84** (1), 47—65.

Issing, O. (1992), 'Theoretical and Empirical Foundations of the Deutsche Bundesbank's Monetary Targeting', *Intereconomics*, pp. 289—300.

Issing, O. (1994), 'Monetary Policy Strategy in the EMU', in J.A.H. de Beaufort Wijnholds, S.W.C. Eijffinger and L.H. Hoogduin (eds), *A Framework for Monetary Stability*, Dordrecht, Kluwer Academic Publishers, pp. 135—48.

Jacquemin, A. and A. Sapir (1996), 'Is a European Hard Core Credible? A Statistical Analysis', *Kyklos*, **49** (2), 105—17.

Jozzo, A. (1993), 'Survey: The Central Bank's operating procedures and the transmission of monetary policy in France', *ECU Newsletter*, **45**, 18—28.

Judd, J.P. and J.L. Scadding (1982), 'The Search for a Stable Money Demand Function: A Survey Of the Post-1973 Literature', *Journal of Economic Literature*, **20** (3), 993—1023.

Kendall, M. (1980), *Multivariate Analysis*, Charles Griffin & Company Limited.

Kenen, P.B. (1969), 'The Theory of Optimum Currency Areas: An Eclectic View', in R. Mundell and A. Swoboda (eds), *Monetary Problems of the International Economy*, Chicago, University of Chicago Press, pp. 41—60.

King, R.G. and S.T. Rebelo (1992), 'Low frequency filtering and real business cycles', *Banco de Portugal Research and Statistics Department*, Working Paper 4—92.

Knot, K.H.W. (1995), 'On the Determination of Real Interest Rates in Europe', *Empirical Economics*, **20**, 479—500.

Knot, K.H.W. (1996), *Fiscal Policy and Interest Rates in the European Union*, Aldershot, Edward Elgar.

Koedijk, K.G. and C.J.M. Kool (1992), 'Dominant interest and inflation differentials within the EMS', *European Economic Review*, **36**, 925—43.

Koedijk, K.G. and C.J.M. Kool (1994), 'Dominant interest and inflation differentials within the EMS: A Reply', *European Economic Review*, **38**,1665—66.

Koedijk, K.G., C.J.M. Kool and T.R.P.J. Kroes (1994), 'Changes in World Real Interest Rates and Inflationary Expectations', *Weltwirtschaftliches Archiv*, **130**, 712—29.

Kole, L.S. and M.P. Leahy (1991), 'The Usefulness of P* Measures for Japan and Germany', *Board of Governors of the Federal Reserve System*, International Financial Discussion Papers Number 414.

Kole, L.S. and E.E. Meade (1995), 'German Monetary Targeting: A Retrospective View', *Federal Reserve Bulletin*, pp. 917—31.

Kool, C.J.M. (1989), *Recursive Bayesian Forecasting in Economics: The Multi State Kalman Filter Method*, Thesis Erasmus University Rotterdam.

Kool, C.J.M. and J.A. Tatom (1994), 'The P-star Model in Five Small Economies', *Federal Reserve Bank of St. Louis Review*, **76** (3), 11—29.

Kremers, J.M. (1990), 'Gaining Policy Credibility for a Disinflation: Ireland's Experience in the EMS', *IMF Staff Papers*, **37** (1), 116—45.

Kremers, J.J.M. and T.D. Lane (1990), 'Economics and Monetary Integration and the Aggregate Demand for Money in the EMS', *IMF Staff Papers*, **37**, 777—805.

Kremers, J.J.M. and T.D. Lane (1992), 'The Implications of Cross-Border Monetary Aggregation', *IMF Working Paper*, WP/92/71.

Kröger, J. and M. Teuteman (1992), 'The German Economy after Unification: Domestic and European Aspects', Commission of the European Communities, *Economic Papers*, No. 91.

Kydland, F.E. and E.C. Prescott (1977), 'Rules Rather than Discretion: The Inconsistency of Optimal Plans', *Journal of Political Economy*, **85** (3), 473—91.

Lane, T.D. and S.S. Poloz (1992), 'Currency Substitution and Cross-Border Monetary Aggregation: Evidence from the G-7', *IMF Working Paper*, WP/92/81.

Lane, T.D., A. Prati and M.E.L. Griffiths (1995), 'An Inflation Targeting Framework for Italy', *IMF Paper on Policy Analysis and Assessment*, PPAA/95/4.

Laxton, D. and R. Tetlow (1992), 'A Simple Multivariate Filter for the Measurement of Potential Output', Bank of Canada, Technical Report No. 59.

Leiderman, L. and L.E.O. Svensson (1995), *Inflation Targets'* Centre for Economic Policy Research, London.

Loureiro, J. (1992a), 'The EMS Discipline Hypothesis: Is It EMS Specific?', Gothenburg University, mimeo.

Loureiro, J. (1992b), 'In Search of a Credible EMS', *Gothenburg Studies in Financial Economics*, Study No. 1992/1.

Lucas, R.E. Jr. (1976), 'Econometric Policy Evaluations: A Critique', in K. Brunner and A.H. Meltzer (eds), *The Phillips Curve and Labor Markets*, Carnegie-Rochester Conference Series on Public Policy, **1**, 19—46.

Masson, P.R. (1996), 'Fiscal Dimensions of EMU', *Economic Journal*, **106**, 996—1004.

Mayer, T. and J. Fels (1994), 'Bundesbank Adrift: German Economic Commentary', *Goldman Sachs*, 11 February 1994.

Mayer, T. and J. Fels (1995), 'Money and Prices in a Mini-EMU', *Goldman Sachs*, 10 February 1995.

Mayer, T. (1995), 'P-star as a Link Between Money and Prices in Germany — A Comment', *Weltwirtschaftliches Archiv*, **131** (1), 149—54.

McCallum, B.T. (1994), 'Monetary Policy Rules and Financial Stability', *NBER*, Working Paper, No. 4692.

McCallum, B.T. (1995), 'Inflation Targeting in Canada, New Zealand, Sweden, the United Kingdom, and in General', paper presented at the Bank of Japan's 7th International Conference October 26—27, 1995, Tokyo.

McKinnon, R.I (1982), 'Currency Substitution and Instability in the World Dollar Standard', *American Economic Review*, **72** (3), 320—33.

Milligan, G.W. (1981), 'A Review of Monte Carlo Tests of Cluster Analysis', *Multivariate Behavioral Research*, **16**, 379—407.

Monticelli, C. (1993a), 'All the money in Europe?: An investigation of the economic properties of EC-wide extended monetary aggregates', Economic Unit of the Committee of Governors of EC central banks, mimeo.

Monticelli, C. (1993b), 'Monetary Coordination under an Exchange Rate Agreement and the Optimal Monetary Instrument', Banca d'Italia, *Temi di discussione del Servizio Studi*, No. 214.

Monticelli, C. (1995), 'Policy Consequences of Money Demand (In)Stability: National vs. European', paper prepared for the workshop 'Monetary Policy in a Converging Europe', Amsterdam, 22—24 February, 1995.

Monticelli, C. and M.O. Strauss-Kahn (1991), 'European Integration and the Demand for Broad Money', *BIS Working Papers*, No. 18.

Monticelli, C. and J. Viñals (1993), 'European Monetary Policy in Stage Three: What are the Issues?', *CEPR*, Occasional Paper, No. 12.

Nationale Bank van België, Annual Report, various issues.

Nelson, C.R. and C.I. Plosser (1982), 'Trends versus random walks in macroeconomic time series: some evidence and implications', *Journal of Monetary Economics*, **10**, 139—62.

Obstfeld, M. and K. Rogoff (1995), 'The Mirage of Fixed Exchange Rates', *NBER*, Working Paper, No. 3603.

OECD, '*Economic Surveys*', various issues.

Okun, A. (1971), 'The Mirage of Steady Inflation', *Brookings Papers on Economic Analysis*, **2**, 435—98.

Orphanides, A. and R. Porter (1996), 'P^* Revisited: Money Based Inflation Forecasts with a Changing Equilibrium Velocity', Board of Governors of the Federal Reserve System, mimeo.

Orr, A., M. Edey and M. Kennedy (1995), 'Real Long-Term Interest Rates: The Evidence from Pooled-Time-Series', *OECD Economic Studies*, **25**, 75—107.

Padoa-Schioppa, T. (1988), 'The European Monetary System: A Long-term View', in F. Giavazzi, S. Micossi and M. Miller (eds), *The European Monetary System*, Cambridge University Press, Cambridge, pp. 369—84.

Pauer, F. (1996), 'Will Asymmetric Shocks Pose a Serious Problem in EMU?', *Oesterreichische Nationalbank*, Working Paper 23, Vienna.

Pecchenino, R.A. and R.H. Rasche (1990), 'P^* type models: evaluation and forecasts', *NBER*, Working Paper, No. 3406.

Perron, P. (1988), 'Trends and random walks in macroeconomic time series: further evidence from a new approach', *Journal of Economic Dynamics and Control*, **12**, 297—332.

Persson, T. and G. Tabellini (1993), 'Designing Institutions for Monetary Stability', *Carnegie-Rochester Conference Series on Public Policy*, **39**, 53–84.

Persson, T. and G. Tabellini (1996), 'Monetary Cohabitation in Europe', *CEPR*, Discussion Paper Series, No. 1380.

Poeck, A. van and J. van Gompel (1994), 'Dominant interest and inflation differentials within the EMS: A Comment', *European Economic Review*, **38**, 1661–63.

Quintyn, M. (1993), 'Managing Monetary Policy Reforms. Lessons from the French Experience', Banca Nazionale del Lavoro, *Quarterly Review*, **186**, 275–98.

Quirk, P.J. (1994), 'Fixed or Floating Exchange Regimes: Does it Matter for Inflation?', *IMF Working Paper*, WP/94/134.

Rasche, R.H. (1987), 'M1-velocity and money demand functions: do stable relationships exist?', *Carnegie-Rochester Series on Public Policy*, **27**, 9–88.

Reagan, P. and R.M. Stulz (1993), 'Contracting Costs, Inflation, and Relative Price Variability', *Journal of Money, Credit and Banking*, **25** (3), 585–601.

Reimers, H.E. and K.H. Tödter (1992), 'The price gap concept for Germany', Deutsche Bundesbank (in German), mimeo.

Reimers, H.E. and K.H. Tödter (1994), 'P-Star as a Link Between Money and Prices in Germany', *Weltwirtschaftliches Archiv*, **130**, 273–89.

Reserve Bank of New Zealand (1993) Post Election Briefing Paper for the Incoming Minister of Finance.

Rogoff, K. (1985), 'The Optimal Degree of Commitment to an Intermediate Monetary Target', *Quarterly Journal of Economics*, **100** (4), 1169–90.

Roubini, N. (1988), 'Offset and Sterilization under Fixed Exchange Rates with an Optimizing Central Bank', *NBER*, Working Paper, No. 2777.

Sachs, J. and C. Wyplosz (1986), 'The Economic Consequences of President Mitterrand', *Economic Policy*, **2**, 262–322.

Santoni, G.J. (1987), 'Changes in Wealth and the Velocity of Money', *Federal Reserve Bank of St. Louis Review*, **69** (3), 16–26.

Sapir, A. and K. Sekkat (1995), 'Exchange Rate Regimes and Trade Prices: Does the EMS Matter?', *Journal of International Economics*, **38** (2), 75–94.

Sapir, A., K. Sekkat and A.A. Weber (1994), 'The Impact of Exchange Rate Fluctuations on European Union Trade', *CEPR*, Discussion Paper Series, No. 1041.

Sardelis, C. (1993), 'Targeting a European Monetary Aggregate: Review and Current Issues', *Economic Papers*, **102**, Commission of the European Communities.

Sargent, T. (1983), 'Stopping Moderate Inflations: The Methods of Poincaré and Thatcher', in R. Dornbusch and M. Simonsen (eds), *Inflation, Debt, and Indexation*, MIT Press, Cambridge, pp. 54–96.

Schächter, A. and A.C.J. Stokman (1995), 'Interest rate policy of the Deutsche Bundesbank: an econometric analysis for 1975 to 1992', *De Economist*, **143** (4), 475–94.

Schlesinger, H. (1994), 'On the Way to a New Monetary Union: The European Monetary Union', *Federal Reserve Bank of St. Louis Review*, **76** (3), 3–10.

Seitz, F. (1995), 'The Circulation of Deutsche Mark Abroad', Economic Research Group of the Deutsche Bundesbank, *Discussion Paper*, no. 1.

Shiller, R.J. (1996), 'Why do people dislike inflation?', *NBER*, Working Paper, No. 5539.

Söderlind, P. (1995), 'Forward interest rates as indicators of inflation expectations', *CEPR*, Discussion Paper Series, No. 1313.

Stein, J.C. (1989), 'Cheap Talk and the Fed: A Theory of Imprecise Policy Announcements', *American Economic Review*, **79** (1), 32—42.

Stockman, A.C. (1988), 'Sectoral and National Aggregates Disturbances to Industrial Output in Seven European countries', *Journal of Monetary Economics*, **21**, 387—409.

Straaten, A.J. van (1989), *Forty years Monetary and Financial Analysis by the Dutch Central Bank: 1947-1986*, Nederlands Instituut voor het Bank- en Effectenbedrijf, NIBE publications No. 67 (in Dutch).

Svensson, L.E.O. (1992), 'Why Exchange Rate Bands? Monetary Independence in spite of Fixed Exchange Rates', *CEPR*, Discussion Paper Series, No. 742.

Svensson, L.E.O. (1993), 'The Simplest Test of Inflation Target Credibility', *NBER*, Working Paper, No. 4604.

Svensson, L.E.O. (1995), 'The Swedish Experience of an Inflation Target', in L. Leiderman and L.E.O. Svensson (eds), *Inflation Targets*, CEPR, London, pp. 69—89.

Swank, J. (1994), *'Bank Behaviour and Monetary Policy in the Netherlands: Theory and Evidence'*, Thesis Free University of Amsterdam.

Tallman, E.W. (1995), 'Inflation and Inflation Forecasting: An Introduction', *Federal Reserve Bank of Atlanta, Economic Review*, **80** (1), 13—27.

Tatom, J.A. (1992), 'The P-star model and Austrian Prices', *Empirica*, **1**, 3—17.

Tavlas G.S. (1994), 'The Theory of Monetary Integration', *Open Economies Review*, **5**, 211—30.

Tewes, T. (1995), 'P-star as a Link Between Money and Prices in Germany — A Comment', *Weltwirtschaftliches Archiv*, **131** (1), 155—62.

Thygesen, N. (1994), 'European Integration and the Single Currency', *Banque de France*, Cahiers Économiques et Monetaires, No. 43.

Tobin, J. (1956), 'The interest-elasticity of the transactions demand for cash', *Review of Economics and Statistics*, **38** (3), 241—47.

Tobin, J. (1958), 'Liquidity preference as behavior towards risk', *Review of Economic Studies*, **25**, 65—86.

Tommasi, M. (1994), 'The Consequences of Price Instability in Search Markets: Towards Understanding the Effects of Inflation', *American Economic Review*, **84**, 124—43.

Trichet, J.C. (1992), 'Ten years of competitive disinflation in France', *Notes Bleues de Bercy* (in French).

Ungerer, H., O. Evans, T. Mayer and P. Young (1986), 'The European Monetary System: recent developments', *IMF* Occasional Paper, No. 48, Washington DC.

Viñals, J. (1994), 'Building a Monetary Union in Europe: Is it worthwile, where do we stand, and where are we going?', *Banco de España*, Servicio de Estudios, Working Document, No. 9412.

Viñals, J. and J.F. Jimeno (1996), 'Monetary Union and European Unemployment', *Banco de Espana*, Working Paper, No. 9624.

Walsh, C.E. (1995), 'Optimal Contracts for Central Bankers', *American Economic Review*, **85**, 150—67.

Weber, A.A. (1992), 'The role of policymakers' reputation in the EMS disinflations: An empirical evaluation', *European Economic Review*, **36**, 1473—92.

White, H. (1980), 'A Heteroskedasticity-Consistent Covariance Matrix and a Direct Test for Heteroskedasticity', *Econometrica*, **48**, 817—38.

Zijlstra, J. (1985), *Moderate Monetarism, 14 Annual Reports of the Dutch Central Bank 1967-1980*, Leiden/Antwerpen (in Dutch).

Index

accountability 159
aggregation issues 97–101
Argy, V. 39
Arnold, I.J.M. 168, 175
Artis, M.J. 98, 196
Australia 162–3, 192
  inflation in 160, 161, 173, 174, 179,
    183, 185
  interest rates in 161, 179, 183, 185
Austria
  accession to EU 144
  economic growth in 147, 148
  effects of ERM on 144–53, 231–2
  European economic convergence
    and 206, 219
  exchange rates and 145–7
  inflation in 4, 147, 149, 152, 215
  monetary policy in 144, 145–8, 151,
    152–3
  P^*-model and 145–53, 231–2

balance of payments see current
  account deficit
Ball, L. 175
Bank of Canada 160, 161
Bank of Japan 8, 16, 20
Banque de France 75–6
Barro, R.J. 2
Baxter, M. 119
Bayesian learning process 23
Bayoumi, T. 95, 98, 107, 119, 120,
  136, 145
Bekx, P. 98
Belgium
  economic growth in 38, 41, 147, 148
  European economic convergence
    and 198, 199, 203, 207, 214, 219,
    226
  exchange rates and 70, 87, 99, 101,
    145, 147
  inflation in 4, 36, 38, 39, 66–72,
    124, 147, 148
  monetary policy in 37, 70, 87, 121,

126, 145, 148
  output in 51
  P^*-model and 36, 66–72, 87, 118,
    122–6
  velocity of money in 38, 42, 66
Biltoft, K. 196
Bini Smaghi, L. 6, 39, 196, 227
Blanchard, O.J. 75, 176
Boersch, C. 196
Boughton, J.M. 43
Braun, S.N. 20
Brazil, attitudes to inflation in 3
Bretton Woods system 37, 43, 70, 74,
  99, 101, 113
Brown, R.L. 70
budget deficits, European economic
  convergence and 197, 199, 207,
  214
Bundesbank 16, 36–7, 43, 61, 80, 81,
  87–8, 94, 112, 130–131, 133, 192
business cycle theory 14

Campbell, J.Y. 28, 29
Canada 164–5, 191
  inflation in 160, 161, 174, 180, 183,
    186, 190
  interest rates in 161, 180, 183, 186,
    190
  monetary policy in 154, 157, 158,
    159, 160, 161, 168
  price index in 156
Canzeroni, M.B. 156
capital controls, liberalization of 107
Caporale, G.M. 39
Cassard, M. 95, 107
central banks
  accountability of 159
  credibility of 155–6, 157, 159–60,
    175–6
Cesar, H. 86
Chadha, B. 156
Christensen, M. 155
Christiano, L.J. 8, 15, 16, 20, 41